First World War
and Army of Occupation
War Diary
France, Belgium and Germany

11 DIVISION
Headquarters, Branches and Services
Commander Royal Engineers,
Royal Army Ordnance Corps
Deputy Assistant Director Ordnance Services
and Branches and Services Royal Army Veterinary Corps
Deputy Assistant Director Veterinary Services
28 June 1916 - 31 March 1919

WO95/1799

The Naval & Military Press Ltd
www.nmarchive.com
Published in association with The National Archives

Published by

The Naval & Military Press Ltd

Unit 10 Ridgewood Industrial Park,

Uckfield, East Sussex,

TN22 5QE England

Tel: +44 (0) 1825 749494

www.naval-military-press.com

www.nmarchive.com

This diary has been reprinted in facsimile from the original. Any imperfections are inevitably reproduced and the quality may fall short of modern type and cartographic standards.

© **Crown Copyright**
Images reproduced by permission of The National Archives, London, England, 2015.

Contents

Document type	Place/Title	Date From	Date To
Heading	WO95/1799/1		
Heading	11th Division C.R.E. Jun 1916-Jly 1919.		
War Diary	At Sea	28/06/1916	30/06/1916
War Diary	At Sea On Brand	01/07/1916	01/07/1916
War Diary	Hmt. Oriana	03/07/1916	03/07/1916
War Diary	Marseilles	04/07/1916	04/07/1916
War Diary	On Train	05/07/1916	07/07/1916
War Diary	Flers	08/07/1916	14/07/1916
War Diary	Le Cauroy	15/07/1916	15/07/1916
War Diary	Duisans	16/07/1916	29/07/1916
War Diary	Warlus	30/07/1916	21/08/1916
War Diary	Le Cauroy	22/08/1916	31/08/1916
Miscellaneous	11th Division	04/10/1916	04/10/1916
War Diary	Le Cauroy	01/09/1916	02/09/1916
War Diary	Doullens	03/09/1916	03/09/1916
War Diary	Acheux	04/09/1916	06/09/1916
War Diary	V.16.9.	07/09/1916	14/09/1916
War Diary	Camouflage V.16.d	14/09/1916	19/09/1916
War Diary	V.16.d.	20/09/1916	30/09/1916
Heading	War Diary of C.R.E., 11th. Division. For October 1916. Vol 4.		
War Diary	Acheux	01/10/1916	01/10/1916
War Diary	Bernaville	02/10/1916	03/10/1916
War Diary	Domart	04/10/1916	17/10/1916
War Diary	St. Ouen	18/10/1916	10/11/1916
War Diary	Yvrench	11/11/1916	13/11/1916
War Diary	Canaples	14/11/1916	15/11/1916
War Diary	Contay	16/11/1916	16/11/1916
War Diary	Headauville	17/11/1916	30/11/1916
War Diary	Englebelmer	01/12/1916	31/12/1916
Heading	R.E. 11 Div. January 1917 Vol 7		
War Diary	Englebelmer	01/01/1917	19/01/1917
War Diary	Marieux	20/01/1917	20/01/1917
War Diary	Bernaville	21/01/1917	21/01/1917
War Diary	Yvrench	22/01/1917	31/01/1917
Heading	War Diary For Month Of February, 1917. C.R.E. Co. R.E. Co. R.E. Co. R.E. Vol 8		
War Diary	Yvrench	01/02/1917	19/02/1917
War Diary	Canaples	20/02/1917	22/02/1917
War Diary	Marieux	23/02/1917	28/02/1917
War Diary	War Diary. March 1917. C.R.E. Vol 9.		
War Diary	Marieux	01/03/1917	11/03/1917
War Diary	Coigneux	12/03/1917	18/03/1917
War Diary	Marieux	19/03/1917	31/03/1917
Heading	War Diary. April 1917. H.Q., R.E. Vol. 10.		
War Diary	Marieux	01/04/1917	11/04/1917
War Diary	Acheux	12/04/1917	19/04/1917
War Diary	Ovillers	20/04/1917	20/04/1917
War Diary	N. 11 Centre	21/04/1917	30/04/1917
War Diary	Sheet 57C. N 11 Centre	01/05/1917	14/05/1917

War Diary	Albert.	15/05/1917	18/05/1917
War Diary	St Jans Cappel	19/05/1917	31/05/1917
Miscellaneous	Handing Over Notes. Vide Map Attached.	14/05/1917	14/05/1917
War Diary	Handing Over Report.		
Miscellaneous	List Of Maps And Plans With Handing Over Reports.		
Miscellaneous			
Miscellaneous	Water Supply.		
War Diary	St Jans Cappel	01/06/1917	13/06/1917
War Diary	Dranoutre	13/06/1917	19/06/1917
War Diary	Merris	20/06/1917	22/06/1917
War Diary	Renescure	23/06/1917	23/06/1917
War Diary	Eperlecques	24/06/1917	30/06/1917
Heading	War Diary. July, 1917. C.R.E. 11th Division. H.Q. Vol 13.		
War Diary	Eperlecques	01/07/1917	22/07/1917
War Diary	Wormhaudt	23/07/1917	24/07/1917
War Diary	Poperinghe	25/07/1917	31/07/1917
Heading	War Diary. Augt. 1917 C.R.E. 11th Division. Vol 14.		
Miscellaneous	Poperinghe	01/08/1917	07/08/1917
War Diary	X Camp A.16.c.2.3. Sheet 28.	08/08/1917	16/08/1917
War Diary	A.16.c.2.3. Sheet 28.	16/08/1917	23/08/1917
War Diary	Border Camp A.30.b.2.3.	24/08/1917	28/08/1917
War Diary	X Camp	29/08/1917	31/08/1917
War Diary	X Camp A.16.c.2.3. Sheet 27.	01/09/1917	10/09/1917
War Diary	X. Camp.	10/09/1917	18/09/1917
War Diary	Poperinghe	19/09/1917	24/09/1917
War Diary	Border Camp	25/09/1917	10/10/1917
War Diary	Poperinghe	11/10/1917	14/10/1917
War Diary	Eperlecques	15/10/1917	17/10/1917
War Diary	Norrent Fontes	18/10/1917	22/10/1917
War Diary	Braquemont	23/10/1917	22/12/1917
War Diary	Labeuvriere.	23/12/1917	22/01/1918
War Diary	Sailly-Labourse	23/01/1918	24/02/1918
War Diary	Verquin	25/02/1918	28/02/1918
Heading	War Diaries For Month Of March 1918 Of H.Q., R.E. Vol 21.		
War Diary	Verquin	01/03/1918	31/03/1918
Heading	11th Divisional Engineers C.R.E. 11th Division. April 1918.		
War Diary	Verquin	01/04/1918	14/04/1918
War Diary	Bracquemont	15/04/1918	31/05/1918
Heading	War Diaries C.R.E. June 1918 HQ RE 11 D. Vol 24		
War Diary	Braquemont	01/06/1918	30/06/1918
Heading	C.R.E. War Diary July 1918 Vol 25		
War Diary	Braquemont	01/07/1918	25/08/1918
War Diary	Hermin	26/08/1918	28/08/1918
War Diary	Arras	29/08/1918	20/09/1918
War Diary	Frevillers	20/09/1918	25/09/1918
War Diary	Vis-En-Artois	26/09/1918	26/09/1918
War Diary	Arras-Cambrai Road	27/09/1918	28/09/1918
War Diary	Baralle	29/09/1918	30/09/1918
Miscellaneous		30/09/1918	30/09/1918
Miscellaneous	The detail of the work carried out by the various units is as follows:-		
Miscellaneous	86th Field Company, R.E.		
Miscellaneous			

War Diary	Baralle	01/10/1918	20/10/1918
War Diary	Naves	21/10/1918	02/11/1918
War Diary	Haspres	03/11/1918	03/11/1918
War Diary	Preseau	04/11/1918	08/11/1918
War Diary	Roisin	09/11/1918	09/11/1918
War Diary	Aulnois	10/11/1918	26/11/1918
War Diary	Hasnon	27/11/1918	31/01/1919
Miscellaneous	11 Division.		
War Diary	Hasnon	01/02/1919	27/02/1919
War Diary	Denain.	28/02/1919	31/03/1919
War Diary	Rue De St Amand Denain	17/03/1919	20/03/1919
War Diary	Denain	01/05/1919	02/07/1919
Miscellaneous	Short Account Of Operations Carried Out By Royal Engineers And Pioneers Of The 11th Division From 2nd November 1918.	02/11/1918	02/11/1918
Heading	WO95/1779/2		
Heading	11th Division D.A.D.O.S. Sep 1916-Jun 1919.		
War Diary	Le Cauroy	01/09/1916	02/09/1916
War Diary	Doullens	03/09/1916	03/09/1916
War Diary	Acheux	04/09/1916	06/09/1916
War Diary	Senlis	07/09/1916	01/10/1916
War Diary	Acheux	02/10/1916	02/10/1916
War Diary	Bernaville	03/10/1916	25/10/1916
Miscellaneous	Headquarters, 11th Division.	05/12/1916	05/12/1916
Heading	War Diary D.A.D.O.S. 511th Division. Octr. & Novr. Vol 5		
War Diary	Senlis	01/10/1916	01/10/1916
War Diary	Acheux	02/10/1916	02/10/1916
War Diary	Bernville	03/10/1916	04/10/1916
War Diary	Domart	05/10/1916	25/10/1916
War Diary	Domart	01/11/1916	10/11/1916
War Diary	Yufrencheux	11/11/1916	15/11/1916
War Diary	Confay	16/11/1916	16/11/1916
War Diary	Hedauville	17/11/1916	26/11/1916
War Diary	Forceville	27/11/1916	31/01/1917
Heading	War Diary For Month Of February, 1917. D.A.D.O.S. Vol 9		
War Diary	Yvrench	01/02/1917	09/02/1917
War Diary	Contterille	01/02/1917	23/02/1917
War Diary	Canaples	24/02/1917	25/02/1917
War Diary	Raincheval	26/02/1917	31/03/1917
Heading	War Diary. April 1917. D.A.D.O.S. Vol XI		
War Diary	Raincheval	01/04/1917	20/04/1917
War Diary	N C7 4	21/04/1917	25/04/1917
War Diary	H.30.a.1.2.	26/04/1917	30/04/1917
Heading	War Diary. May 1917. D.A.D.O.S., 11th. Divn. Vol 12		
War Diary	H.30.a.1.2.	01/05/1917	19/05/1917
War Diary	St Jans Cappel	20/05/1917	31/05/1917
Heading	D.A.D.O.S. 11th Division. Vol 13		
War Diary	St Jans Capel	01/06/1917	08/06/1917
War Diary	Dranoutre	09/06/1917	19/06/1917
War Diary	Merris	20/06/1917	20/06/1917
War Diary	Renescure	22/06/1917	22/06/1917
War Diary	Eperlecques	24/06/1917	30/06/1917
War Diary	War Diary. July, 1917. D.A.D.O.S. 11th Division. Vol 14		

War Diary	Eperlecques	01/07/1917	22/07/1917
War Diary	Wormhoudt	23/07/1917	24/07/1917
War Diary	Poperinghe	25/07/1917	31/07/1917
Heading	War Diary Augt. 1917. D.A.D.O.S. 11th Div. Vol 15		
War Diary	Poperinghe L.11.b.1.8.	01/08/1917	20/08/1917
War Diary	Poperinghe A.22.d.6.5. Sheet 28.	21/08/1917	31/08/1917
Heading	Confidential War Diary of D.A.D.O.S. 11th Division From Sept. 1st To Sept. 30th 1917. Vol 16		
War Diary	A.22.d.6.5. Sheet 28	01/09/1917	30/09/1917
Heading	Confidential War Diary of D.A.D.O.S. 11th Division. From October 1st To October 31st 1917. Vol 17		
War Diary	A.22.d.6.5.	01/10/1917	10/10/1917
War Diary	Eperlecques	11/10/1917	17/10/1917
War Diary	Norrent Fontes	18/10/1917	21/10/1917
War Diary	Bracquemont	23/10/1917	31/10/1917
Heading	War Diary of D.A.D.O.S. 11th Div. Date. From November 1st 1917 To November 30th 1917. Vol 18		
War Diary	Bracquemont	01/11/1917	30/11/1917
Heading	Confidential War Diary of D.A.D.O.S. 11th Division. From Decr. 1st To Decr. 31st 1917. Vol 19		
War Diary	Bracquemont	01/12/1917	22/12/1917
War Diary	La Beuvriere	23/12/1917	31/12/1917
Heading	War Diary of DADOS. 11th Division For Period Jan. 1st To 31st 1918 Vol 20		
War Diary	Labeuvriere	01/01/1918	22/01/1918
War Diary	La Bourse	23/01/1918	28/02/1918
Heading	War Diary of D.A.D.O.S. 11th Div. For March 1918. Vol 22		
War Diary	La Bourse	01/03/1918	05/03/1918
War Diary	La Bourse	06/02/1918	10/02/1918
War Diary	La Bourse	12/03/1918	31/03/1918
Heading	DADOS War Diary 1st 4/18-30th 4/18 Vol 23		
War Diary	La Bourse	01/04/1918	08/04/1918
War Diary	Verquin	09/04/1918	15/04/1918
War Diary	Braquemont	16/04/1918	30/04/1918
Heading	War Diary DADOS May 1918 Vol 24		
War Diary	Bracquemont	01/05/1918	31/05/1918
Heading	War Diary DADOS June 1918 Vol 25		
War Diary	Bracquemont	01/06/1918	30/06/1918
Heading	D.A.D.O.S. War Diary July 1918 Vol 26		
War Diary	Bracquemont	01/07/1918	25/08/1918
War Diary	Kingoval	26/08/1918	28/08/1918
War Diary	Moroeuil	29/08/1918	30/08/1918
War Diary	Arras	01/09/1918	19/09/1918
War Diary	Kingoval	20/09/1918	25/09/1918
War Diary	Arras	26/09/1918	26/09/1918
War Diary	O.34.b.9.5. Sheet 51 B.	27/09/1918	28/09/1918
War Diary	Buissy V.18.d.2.7.	29/09/1918	30/09/1918
Heading	War Diary of DADOS 11th Divn. October 1918. Vol 29		
War Diary	Buissy	01/10/1918	02/10/1918
War Diary	Baralle	03/10/1918	20/10/1918
War Diary	Naves	21/10/1918	31/10/1918
Heading	War Diary of D.A.D.O.S. 11th Divn. November 1918. Vol 30		
War Diary	Naves	01/11/1918	02/11/1918

War Diary	Aaspres	03/11/1918	06/11/1918
War Diary	Curgies	07/11/1918	08/11/1918
War Diary	Roisin	09/11/1918	09/11/1918
War Diary	Aulnois	10/11/1918	26/11/1918
War Diary	Denain	27/11/1918	30/11/1918
Heading	War Diary of D.A.D.O.S. 11th Division Dec 1st To 31st 1918. Vol 31		
War Diary	Denain	01/12/1918	30/06/1919
Heading	WO95/1799/3		
Heading	11th Division D.A.D.V.S. Jly 1916-Mar 1919		
War Diary	Flers	04/07/1916	14/07/1916
War Diary	Le Cauroy	15/07/1916	15/07/1916
War Diary	Duisans	16/07/1916	29/07/1916
War Diary	Warlus	30/07/1916	31/07/1916
War Diary	Le Cauroy	01/09/1916	01/09/1916
War Diary	Doulens	02/09/1916	02/09/1916
War Diary	Acheux	03/09/1916	06/09/1916
War Diary	Senlis	07/09/1916	29/09/1916
Heading	War Diary of A.D.V.S, 11th. Division. For October 1916. Vol 3		
War Diary	Senlis	01/10/1916	01/10/1916
War Diary	Acheux	02/10/1916	02/10/1916
War Diary	Bernaville	03/10/1916	04/10/1916
War Diary	Domart	05/10/1916	21/10/1916
War Diary	St Ouen	22/10/1916	31/10/1916
Heading	War Diary. Vol 5		
War Diary	S. Ouen	07/11/1916	11/11/1916
War Diary	Yvrench	12/11/1916	16/11/1916
War Diary	Contay	17/11/1916	23/11/1916
War Diary	Hedauville	24/11/1916	27/11/1916
War Diary	Forceville	28/11/1916	30/11/1916
Heading	War Diary. A.D.V.S. 11th Div. Vol 6.		
War Diary	Engiebelmer	22/12/1916	25/01/1917
War Diary	Yvrench	26/01/1917	31/01/1917
Heading	War Diary For Month Of February, 1917. A.D.V.S. 22nd Mobile Vet. Section. Vol 8		
War Diary	Yvrench	10/02/1917	28/02/1917
Heading	War Diary. March 1917. A.D.V.S. Vol 9		
War Diary	Marieux	01/03/1917	31/03/1917
Heading	War Diary. April 1917. A.D.V.S., 11th. Div. Vol 10		
War Diary	Marieux	01/04/1917	11/04/1917
War Diary	Acheux	12/04/1917	19/04/1917
War Diary	Ovillers Huts	20/04/1917	20/04/1917
War Diary	N 11 Central	21/04/1917	30/04/1917
Heading	War Diary. May 1917. A.D.V.S., 22nd. Mob. Vet. Section. Vol. XI		
War Diary	N 11 Central	01/05/1917	14/05/1917
War Diary	Usna Hill	18/05/1917	19/05/1917
War Diary	St Jans Cappel	20/05/1917	31/05/1917
Heading	D.A.D.V.S. Vol 12.		
War Diary	St. Jans Cappel	01/06/1917	09/06/1917
War Diary	Dranoutre	10/06/1917	20/06/1917
War Diary	Merris	21/06/1917	23/06/1917
War Diary	Renescure	24/06/1917	24/06/1917
War Diary	Eperlecques	25/06/1917	30/06/1917

Heading	War Diary. July, 1917. D.A.D.V.S. 11th Division. Vol 13.		
War Diary	Eperlecques	01/07/1917	23/07/1917
War Diary	Wormhoudt	24/07/1917	25/07/1917
War Diary	Poperinghe	26/07/1917	31/07/1917
Heading	War Diary of Major J.W. O'Kelly D.A.D.V.S. 11th Division From 1-8-17 To 31-8-17. Vol 14.		
War Diary	Poperinghe	01/08/1917	22/08/1917
War Diary	X Camp A.16.c.2.5.	23/08/1917	23/08/1917
War Diary	Border A.30.B2.3.	24/08/1917	29/08/1917
War Diary	X Camp A.16.c.2.5.	30/08/1917	31/08/1917
Heading	War Diary of Major J.W. O'Kelly A.V.C. D.A.D.V.S. 11th Division. From 1-9-17 To 30-9-17. Vol 15		
War Diary	X Camp	01/09/1917	03/09/1917
War Diary	Poperinghe	13/09/1917	19/09/1917
War Diary	Wormhoudt	20/09/1917	25/09/1917
War Diary	Border Camp	26/09/1917	30/09/1917
Heading	War Diary of Major J.W. O'Kelly D.A.D.V.S. 11th Div. From 1-10-17 To 31-10-17. Vol 16.		
War Diary	Border Camp	01/10/1917	11/10/1917
War Diary	Eperlecques	12/10/1917	18/10/1917
War Diary	Norrent Fontes	19/10/1917	23/10/1917
War Diary	Braquemont	24/10/1917	31/10/1917
Heading	War Diary of Major J.W. O'Kelly D.A.D.V.S. 11th Divn. From 1-11-17 To 30-11-17. Vol 17.		
War Diary	Braquemont	01/11/1917	22/12/1917
War Diary	Labeuvriere	23/12/1917	31/12/1917
Heading	War Diary of Major J.W. O'Kelly D.A.D.V.S. 11th Division 1-1-18 To 31-1-18. Vol 19.		
War Diary	Labeuvriere	01/01/1918	23/01/1918
Heading	War Diary of Major J.W. O'Kelly. A.V.C. DADVS. 11. Divn. February 1918. Vol 20		
War Diary	Sailly La Bourse	06/02/1918	24/02/1918
War Diary	Verquin	25/02/1918	28/02/1918
Heading	War Diary of D.A.D.V.S. 22nd Mob. Vet. Section For March 1918 11th Division. DADVS 11 D Vol 21.		
War Diary	Verquin	01/03/1918	31/03/1918
Heading	War Diary of Major J.W. O'Kelly A.V.C. DADVS 11th Divn. From 1/4/18-30/4/18. Vol 22.		
War Diary	Verquin	01/04/1918	15/04/1918
War Diary	Bracquemont	16/04/1918	30/04/1918
Heading	War Diary DADVS May 1918 Vol 23.		
War Diary	Bracquemont	01/05/1918	31/05/1918
Heading	War Diaries. DADVS. June 1918 Vol 24		
War Diary	Bracquemont	01/06/1918	07/06/1918
War Diary		08/01/1918	10/01/1918
War Diary	Bracquemont	11/06/1918	30/06/1918
War Diary	DADVS. & War Diary July 1918 Vol 25.		
War Diary	Bracquemont	01/07/1918	31/08/1918
War Diary	Maroeuil	01/09/1918	02/09/1918
War Diary	Arras	03/09/1918	09/09/1918
War Diary	Villers Chatel	24/09/1918	26/09/1918
War Diary	Arras	27/09/1918	29/09/1918
War Diary	Baralle	30/09/1918	21/10/1918
War Diary	Naives	22/10/1918	02/11/1918
War Diary	Haspres	03/11/1918	03/11/1918

War Diary	Preseau	04/11/1918	07/11/1918
War Diary	Curgies	08/11/1918	08/11/1918
War Diary	Roisin	09/11/1918	09/11/1918
War Diary	Aul Nois	10/11/1918	30/11/1918
War Diary	Denain	01/12/1918	31/03/1919

wops/1799(1)

wops/1799(1)

11TH DIVISION

C. R. E.
JUN 1916 - JLY 1919

Army Form C. 2118.

WAR DIARY
or
INTELLIGENCE SUMMARY.   CRE 1st Division
(Erase heading not required.)

Instructions regarding War Diaries and Intelligence Summaries are contained in F. S. Regs., Part II. and the Staff Manual respectively. Title pages will be prepared in manuscript.

Place	Date	Hour	Summary of Events and Information	Remarks and references to Appendices
At Sea	28.6.16		Left ALEXANDRIA at 06.00. Strength 3 O. + 6 O.R.	6/13
	29.6.16		At sea weather fine.	
	30.6.16		" "	

Army Form C. 2118.

WAR DIARY
or
INTELLIGENCE SUMMARY.
(Erase heading not required.)

CRE 11 (D) Division

Instructions regarding War Diaries and Intelligence Summaries are contained in F. S. Regs., Part II. and the Staff Manual respectively. Title pages will be prepared in manuscript.

Place	Date	Hour	Summary of Events and Information	Remarks and references to Appendices
At sea HMT ORIANA	1.7.16		Arrived MALTA 06.00m. Left again at 10.a.m accompanied by escort.	
MARSEILLES	3.7.16		" MARSEILLES at 1 p.m.	
	4.7.16		Disembarked 8m prisoners & went road to Camp FOURNIER arriving at 10.30 p.m. including 7 horses + 4 grooms + 1 mules cart. Shot arrival by HAVERFORD. Major DENISON A/CRE apprise O.C. Train. Left MARSEILLES at 1.30 a.m.	
On Train	5.7.16		Admin of D.H.Q. fell off train in travel near VIENNE; injured by French authorities at LYONS VAISE as having been taken to hospital badly injured on head.	
"	7.7.16		Arrived ABBEVILLE 3.30 a.m. Offloaded 1st two troops of various units: left again at 06.45 am arriving PRÉVENT at 10.00.	
FLERS	8.7.16		Marched to FLERS (D.H.Q.) in the afternoon to billets	
	9.7.16		at FLERS. 67 Field Co line troops at FRANCOURT.	
			67 " " marches to MAIZIÈRES. 68 arrived at	
"	10.7.16		MAIS-NIL-ST-POL. Reports to C.E. vi Corps at NOYELLE-VION.	Sub

Army Form C. 2118.

WAR DIARY
or
INTELLIGENCE SUMMARY.   CRE 11 Division
(Erase heading not required.)

Instructions regarding War Diaries and Intelligence Summaries are contained in F. S. Regs., Part II. and the Staff Manual respectively. Title pages will be prepared in manuscript.

Place	Date	Hour	Summary of Events and Information	Remarks and references to Appendices
FLERS	11.7.16		Lt Col F.A.K.WHITE rejoins from duty on detachmt in EGYPT.	
	13.7.16		Major DENISON rejoined 68 Field Co. at MAIS-NIL	
	13.7.16		11 Div Signal Co. + M.W. Cable section arrived at FLERS	
	14.7.16		at FLERS	
Le CAUROY	15.7.16		Marched to Le CAUROY to billets for the night	
DUISANS	16.7.16		" DUISANS. baggage waggon attacked today: 67 Field Co at MONTENESCOURT (1 room in ARRAS). 68 Coy at AGNEZ. 86	
"	17.7.16		Coy at GRAND RULLE COURT. 2/Lt H.D.M. POULTER (68 Coy) killed (G.S.W abdomen) on front line trench while with 62nd Field Coy.	
"	18.7.16		} leaving the ground.	
"	19.7.16			
"	20.7.16		Took over water supply from Park Coy, march vill	
"	21.7.16		Took over all paper etc from CRE 33 Division also Park at LAHERLIERE + workshops 67 Coy at AGNY, 68 at AGNEZ, 86 F at LE FERMONT.	

Army Form C. 2118.

WAR DIARY
or
INTELLIGENCE SUMMARY.
(Erase heading not required.)

CRE 11 Division

Instructions regarding War Diaries and Intelligence Summaries are contained in F. S. Regs., Part II. and the Staff Manual respectively. Title pages will be prepared in manuscript.

Place	Date	Hour	Summary of Events and Information	Remarks and references to Appendices
DUISANS	22.7.16		Capt YORKE-ELIOT remained in charge of machinery in shops at LAHERLIERE. Lt WHITE (81st Field Co) in charge of RE Park.	
"	23.7.16		Arranged how Brigades should be responsible for arranging transport for all RE stores from the Park.	
"	24.7.16		Arranged for trucks (3) to go down into ARRAS for use of 67 Coy in gun emplacements.	
"	25.7.16		Trenches cancelled: considerable trouble with pumps begun at SIMENCOURT + FOSSEUX: shipping.	
"	26.7.16		In obtaining spares + renewals + took over no 106 Manoeuvres from 53 Division.	
"	27.7.16		Headquarters of Field Coys as follows: 67th AGNY (shed-51B) M.8.b.63. 68 ARRAS ("51.C.) C 21.a.2.2. 81st LE FERMONT R 26.c.8.9.	
"	28.7.16		Routine work, chiefly improving dugouts in	
"	29.7.16		" " " " obtained RE's + upon part for fronts reported by fronts at DOULLENS : trouble with water supply still extremely irregular in BARLY, FOSSEUX + SIMENCOURT.	
WANQUETIN	30.7.16		Ordinary routine. 236 Tunnelling Coy survey comm in ADONVILLE church	
"	31.7.16		" "	S.E.S.

Signed,
Lt Col. R.E.
CRE 11 Div

Army Form C. 2118.

CRE 11 Div ---- Vol 2

WAR DIARY
or
INTELLIGENCE SUMMARY.
(Erase heading not required.)

Instructions regarding War Diaries and Intelligence Summaries are contained in F. S. Regs., Part II. and the Staff Manual respectively. Title pages will be prepared in manuscript.

Place	Date	Hour	Summary of Events and Information	Remarks and references to Appendices
WARLUS	1-6-16		Pump at MONCHIET WARLUS ~~Britist~~ both out of water. New police above pump at BARLY nearly complete.	
"	2-6-16		BARS (Shower) attended & talks to GOUY; Eng employed chiefly in urgent M.G. improvements etc.	
"	3-6-16 to 5-6-16		Routine work. Pumping Station at BARLY nearly complete.	
"	6-6-16		Well at MONCHIET repaired; new store & opened attn's pattn in prog. Bomb ... out of order. 216 Tunnelling Coy Captain very appreciate to be getting water flow in.	
"	7-6-16		H 33 & 38. Decauville ... sent up to ARMY	
"	7-6-16		Request went to AMIENS to buy eng'rm fittings & parts for water supply	
"	8-6-16		Ordinary routine	
"	9-6-16		"	
"	10-6-16		"	
"	11-6-16		" " ; trouble with 2 chlorin engines in SIMENCOURT	
"	12-6-16		M. HAUTIER, french intendu occasionally attn & killed by bosche intrepide	
"	13-6-16		Routine	

Army Form C. 2118.

WAR DIARY
or
INTELLIGENCE SUMMARY.
(Erase heading not required.)

CRE 11 Div.

Instructions regarding War Diaries and Intelligence Summaries are contained in F.S. Regs, Part II. and the Staff Manual respectively. Title pages will be prepared in manuscript.

Place	Date	Hour	Summary of Events and Information	Remarks and references to Appendices
WARLUS 14.8.16	14/8/16		Funeral of M. HAUTIER; the architect of late whose abandoned to nothing the by French Mission, who undertake to have it returned	
"	15/8/16		nothing much. CRE 21st Div went round the 1 section	
"	16/8/16		CRE of 12 Div looked over H section; arranged between DAINVILLE & BERNEVILLE section ones	
"	17/8/16		CRE 12 Div inspected on G section	
"	18/8/16			
"	19/8/16		Dainville hutts sent up to DAINVILLE for trench tramway	
"	20/8/16		Routine work & preparing to hand over	
"	21/8/16		" " " Capt BUDDLE left on 7 days leave	
Le Cauroy	22/8/16		Moved to Le Cauroy & handed over to 12th Division	
	23/8/16 31/8/16		Coy training; bayonet fighting, bombing, musketry, physical exercise etc. weather very wet. limited training a great deal	

11th Division

Herewith War Diaries of Hd Qrs R.E. & B Field Coy. for month of September.

4/10/16

G.W. Burdett
Captain
for CRE 11 Div

Army Form C. 2118.

WE 3

CRE 11 Div

WAR DIARY
or
INTELLIGENCE SUMMARY.
(Erase heading not required.)

Place	Date	Hour	Summary of Events and Information	Remarks and references to Appendices
Le CAUROY	1/9/16		Training; weather very bad	
"	2/9/16		" " " "	
DOULLENS	3/9/16		Moved to DOULLENS; 3 Coys train via CROUCHES	
ACHEUX	4/9/16		" " ACHEUX: 67 Field's RAINCHEVAL: 68 at LEALVILLERS	
"			86 = at PUCHEVILLERS	
"	5/9/16		bearing the ground to be taken over from 25 Div	
"	6/9/16		" " " " "	
V.16.9	7/9/16		Moved to CAMOUFLAGE V.16.9. 86 Coy to AVELUY: 86 to W.9.d.7.6.	
"	8/9/16		67 = to AVELUY: getting stores up to forward area. O Coy in the line	
"	9/9/16		Consolidating the line.	
"	10.9.16		Commenced getting more of material and mining material to AVELUY. 67 Coy casualties	
"	11.9.16		Continued as above.	"
"	12.9.16		" " "	
"	13.9.16		Opening up dugouts and communication between HINDENBURG and MUSSLIENT LEIPZIG	
"	14.9.16		" " " "	

Army Form C. 2118.

WAR DIARY
or
INTELLIGENCE SUMMARY.   C.R.E. 11 Div.
(Erase heading not required.)

Place	Date	Hour	Summary of Events and Information	Remarks and references to Appendices
CAMOUFLAGE	14/9/16		Deepening of Fire trench for attack on WONDER WORK + in R.31.d.9.8. to C.7.8. (S=7.D.S.E. Ed 2d.) 1 sectn 86 to consolidate at R.31.a.9.1.; 1 sectn 67 to consolidate R.31.d.9.8. + R.31.b.6.1.; 1 sectn 67 to consolidate R.31.b.2,3. + 0.3.; 1 sectn 67 RE + 1 Coy 6 E.Yorks consolidate R.31.d.0.7. to centre of WONDER WORK and R.31.b.9. communication trench R.31.d.0.7. to centre of CRUCIFIX to R.31.d.7.9. 1 sectn 67 RE to be in reserve in dugouts at BLUFF. Comm: 86 Field Coy find 1 sectn in reserve in dugouts at BLUFF. East end of BLACK HORSE BRIDGE, RE DUMPS near Brigade Hd Qrs at W.12.a.6.6. and in AVELUY.	
"	15.9.16		Lt A.F. REID and 4 nappr wounded by shrapnel. Work of consolidation successfully carried out. Coys moved back to their normal billets	
"	16.9.16		Handed over work in hyr Sectn to 49th Div; 132 Bde overran Contain + DANUBE trenches. G7 + 86 Coy awaiting orders. 34 Bde took on for of Like on right.	
"	17/9/16		Consolidating + making good communication " weather very bad.	
"	18/9/16		" " " " " "	
"	19/9/16		" " " " " " weather very bad.	

Army Form C. 2118.

WAR DIARY
or
INTELLIGENCE SUMMARY.
(Erase heading not required.)

CRE 11 Div

Place	Date	Hour	Summary of Events and Information	Remarks and references to Appendices
V.16.d.	20.9.16		Weather very bad: all operations suspended: work on dugouts & communications continued.	
"	21.9.16		Weather still bad: mud too heavy to allow much work to be done.	
"	22.9.16		Weather improving, ground drying up: communications & assembly trench well in hand	
"	23.9.16		"	
"	24.9.16		Forward Divisional Dump of RE rsn at FRITZ WELL W.9.a.1.6 in use, formed by of Railway mining material & dugout frames + props etc etc.	
"	25.9.16.		Fine day: Dmn moved to Cmy for construction of strong points after the infantry assault. 86.7 cm night & 6.8 cm Sept. 17th in Reserve	
"	26.9.16		Advanced Div HQrs formed at DONNETS POST. Assault carried out at 12.35 p.m. Section of field Coy attached for strong points in 32 Objective. Work to get up. Work in communications & roads commenced in an afternoon - also construction in ZOLLERN REDOUBT and an left flank in ZOLLERN TRENCH	
"	27.9.16		Work of consolidation carried on : clearing of MOUQUET FARM taken in hand by 82 Field Co.	

Army Form C. 2118.

WAR DIARY
or
INTELLIGENCE SUMMARY.
(Erase heading not required.)

CRE 11 Div

Place	Date	Hour	Summary of Events and Information	Remarks and references to Appendices
V.R.G.	28.9.16		Constructing entrance walk. Parapets to work	
	29.9.16		Work on road up NABSVALLEY. Walk to bank also on right road through POZIERES.	
"	30.9.16		Field Coys relieved by those of 25th Division : Coys moves to bivouac near BOUZINCOURT and billets in SENLIS. Casualties during the operation very small : 67 of AVELUY : 68 HERRINVILLE : 86 in bivouac nr BOUZINCOURT	3,4,5

Vol 4

WAR DIARY

of

C.R.E., 11th. Division.

for October 1916.

Army Form C. 2118.

WAR DIARY
or
INTELLIGENCE SUMMARY.
(Erase heading not required.)

CRE 11 DIV

Place	Date	Hour	Summary of Events and Information	Remarks and references to Appendices
ACHEUX	1/10/16		Div Hd Qrs move to ACHEUX: dismounted personnel of field coys marched to ACHEUX & entrained to CANDAS; marching thence to billets 67 & 68 at OUTREBOIS: 86 at OCCOCHES	
BERNAVILLE	2/10/16		Transport of field coys moved on to OUTREBOIS & OCCOCHES. Hd Qrs moved to BERNAVILLE. Capt Rogers 67 Field Co proceeded on leave. Weather very bad	
"	3/10/16		All Field Coys marched to ST OUEN; weather very bad	
DOMART	4/10/16		Moved to DOMART: Lieut FAR WHITE 14th for England on 10 days leave: Coys commenced training	
"	5/10/16		Training continued: Capt REIS PRATT (86 Fd Co) attached to 6" 11 Div for instruction in riff work.	
"	6/10/16		Training (chiefly marching, physical exercises & rifle exercises) continued	
"	7/10/16		" "	
"	8/10/16		Commenced reports on hutting accommodation for Reserve Army Q. who contracts of P.O.W. cage at ST OUEN	
"	9/10/16		Commenced work on hut standings at ST OUEN, continued on Prisoners of War cage	
"	10/10/16		Carried out for Divisional Gas school at DOMART. Training continued	Z.2.3

Army Form C. 2118.

WAR DIARY
or
INTELLIGENCE SUMMARY.
(Erase heading not required.)

CRE 11 Division

Instructions regarding War Diaries and Intelligence Summaries are contained in F. S. Regs., Part II. and the Staff Manual respectively. Title pages will be prepared in manuscript.

Place	Date	Hour	Summary of Events and Information	Remarks and references to Appendices
DOMART 11.10.16	11.10.16		Training continued: also construction of gun sector; POW cage; horse standings etc:	
"	12.10.16		"	
"	13.10.16		Ditto: Lt Col FAIRWHITE returned from leave: companies at full strength: report to billets, horse	
"	14.10.16		"	
"	15.10.16		"	
"	16.10.16		"	
"	17.10.16		Received orders that 11 Field Coy was placed in disposal of 2 I Corps	
ST OUEN 18.10.16	18.10.16		Moved to ST OUEN: 3 Field Coys of 11 Div ST OUEN to march to Pac de MAISON	
"	19.10.16		mining support: 67 + 68 Field Coys attached to Divison employed moving cable and laying tramway etc: 86 Field Coy attached 2 I Div employed	
"	29/10/16		similar work.	
"	30/10/16		"	
"	31/10/16		"	

Army Form C. 2118.

WAR DIARY
or
INTELLIGENCE SUMMARY.
(Erase heading not required.)

CRE 11th Division

Place	Date	Hour	Summary of Events and Information	Remarks and references to Appendices
ST OUEN	1/11/16		Work in hand drawings on hand; Field Coys attached 67th Div to 18 Div	
			56 to 19th Division in Divnl. Horse AVELUY - POZIERES area working	
			on roads and tramways	
	6/11/16		"	
	7/11/16		"	
	10/11/16		"	
YVRENCH	11/11/16		Brought to YVRENCH	
"	12/11/16		Bought materials for horse standings and return of stores	
"	13/11/16		"	
CANAPLES	14/11/16		Moved to CANAPLES	
"	15		at CANAPLES RAMC.	
CONTAY	16		moved to CONTAY: Capt- AG CLASS joined. Capt PR A AUSTIN, RAMC. am/c to 33 Field Amb.	
HEDAUVILLE	17		Moved to HEDAUVILLE; 3 Field Coys moved to FORCEVILLE and came under	
			orders of CRE 11th Division	
"	18/11/16		Coys wiring & clearing for 39 I.D. mar	
"	19/11/16		Came under orders of II Corps	

Army Form C. 2118.

WAR DIARY
or
INTELLIGENCE SUMMARY.
(Erase heading not required.)

CRE 11 Division   Vol 5

Place	Date	Hour	Summary of Events and Information	Remarks and references to Appendices
MEDAUVILLE	20/11/16		67 Field Co moved up to huts nr Wq b g r. 68 + 81 Coys remain at FORCEVILLE	
"	21/11/16		68 Field Co moved to Martinsart + took over from 152 "Field Co" 11 Div of ANCRE. 81 Field Co moved to BOUZINCOURT	
"	22/11/16		86 Field Co moved to North BLUFF. THIEPVAL area.	
"	24/11/16		68" Field Coy moved to HAMEL	
"	26/11/16		CRE Hd Qrs moved to ENGLEBELMER	
"	28/11/16		67th Field Coy moved to vicinity of HAMEL	
"	30/11/16		The 67th Field Coy relieved 68th Field Coy in Left Section, 68 Field Coy came into reserve Pole area	

Arafodon
Capt & Adjt "   "

Army Form C. 2118.

Vol 6

C R E 11th Division

WAR DIARY
or
INTELLIGENCE SUMMARY
(Erase heading not required.)

Instructions regarding War Diaries and Intelligence Summaries are contained in F. S. Regs., Part II. and the Staff Manual respectively. Title pages will be prepared in manuscript.

Place	Date	Hour	Summary of Events and Information	Remarks and references to Appendices
ENGLEBELMER	1.12.16		200 yds of Tramway (East of main Rly) relaid to duckwalk.	
"	2.12.16		Work proceeding on Tramway. Stables out & panniers made in AVELUY wood.	
"	3.12.16		Tramway relaid. Knocked up Jun LANCASHIRE dump tramway Rly Line.	
"	4.12.16		Tunnel under main Ry line needs repairs.	
"	5.12.16		Work on hut at R.M.O. and both at ENGLEBELMER.	
"	6.12.16		Capt. P.T. Joyston & Lieut G.T.F. White wounded.	
"	7.12.16		Work on Lewiston proceeded in front. This work on dugouts cont'd.	
"	8.12.16		Capt E Rogers died of wounds.	
"	9.12.16		Repairs to St Pierre - Divion well continued.	
"	10.12.16		2/Lieut H.N Contain killed, 2/Lieut M.O Lewis wounded; 2/Lt E.R Cantlem admitted to Hospital.	
"	11.12.16		Work continued on front line dugouts.	
"	12.12.16		2/Lt A. Leir joined 67 F. Coy. Capt. G.A. Burkitt admitted Hospital. Lieut CAHILL E. York R. acting adjutant.	
"	13.12.16		Work continued on RAILWAY ALLEY & ENGINE TRENCH.	
"	14.12.16		Conference of Cov. Perrers Lof. Division on establishment.	

T134. Wt. W708—776. 500000. 4/15. Sir J. C. & S.

Army Form C. 2118.

WAR DIARY
or
INTELLIGENCE SUMMARY.
(Erase heading not required.)

CRE 11th Division

Instructions regarding War Diaries and Intelligence Summaries are contained in F. S. Regs., Part II. and the Staff Manual respectively. Title pages will be prepared in manuscript.

Place	Date	Hour	Summary of Events and Information	Remarks and references to Appendices
		December		
ENGLEBELMER	15.12.16		2/Lt. G.V. Robinson & 2/Lt. T.L. Brown joined 67 Coy. Capt. P.T. Foulds died of wounds.	
"	16.12.16		Work carried on on Dugouts Trench revetting. State of ground very bad, owing to inclement rains.	
"	17.12.16		Work on pump stations, & clearing dugouts in BEAUCOURT trench.	
"	18.12.16		26 Coy. relieved 67 Coy. on LEFT SECTOR.	
"	19.12.16		Work on Dugouts continued for dugouts.	
"	20.12.16		Report received that BEAUCOURT CAVE was dangerous. Work on shoring up started. Work 20/21 by 175 Tunnelling Coy.	
"	21.12.16		Lt. J.I.H. Robinson joined 67 Coy.	
"	22.12.16		2/Lt. T.L. Brooks & 2/Lt. H.E. Bundle joined 67 Coy. 2/Lt. O.C.G. Mott joined 68 Coy. Work allotted on THIEPVAL - MOUQUET FARM Road.	
"	23.			
"	23.12.16		Work continued on THIEPVAL - MOUQUET FARM road and dugouts. One party making O.P.	
"	24.12.16		Work continued on Tramway, making of ENGINE TRENCH.	

Army Form C. 2118.

WAR DIARY
or
INTELLIGENCE SUMMARY.
(Erase heading not required.)

CRE 11 Division

Place	Date	Hour	Summary of Events and Information	Remarks and references to Appendices
ENGLEBELMER	24/12/16 contd.		The resetting of timbers was also continued; plus bakers well employed on dist. dugouts.	
"	25.12.16		Work proceeding on Observation Post, Beaucourt By from Q.2 a.a.2.5 to Q.18.6.88. About 300 yds. laid. 67OTAH. 116 - 5' frames made - 6' plates were made.	
"	26.12.16		Work proceeding on observation post dugouts. 67 Field Coy. Relief 86 Field Coy carried out. A few	
"	27.12.16		Work continued in sundry ENGINE TRENCH and in Gallery from HAMEL to bottom of ENGINE TRENCH. 67 Coy. 2/Lieut O.C GILLOTT 2/Lt E.T. DAVIES joined 67 Coy. joined 68 F. Coy.	
"	28.12.16 to 30.12.16		Work continued as on 27th. Labs on Communication Trench to SHVL A TRENCH. Clearing proceed in dug-out in ENGINE TRENCH.	
"	31.12.16		Dug-out commenced in BEAUCOURT SWITCH. Our N.C.O and 3 men with 4 - 36 Charge of Gun cotton went out with wiring party on night 31/1. They had instructions to blow up any machine guns.	

Army Form C. 2118.

WAR DIARY
or
INTELLIGENCE SUMMARY
(Erase heading not required.)

C R E 11 Division

Place	Date	Hour	Summary of Events and Information	Remarks and references to Appendices
ENGLEBELMER	December			
	31.12.16		Gun emplacements completed. Also to blow in any dugouts. Referred was not successful as nothing was done. Capt. WYATT attached to 58 F.Coy for 10 days from 30.12.16.	

G.W.Wilby? Lt. Col.
C.R.E. 11 Division.

Vol 7.

R.E. 11" Div
January 1917

Army Form C. 2118.

WAR DIARY
or
INTELLIGENCE SUMMARY.
(Erase heading not required.)

Instructions regarding War Diaries and Intelligence Summaries are contained in F. S. Regs., Part II. and the Staff Manual respectively. Title pages will be prepared in manuscript.

Place	Date	Hour	Summary of Events and Information	Remarks and references to Appendices
ENGLEBELMER	1/1/17		Major PRATT. O.C. 86th Field Co. assumed command. The following work in progress - repairs to various dug-outs, Pees Trench, Scar Read & Leslie Trench; Dugouts in Engine Trench, Beaucourt Smith Criticality, Honor Trim & Frankfurt Trench; Tunnel Tramway Lt from HAMEL to BEAUMONT HAMEL station.	
"	2/1/17		Lieut. Jones 86th Fld. Co. proceeded on 10 days leave. Lt. H. READ attached to Fld.Co. returned from leave & proceeded to join his Battalion. 6 other R.E.	
"	3/1/17		86 Fld. Co. completed taking over new lines from 67 Fld. Co. to letter going into reserve. Dug-outs near MARTIN SAPT.	
"	4/1/17		Work continue on repairs & erecting of Communication Trenches & construction of dug-outs.	
"	5-10/1/17		do. do.	
"	11/1/17		1/7 Fld. Co. relieved 86 Fld. Co. at MESNIL.	
"	12/1/17		Have sent tinned in repairs to Communication Trenches & cross-in-fire	
"	13/1/17		& dug-outs	
"	14/1/17		do do. Capt. FEARFIELD attached 86th Fld. Co. returned.	

T2134. Wt. W708—776. 500000. 4/15. Sir J. C. & S.

WAR DIARY
or
INTELLIGENCE SUMMARY.
(Erase heading not required.)

Army Form C. 2118.

Place	Date	Hour	Summary of Events and Information	Remarks and references to Appendices
ENGLEBELMER			This unit in the 689. Outposts on north of GRANCRE advanced to new line. Two sections successfully carried out the consolidation of two strong points. A communication to French connecting trench advance was not dug.	
"	18/1/17		One section R.E. assisted infantry parties in making 3 Trs/m advanced posts.	
			Field Co. completed trenches over L 53rd Div. 7th Bn. to unite to dugouts at CRUCIFIX CORNER for work under C.R.E. 3rd Div One. Handing over to C.R.E. 53rd Division.	
"	19/1/17		Handing over completed + H.Q. moved to MARIEUX.	
MARIEUX	20/1/17		Major DENISON O.C. 68 F.d Co. left to take up appointment as C.R.E. 30th Division.	
BERNAVILLE	21/1/17		Moved to BERNAVILLE.	
YVRENCH	22/1/17		Moved to YVRENCH. Q.M.S.M. TREMAIN firing.	
"	23/1/17		Arranging to supply of materials. H.E. LITTLE proceed on leave.	
"	24/1/17		Parties of attached 280 & A.T. Co. working on consolidation of material.	

Army Form C. 2118.

WAR DIARY
or
INTELLIGENCE SUMMARY.
(Erase heading not required.)

Instructions regarding War Diaries and Intelligence Summaries are contained in F. S. Regs., Part II. and the Staff Manual respectively. Title pages will be prepared in manuscript.

Place	Date	Hour	Summary of Events and Information	Remarks and references to Appendices
YVRENCH 20E	26/1/17		Continuous & repairs to billets in Div: Area assisted by infantry working parties.	
"	27/1/17		288ª A/T. Co. detached for work at R.E. Dump AUX1. Leave = 1 N.C.O. + 10 sappers attached to H.Q. - Major SOMERVILLE, 573 Co. proceed on leave. Relieving & bathing accommodation at YVRENCH in progress.	
"	28/1/17		Lt. Col. F.A.K. WHITE proceeded on 14 days leave to U.K.	
"	29-30/1/17		Repairs to billets & construction of gas chamber at YVRENCH in progress.	
"	31/1/17		do. do. Sunl. hill, 6 E.YORKS R. transferred to R.E. & proceed to POPERINGHE on duty.	

C P Hingford
Captain & Adjutant, R.E.
11th Division.

WAR DIARY for month of February, 1917.

C.R.E.

~~67th Fd.~~ Co. R.E.

68th Fd. Co. R.E.

~~86th Fd.~~ Co. R.E.

Army Form C. 2118.

WAR DIARY
or
INTELLIGENCE SUMMARY.
(Erase heading not required.)

C.R.E. 11th Division

Place	Date	Hour	Summary of Events and Information	Remarks and references to Appendices
YVRENCH	1/2/17		Work on improvements to billets at YVRENCH in progress. Major BRATT 88th	
"	2/2/17		Fd. Co. left for course at R.E. School. Four Men in hosp. received from Field Cos.	
"	3/2/17		Two men inoc. hosp. received. 11 Rt. LISLE 67 Fd. Co. left to join R.M.O.	
"	5/2/17		Field Co. moved from Cunifu Corner to EIENVILLERS, distribution as per Form from ACHEUX to CANDAS.	
"	6/2/17		Field Co. marched from EIENVILLERS to the following locations:- 67 F.C. to LONGVILLERS, 68 F.C. to MAISON ROLLAND and 85 F.C. to NESVIL DOMQUEUR. Major SOMERVILLE returned from leave. Two men in hosp. at YVRENCH complete, work on the improvements continued as they are not now required.	
"	9/2/17		Division Horseshow from 4th to 13th Corps. Election of 1st Divisional Camp Commandant in progress Horses & Carcases paraded at CRAMONT.	
"	10/2/17		Capt. BUDDLE returned from sick leave.	
"	11/2/17		Nissen huts returned to Army.	203

Army Form C. 2118.

WAR DIARY
or
INTELLIGENCE SUMMARY.
(Erase heading not required.)

Instructions regarding War Diaries and Intelligence Summaries are contained in F.S. Regs., Part II. and the Staff Manual respectively. Title pages will be prepared in manuscript.

Place	Date	Hour	Summary of Events and Information	Remarks and references to Appendices
YVRENCH	12/2/17		Major R.E.B. PRATT returned from R.E. short L/t Course. Capt. BEAUFIELD returned from leave; Lt. Col. WHITE returned from leave; Capt. TOWNSEND attached for instruction.	
"	13/2/17		Lt. KINGSFORD rejoined 66 Field Coy, arranged work to start work at LONGVILLERS sawmill.	
"	14/2/17		Made efforts to purchase forest timber for purpose of erecting to front by road and local owners are not willing to sell. Field Companies occupied in training.	
"	15"		" "	
"	16/2/17		Capt. R.E.B. PRATT left for Junior Staff Course at HESDIN; training cond. Capt. TOWNSEND made a farewell inspection, visits intended to 66 Coy for instruction. Demonstration of trench diggings with use of explosives on fresh ground by 66 Field Co.	
"	17/2/17			
"	18/2/17		Training continued	
"	19/2/17		" "	
CANAPLES	20/2/17		Moved to CANAPLES; 3 Field Companies to PERNOIS.	
"	21/2/17		Capt. CANNELL (Lineham) attached for instruction.	
"	22/2/17		Infantry parties attached to 67 & 68 Coys reported for instruction.	

Army Form C. 2118.

WAR DIARY
or
INTELLIGENCE SUMMARY.
(Erase heading not required.)

Instructions regarding War Diaries and Intelligence Summaries are contained in F.S. Regs., Part II. and the Staff Manual respectively. Title pages will be prepared in manuscript.

Place	Date	Hour	Summary of Events and Information	Remarks and references to Appendices
MARIEUX	23/2/17		Moved to MARIEUX. 67th to BEAUQUESNE. 68th MARIEUX. 58 to PAINCHEVAL.	
"	25/2/17		Major SOMERVILLE and Capt. G.A. BUDDLE proceeded to R.E. School of Instruction LE PATCQ. Lieut. G.N. KINGSFORD took over duties as Acting Adjt.	
"	26/2/17		Capt. A.C. GLASS R.A.M.C. returned from leave. 2Lt. A.F. REID and 11th Rft. J.N. FOX joined, posted to 68th Coy. & 57th Coy. respectively.	
"	27/2/17		83 Field Coy. moved to 62 Div. Area for work in craters under C.C. S.T. Corps located in shelters near HAMEL.	
"	28/2/17		67th & 68th Field Cos. engaged in training.	

C.M. Kingsford
Lieut. & Adjt.
1/3/17

WAR DIARY.

March 1917.

C.R.E.

67th. Fd. Coy.
68th. "   "
86th. "   "

Army Form C. 2118.

WAR DIARY
or
INTELLIGENCE SUMMARY.

C.R.E. 11th Division

(Erase heading not required.)

Instructions regarding War Diaries and Intelligence Summaries are contained in F. S. Regs., Part II. and the Staff Manual respectively. Title pages will be prepared in manuscript.

Place	Date	Hour	Summary of Events and Information	Remarks and references to Appendices
MARIEUX	1/3/17		67th and 58th Field Co. training at BEAUQUESNE and MARIEUX respectively. 88 F Co. near HAMEL on road-repairs. Q.18498.	
"	3/3/17		3 Officers and 120 O.R.s of 87th F.A. Co. attached to VARENNES. Working in mud. French trenches.	
"	6/3/17		Lieut. S. HERMAN joined 88 I Field Co.	
"	8/3/17		1 Section of 88th F.M. Co. attached to I Army Infantry School at DOMART. Maj. S. DAVIES & Capt. BUDDLE returned from R.E. school	
"	9/3/17		Remainder of 68 F Co. proceeded to BERTANGLES	
"	10/3/17		HQ. & remaining personnel of 67 Field Co. proceeded to LOUVENCOURT to man newer cost.	
"	11/3/17		C.E.E. Corps: Lt Col WHITE proceeded to COISY to collect H. ready information	
COIGNEUX	12/3/17		R.E. HdQrs moved to COIGNEUX; Lieut. A.F. REID transferred from 68 to 67 Field Co. Lt E. RIMMINGTON transferred from 67th to 68th Field Co to date 15/3/17	
"	13/3/17			
"	14/3/17		Barracks unite through GOMMECOURT	
"	17/3/17		nil	
"	18/3/17			

Army Form C. 2118.

WAR DIARY
or
INTELLIGENCE SUMMARY.
(Erase heading not required.)

CRE 11th Division

Instructions regarding War Diaries and Intelligence Summaries are contained in F. S. Regs., Part II. and the Staff Manual respectively. Title pages will be prepared in manuscript.

Place	Date	Hour	Summary of Events and Information	Remarks and references to Appendices
MARIEUX	19/3/17		HQrs moved back to MARIEUX	
"	20/3/17		nil	
"	21/3/17		2/Lt RADCLIFFE attached for instruction. Capt. MAY attached to 67th Field Co. for instruction	
"	22.3.17			
"	23.3.17		2/Lt RADCLIFFE returned to DHQ	
"	24.3.17		All Field Company moved to MARIEUX. Attached officers rejoined their units	
"	25.3.17		Parade of all companies for divine service	
"	26.3.17		Lt DUFF left unit to proceed on leave	
"	27.3.17		Training. Lt. MAY attached for instruction	
"	28.3.17		"	
"	29.3.17		"	
"	30.3.17		Lt. MAY returned to DHQ. 2/Lt. CLAM attached to Field Coys.	
"	31.3.17		"	

W A R   D I A R Y.

April 1917.

H.Q., R.E.

~~87th. Field Coy.~~
~~88th.   "   "~~
~~86th.   "   "~~

Army Form C. 2118.

WAR DIARY
or
INTELLIGENCE SUMMARY.
(Erase heading not required.)

CRE. 11th Division

Instructions regarding War Diaries and Intelligence Summaries are contained in F. S. Regs., Part II. and the Staff Manual respectively. Title pages will be prepared in manuscript.

Place	Date	Hour	Summary of Events and Information	Remarks and references to Appendices
MARIEUX	1/4/17		Company training. Improved pack road being made. Also RAINHAM fan camp.	
"	2/4/17		Quiet day – a pack arrival.	
"	5/4/17		" "	
"	6/4/17		124 KAJMAHS handed over to S M A Sub-sec D.A.C. 13 improvised pack-saddles for camps.	
"	7-9/4/17		Non active – weather. Training continued.	
"	11/4/17		67 Coy moved to MAILLY MAILLET + 86 Coy to ACHEUX doing road work. 9 officers, horses on arrival. (I Corp area)	
ACHEUX	12/4/17		Moved to ACHEUX.	
"	13/4/17		86 Field Coy commenced work on improvement of tracks for Divisional Report FORCEVILLE. Major PRATT returned from leave – pursuing employment of Sunken Shaft Shoot ?	
"	14/4/17		CRE visited bridging school at AILLY.	
"	15/4/17		67 Coy + 1 battalion of pack cont. employed carrying pipe line in vicinity of MAILLY MAILLET – contracts roadway & culvert at ATTIE	
"	16.4/17 to 18/4/17		Work on report + roadway work continued.	
"	19/4/17		67 Coy moved to AVELUY – 6 & 8 Coy to BUZINCOURT. 86 Coy to huts in W.10.	

Army Form C. 2118.

WAR DIARY
or
INTELLIGENCE SUMMARY.
(Erase heading not required.)

Instructions regarding War Diaries and Intelligence Summaries are contained in F. S. Regs., Part II. and the Staff Manual respectively. Title pages will be prepared in manuscript.

Place	Date	Hour	Summary of Events and Information	Remarks and references to Appendices
OVILLERS	20/4/17		Moved to huts at OVILLERS	
N. 11 Cohen	21/4/17		Moved to huts at Nicotine (sheet 57C), taking over from II Aust. Division. 67 Field Co. BEAULENCOURT. 68 Field Co in BAPAUME. 86 Field Co at AVESNES	
	22/4/17		Work on roads & salvage of shelters	
	24.4.17		Took over from CRE 1st Aust. Division; 67th Coy moved to LEBUCQUIERE. 68 Coy to BEUGNY & moved up to FREMICOURT. (tents & huts)	
	25/4/17		86 Field Co moved up to FREMICOURT. (tents & huts)	
	26/4/17		67 & 86 Coy engaged in repair of forward village tracks, Organi, Damicourt, MORCHIES & LOUVERVAL, also in opening up wells; 86 Coy engaged on return of country tracks etc & repair of Beaumetz - Morchies line of defence. Division RE Dump established on new BAPAUME - CAMBRAI Rd. between BEUGNY & FREMICOURT, stone brought by by/night from transfer from BAPAUME railway & from existing dumps in barracks.	
	27/4/17		Capt. ACT. WHITE 1st Yorkshire Regt attached for instruction	
	28/4/17 to 30/4/17		Work continued as above	

Somewhat shortened. 11th Div.

WAR DIARY or INTELLIGENCE SUMMARY

Army Form C. 2118.

CRE 11th Division

Place	Date	Hour	Summary of Events and Information	Remarks and references to Appendices
Sheet 57C				
N11 central	1/5/17		Companies employed on upkeep of forward villages (67th Coy HERMES, DOIGNIES & DEMICOURT)	
			68 Coy LOUVERAL & BOURSIES) 66 Coy in reserve quarters Dick Bush.	
			Learning & Craons etc & repairing work of 34 Brigade on Bisamu sidings.	
			line of defences. All companies also employed in opening up mills especially	
			Marcoits, Bergny, DOIGNIES & HAPLINCOURT. Dugouts & TM dug at	
			1.20.6.6.6. Stores sent up by horse & lorry transport from lines at	
			dumps at BEAUMENCOURT GUEUDECOURT etc in L/R Sector (work of Canadian Rly)	
"	2.5.17		67 Coy relieved by 81 ? in L/R Sector (work of Canadian Rly)	
"	3.5.17 to		Work as usual.	
"	8.5.17		67 Field relieved by 68 Coy	
"	9.5.17		Work as usual	
"	10/5/17		Arrangements for 2 hrs for day on ANZAC LIGHT Railway to take relief for Rinin railway	
"	11-5-17		Bapaume to Bertyny & Velu in alternate days.	
"	12-5-17		Work as usual: cutting gangways at New DHQ 1.26 central	EMS
"	14-5-17		CRE 48 Div came up in preparation for taking over	
			Handed over to CRE 48 Division	

Army Form C. 2118.

WAR DIARY
or
INTELLIGENCE SUMMARY.
(Erase heading not required.)

CRE 11th DIVISION

Place	Date	Hour	Summary of Events and Information	Remarks and references to Appendices
ALBERT	14/5/17 to 16/5/17		Moved to ALBERT in preparation for entrainment to new area.	
	16/5/17		Capt GLASS R.A.M.C. left for England on 17th	
	18/5/17		Entrained at EDGEHILL 3 miles from ALBERT on	
	19/5/17		morning of 19th. 2nd ARMY area. Joined 9th Corps on arrival. 3 T.S.T.M.	
St JANS CAPPEL			Coy billeted in this area. Division in Corps Reserve	
	20/5/17		Lt KINGSFORD left for England on short leave	
	21/5/17		Capt MEEK R.A.M.C. joined as M.O. ¹⁄c R.E.	
			C.R.A. for preparation of gun positions etc.	
	22/5/17		Dismounted portion of 68 & 86 Field Coys attached to 58 & 59 Bdes R.F.A. for work on construction	
			of gun pits in 16th Div area in which 11 Div Arty are located.	
	23/5/17	"	" Lt A.F. REID rejoined 67 Coy from hospital	
	24/5/17	"	67 Field Coy commence work in 9 Corp Reinforcement Camp at BERTHEN	
	25/5/17	"	H.P. of all field companies moved into Brigade groups in 9 Corp Reserve area.	
	26/5/17 to 29/5/17	"	67 Coy continue work in 9 Corp Reinforcement Camp.	
		"	" Commenced work on Divl. Baths at ST JANS CAPPELL	
	30/5/17 31/5/17	"	86 Coy returned from work with R.A. 68 " " " " " "	

BAPBERNARD
Capt + adj R.E.
fr CRE. 11th Div

T134. Wt. W708-776. 500000. 4/15. Sir J. C. & S.

HANDING OVER NOTES.　　　　　　14.5.17.

DEFENCES.　　　　　Vide Map attached.

The defences consist of a series of detached posts and are divided up as under :-

(a) Front system consisting of Front line, Support line and Reserve line.
(b) The BEAUMETZ-MORCHIES line.
(c) The BEAUMETZ and MORCHIES village defences.
(d) The Corps (YTRES-BEUGNY) line.

As regards the posts in (a) they require e improvement which should be carried out by the Garrisons holding them. The front line posts in the Left Sector have been to a large extent joined together by communication trenches and this should be continued throughout both Sectors.

As regards (b) the posts are completed but the wire wants improving. As regards (c) the posts have been dug, but they require extension to bring more flanking fire to cover one another and communication trenches are required from all back into the villages. Only a small portion of the wiring has been started. *Plan showing proposals is attached.*
(d) This is the Corps line and work required on it is carried out by Division in Corps reserve.
new scheme for extension of this line vide notes by C.E. V. Army is attached marked. Z.

DUGOUTS.　　　　　Sketches attached.

Two Sections of the 258th Tunnelling Coy are available for work in the Division Area. These are employed on dugouts as under :-

1 Section (less party of 24 making dugout for Railway Control Officer at FREMICOURT) with Left Brigade.
　　New Brigade Headquarters at I.12.b.7.3.
　　Headquarters for M.G.Coy at I. 6.c.2.5.

1 Section with Right Brigade.
　　Battalion Headquarters　　at J.18.b.3.0.
　　　　"　　　　"　　　　　at J.29.b.5.5.
　　　　"　　　　"　　　　　at J.20.c.8.8.
　　　　"　　　　"　　　　　at J.34.d.2.4.
　　Divnl O.P.　　　　　　　at K.25.a.8.2.

Inaddition the following dugouts are in hand under the supervision of the Field Companies, for the accommodation of Battalion and Coy Headquarters. (Sketches attached)

　　Battalion Headquarters　　at C.30.d.5.5.
　　Battalion Headquarters　　at J.10.a.9.8.
　　Battalion Headquarters　　at J. 4.b.7.1.
　　Battalion Headquarters　　at J.17.a.7.7.
　　Company　 Headquarters　　at J. 2.a.5.5.
　　Company　 Headquarters　　at J. 2.b.2.8.
　　Company　 Headquarters　　at C.30.d.7.3.
　　Company　 Headquarters　　at J. 1.d.2.3.

One Platoon of Pioneers is allotted for work in each Sector for assistance with dugouts.

NEW DIVISIONAL HEADQUARTERS.

Site for a new Divisional Headquarters has been selected in the hollow road running from I.36.a.9.3. to b.1.9. Sites for huts have been cut into bank and the erection of 6 Greenlees Huts is inhand, and Signal Office has been erected. Three dugouts as shown on plan have been commenced, the work being carried out by 2 Platoons of Pioneers.

The Location of the three Field Companies is as under :-

    a.   LEBUCQUIERE   I.30.a.7.7. for work in the Right Sector
    b.   BEUGNY   I.22.a.9.9. for work in the Left Sector
    c.   I.27.c.1.8.   for work in the Reserve Brigade Area

Details of work in hand by the Companies have been handed over to relieving Company.

The Pioneers are in Camp at I.33.d.7.0.
They are employed as follows :-

    1 Platoon   dugout shelters in Right Sector
    1 Platoon   dugout shelters in Left Sector
    2 Platoons dugouts in new D.H.Q.
    2 Platoons erection of huts and draining of new D.H.Q.
    Remainder on roads (vide road report attached)

Separate reports on ROads, Water Supply, Dumps and Supply of R.E. material are attached.

BRIDGES.

Materials and trestles for two foot bridges over the CANAL DU NORD which it is proposed should be erected if more ground be gained about K.31.b.5.6. have been collected and stored by the side of the road in K.36.b.

F. A. K. White Lt Col
CRE XI Div
14/5/17

HANDING OVER REPORT.

F Coy

BATH VELU

These are practically finished.
The ironing arrangements want completing and possibly some furniture for store room also the flooring is not finished. I attach a plan of Baths but this does not show an ironing room. I propose turning one of the store rooms into an ironing room. Twenty men have been employed on this.

DAM ON CANAL. J.35.a.31.

This is to prevent water in Canal being drained out by the enemy. There is some work to be done in completing this. About two courses of sandbags have been added above level of shell way and earth filling between these bags is not complete. As any shell may destroy this dam I suggest another dam should be built a couple of hundred yards from this.

WELLS.

J.16.a.8.6. at DOIGNES (Map 57c)
This well has now about 3 feet of water standing and a pump will be required before further clearing is done. A lift and force pump, if in good working order, may clear this but work will probably have to be continuous for the 24 hours.

J.30.a.2.9. (Map 57c). J.29.b.9.1. (Map 57c).
Both these wells in HERMIES.
Water has not been struck yet and wells contain debris of varying kinds, mostly bricks and soil from the spoil of craters blown in top.
Five men have been working on each of these wells.

Spring in Canal at J.3.d.0.0.
A pump (Lift and Force) has been established here to pump up to tank on Canal bank. Capacity of tank about 50 galls.

This point could be used for filling water carts but a road would have to be made from Bridge-head west of Slag Heap to tank. Very little work is required to make it passable. There is an excellent supply of water which has been passed for drinking purposes.

ELEPHANT SHELTERS.

J.18.b.4.1. The excavation for this is about 50% complete. The shelter is to be 16 feet x 9 feet 3". Material is on site. This is intended for an advanced Battalion Headquarters.

J.30.b.7.5. One section of Iron work to be completed and Sandbags put over roof. About 80% complete.
Work for 20 men for one night under R.E. supervision.
This is intended for Company Headquarters. 16 feet x 9 feet 3"

A table shewing state of posts in line (except outposts) is attached.

LIST OF MAPS AND PLANS WITH HANDING OVER REPORTS.

R.   General Map of Defences.

R.1   Notes on conditions of Posts.

S.   Lists of Posts with Garrisons.

T.   Plan of village Defences of BEAUMETZ-MORCHIES.

U.   Plan of BEUGNY-YTRES line.

V.   Details of dugouts under construction.

W.   Plan of new Divisional Headquarters.

X.   Road Map.

Y.   Rough sketches of proposed defence of Slag Heap. K.20 Central.

Z.   Notes by C.E. Fifth Army on proposed extension of the BEAUMETZ-MORCHIES line.

Copies of Field Company handing over reports.

List of stores in Dumps.

ROADS. The repairs to the Roads have been worked on a general scheme of providing three roads running forward viz

1. The BAPAUME-CAMBRAI main road.
2. The FREMICOURT-LEBUCQUIERE-HERMIES road.
3. The BAPAUME-BANCOURT-HAPLINCOURT-BERTINCOURT road.

In addition the following cross roads have been taken in hand :-

4. BANCOURT to FREMICOURT.
5. HAPLINCOURT to BEUGNY.
6. BERTINCOURT-VELU-LEBUCQUIERE.

1. **BAPAUME-CAMBRAI Road.**
Maintenance has been taken over by Corps Roads Officer as far as BEET ROOT Factory in I.17.
Beyond this the road comes into view of the enemy and there are a few shell holes in it.
The crater in J.13 has been filled in and that in J.9 is nearly filled in.
A culvert across the road in J.10. has been blown in and not yet repaired.
The above work can only be executed at night.

2. **FREMICOURT-HERMIES Road.**
Has been taken over by Corps Roads Officer as far as LEBUCQUIERE. From LEBUCQUIERE it is proposed to run the road to VELU then towards BEAUMETZ to J.19.d.41 and thence by a deviation across the fields to J.20.d.03 and thence along the existing road to HERMIES.
The craters at VELU have been filled in also crater at J.20.d.03
The deviation from J.19.d.4.1 to J.20.d.0.3. has been marked out by a ditch cut each side and a portion of the road is covered with broken brick as a foundation. Forward of this point the road is in fair condition except for some shell holes which require filling.

3. **BAPAUME-BERTINCOURT Road.**
Is in fair condition as far as is possible using broken brick only for repairs. Metal is urgently required over the whole length, and Corps Roads Officer should take over this road in order that it may be metalled.

4. **BANCOURT to FREMICOURT.**
In good condition but requires metal in places.

5. **HAPLINCOURT to BEUGNY.**
In good condition except crater in I.34.c. which has been recently filled in and requires metal.

6. **BERTINCOURT-VELU.**
In fairly good condition but requires metal in parts.

7. **HAPLINCOURT-VELU.**
Is now under repair and in fair condition as far as the cross roads at I.29.d.62. From I.d.62 to the cross roads at I.30.d.22 the road is unmetalled and at present impassable except by a dry weather track running alongside. From I.30.d.22 to VELU is in fair condition. Metal is required in all places where holes have been filled in with brick. This road will be the main approach to new Divisional Headquarters at I.36.b.19.

8. **Cross Road from I.29.b.63 to I.29.d.62.**
Is in fair condition but requires side drains clearing.

9. **BEET ROOT Factory (I.17.d.58) to MORCHIES.**
No repairs have been done on this road. The surface is in fair condition but side drains require clearing.

10. **BEAUMETZ to J.8.c.22.**
Is in good condition and no repairs are required at present.

WATER SUPPLY.

1. Corps Systems.

Deep bores have been put down at following points :-

1. FREMICOURT   I.19.b.5.5.   (1000-1500 horses per hour)
2. FREMICOURT   I.26.central   (700- 1000 horses per hour)
3. VELU   J.31.a.3.8.   (1000-1500 horses per hour)
4. HAPLINCOURT   O. 3.d.5.1.

These are all in use at present except No.4 which is expected to be ready about 16th inst.
The wells are fitted with air lifts and water is distributed from reservoirs to 2 or more large horse watering points and to stand pipes for water cart filling.
No long pipe line exists.
Divisions are not concerned with maintenance of these systems except for policing.

2. Divisional.

FREMICOURT I.25.b.0.8. chain helice pump driven by petrol engine used for filling water carts
BEUGNY I.16.c.5.0. chain helice pump hand driven
DOIGNIES J.16.a.central   "   "   "   "

Wells at MORCHIES in use are as follows :-
     I.6.c.1.2.
     I.5.d.8.3.
     I.5.d.3.1.
There are no pumps fitted.
Work is being done at present on the following wells which are being opened up and cleared
     J.16.a.8.6.
     J.30.a.2.9.
     J.29.b.9.7.
Work on wells in HAPLINCOURT has been stopped as the new bore will be ready in a few days.
A large spring at J.34.d.0.0. is being opened up and casing put in.
A dam across the Canal at J.35.a.3.1. is being repaired
The Army are preparing to put in a plant capable of delivering about 6000 gallons per hour about here. The water if chlorinated is fit for drinking purposes.
It is suggested that, when labour is available, a second dam should be put across the Canal near the present one, in case of damage to the latter.

NOTE.   Some wells opened up have not been satisfactory owing to the amount of refuse in them. Continuous pumping would probably clear them.

Army Form C. 2118.

WAR DIARY
or
INTELLIGENCE SUMMARY.
(Erase heading not required.)

CRE 11th Division   Vol 12

Place	Date	Hour	Summary of Events and Information	Remarks and references to Appendices
ST. JANS CAPPEL	1-6-17		Reorganise camp complete.	
"	2-6-17		81 Field Co. commenced work on camp for 1000 slightly wounded at BERTHEN	
			Lt. KINGSFORD returned from leave. Major Frazier 2nd i/c ETAPLES on 21 days leave.	
"	3-6-17		67 Field Coy doing available work on roads; also for sheet iron huts etc: officers	
"	4-6-17		Captains during outdoor schools in Corps area & communication to front line	
"	5-6-17		General instruction for tin roofs issued (extracts from Corps & Divisional orders)	
"	6-6-17		68 Field Coy attached to 16th Division for attack	
"	7-6-17		68 Field Coy employed in construction of starting points in support of near OOSTAVERNE	
			LINE: 2 Lt. GILLOTT killed by shellfire. 3 NCO's wounded.	
"	8-6-17		Work continues on starting points by 68 Field Co. 14 O.R. wounded in enemy barrage.	
"	9-6-17		D.H.Q. moved to DRANOUTRE & took over command of the line for 16th & 36th Division	
			Also part of the line from 25th Div & 4 Aust. Div on right of 9 Corps front	
"	10-6-17		34 Bde relieved part of 33 Bde on left Divisional front	
"	11-6-17		32 Bde " " " & 25th & Aust. Div.	
"	12-6-17		Work of consolidation being pushed forward.	
"	13-6-17		67 Coy employed in fixing up roads & clearing & repairing dugouts once moving to A43	

Army Form C. 2118.

WAR DIARY
or
INTELLIGENCE SUMMARY.
(Erase heading not required.)

C.R.E. 11th Division

Place	Date	Hour	Summary of Events and Information	Remarks and references to Appendices
DRANOUTRE	13.6.17		Forward camp. Also tracing out communication trench in front of Black Line & supervising working parties. 86 Coy on similar work; 68 Coy in Reserve. Pioniers working on road forward from old Bosche front line.	
"	14.6.17		67 & 86 Coys spring up mills, making dugouts in forward areas & supervising work on C.T.s; 68 Field Co supervising working parties on making mule tracks	
"	16.6.17		up to forward area.	
"	17.6.17		Spur on 60 cm light Railway in front of store Farm spur in hand. Also construction of connecting spur from Tramway system to right. Section to run on Rau Die RE Dump now in connection with Zevecoten Corps Park. Consin tracks of workshops at LINDENHOEK matured being moved up from DRANOUTRE. Capt. CABUDDEL left for England on short leave.	EWS
"	18.6.17		2/Lt. BRIDGEWATER joined 68th Field Co. 2/Lt. J.N. FOX attached to R.H.Q.	
"	19.6.17		New Field Co relieved by 30th Div. & moved back to DRANOUTRE and St. JANS CAPEL Areas.	
METRIS	20.6.17		Handed over to 35th Div. O.P. & moved to METRIS. Lt. G. WHITE proceeded to 18th Corps HQ. Pro. near POPERINGHE.	2118

Army Form C. 2118.

WAR DIARY
or
INTELLIGENCE SUMMARY.
(Erase heading not required.)

C.R.E. 11th DIV.

Place	Date	Hour	Summary of Events and Information	Remarks and references to Appendices
MERRIS	21-6-17		The two Field Cos. moved to MERRIS Area.	
"	22-6-17		Lt. Col. WHITE returned from Corps HQ Gas. Two Field Cos. moved to CAESTRE AREA.	
RENESCURE	23-6-17		Head Quarters moved to RENESCURE and 68th Field Co. to LA CROSSE. 67th and 88th Field Co. moved to PESELHOEK for work under orders of C.E. 18th Corps.	
EPERLECQUES	24-6-17		Head Quarters moved to EPERLECQUES.	
"	26-6-17		Arranging for supply of materials - Training also from 10th Corps Park (PESELHOEK) and for a wooden bridge from BOISDINGHAM. 68th Field Co training.	
"	27-6-17		do.	
"	28-6-17		do. Lt. C.H. WHITE proceeded on short leave.	
"	29-6-17		Capt. BUDDLE returned from leave. Lt. FOX returned to 67th Field Co. 68th Field Co training & making settlement tanks for Div. Sawmills.	
"	30-6-17		68th Field Co. do.	

J.M. Kingsford
Captain & Adjutant, R.E.
11th Division

1913.

WAR DIARY.

July, 1917.

C.R.E. 11th Division.

H.Q.

~~67th Field Coy.~~ R.E.

~~68th~~   "   "   "

~~86th~~   "   "   "

Army Form C. 2118.

WAR DIARY
or
INTELLIGENCE SUMMARY.
(Erase heading not required.)

C.R.E. 11 DIV.

Place	Date	Hour	Summary of Events and Information	Remarks and references to Appendices
EPERLECQUES	1-7-17		68th Field Co. training + working in Divisional Parks.	
"	2-7-17		68th Field Co. moved on orders for work under C.R.E. 8th Corps Troops = Head quarters + two sections to ARNEKE, one section to ESQUELBECQ and one section to WATTEN.	
"	3-7-17		Major SOMERVILLE returned from leave.	
"	4-7-17		12 men of 68th Field Co. continued work on setting lambs of Div. Parks. Work delayed for want of transport to obtain bricks etc.	
"	5-7-17		Work on Parks continued.	
"	6-7-17		68th Field Co. moved back to WESTROVE for work on new Headquarters of 5th Corps.	
"	7-7-17		68th Field Co. commenced work on erecting Expansion Huts + Huts at GIVENCHY Château for 5th Corps H.Q. Work on Div. Parks discontinued.	
"	8-7-17		Work on Corps Head Quarters and Div. Parks continued. Lt. Col. WHITE returned from leave.	
"	9.7.17 to 12.7.17		" " " "	
"	13.7.17 to 26.7.17		6's coy employed on construction of Corp. H.Q. Qrs. near EPERLECQUES.	

Army Form C. 2118.

WAR DIARY
or
INTELLIGENCE SUMMARY.
(Erase heading not required.)

CRE 11th DIVISION

Instructions regarding War Diaries and Intelligence Summaries are contained in F.S. Regs., Part II. and the Staff Manual respectively. Title pages will be prepared in manuscript.

Place	Date	Hour	Summary of Events and Information	Remarks and references to Appendices
EPERLECQUES	21.7.17		G & Coy checking & repairing tools, equipment etc.	
"	22.7.17			
WORMHOUDT	23.7.17		Hd Qrs moved to WORMHOUDT.	
"	24.7.17		6 & Field Company moving under orders of 34 Bde. CRE	
POPERINGHE	25.7.17		Hd Qrs moved to POPERINGHE: 67 & 86 Coys come under orders of 11th Division.	
"	26.7.17 to 29.7.17		nil	
"	30.7.17		6 & Field Coy joined 67 & 86; 86, 67, 34(minor) in all under orders to CRE 11th under orders of C.E. 18th Corps for work on roads after gun.	
"	31.7.17		6th East Yorks commenced work on 6 a.m. on road & track between Canal de L'YSER & old No man's land (POND COTTAGE - BURNT FARM - LA BELLE ALLIANCE - BOUNDARY ROAD - FRONT LINE; sheet 28.N.W.2.) 67 & 68 Field Coy commenced work on rear portion of this road at 3 p.m. to arrive 121st Labour company under Lt. MANISTY R.E. Road was passable for guns up to old front line by 9 a.m. work continued repairing & widening.	

T.J.134. Wt. W708—776. 500000. 4/16. Sir J. C. & S.

WAR DIARY. AUGT. 1917

C.R.E. 11th Division.
    ~~67th Field Coy. R.E.~~
    ~~68th Field Coy. R.E.~~
    86th Field Coy. R.E.

August 1917   Volume I

Army Form C. 2118.

WAR DIARY
or
INTELLIGENCE SUMMARY.
(Erase heading not required.)

CRE 11th DIVISION

Place	Date	Hour	Summary of Events and Information	Remarks and references to Appendices
POPERINGHE	1-8-17		6th East Yorks + 67 + 68 Field Coys continued work on POND COTTAGE - BURNT FARM - LA BELLE ALLIANCE - BOUNDARY ROAD. Weather very bad, rain all night. 6th East Yorks took over from 51st Div. consolidation of tracks as far as BELOW FARM.	
"	2/8/17 3/8/17		Ditto. Weather very bad, little progress made.	
"	5/8/17		Weather improved. Little progress made.	
"	6-8-17		"	
"	7-8-17		Field Coys. Pioneers took over from units of 51st Div. 67 Coy & 8th Coy. 4th Pioneers moved into Canal Bank. 67 Coy on left forward sector. 86 Coy on right forward sector. 68 Coy in rear sector. Pioneers in rear + track forward from X on map Besselhoek	
"	8-8-17		Div HdQrs moved to huts at X camp near PESELHOEK	
X Camp A 16 c 2.3 Sheet 28	9-8-17 to 15-8-17		Roads made good up to GOURNIER FARM + HURST PARK. Duck board tracks completed to FRANCOIS FARM + FERDINAND FARM. Dugouts furnished out + repaired wherever possible in the Divisional area.	
"	16-8-17		Work on always forward commenced about 2 hours after Zero. Tracks M.29.d.1.9 + HANIXBEEK FARM completed without trouble completed by about 2.30 p.m. + handed over to Canadians	hits

Army Form C. 2118.

WAR DIARY
or
INTELLIGENCE SUMMARY.
(Erase heading not required.)

CRE. 11th Division

Place	Date	Hour	Summary of Events and Information	Remarks and references to Appendices
A16.c.23 Sheet 28	16.8.17		Section for work on above points in night were not able to get forward of C.5.b.6.0 owing to enemy working parties against our Strong points wandering there & was fired by snipers + working parties against our M.G. + rifle fire of the enemy: casualties 1 O.R. Killed + 4 wounded; it was known that about 7 p.m. to 8 p.m. N.F with a garrison of about 40. MILITARY BRIDGE over STEENBEEK repaired by masonry + bridge M & N were repaired by 5 p.m. 2nd Lt. J. N. Fox slightly wounded. Work on BOECHASTEL - REGINA CROSS ROAD covered two turn of a given; not much progress owing to heavy shell fire. Work on RUDOLPH FARM - VARNNA FARM ROAD carried on subsequently with no casualties.	
"	17.8.17		Coys + Pioneers employed on roads + tracks forward of Corps road limit (RUDOLPH FARM - CHEDDAR VILLA)	
"	16 Aug 18.8.17		Ditto 1 Coy of 6th East Yorks commenced work on Tramway from ADMIRALS Road - HURST PARK	
"	19.8.17		Continuation of above. 1 coy of infantry attached to Pioneers for accumulating materials used up by light Railway to ADMIRALS Road	RWB

Army Form C. 2118.

WAR DIARY
or
INTELLIGENCE SUMMARY.

(Erase heading not required.)

CRE 11th Div.

Instructions regarding War Diaries and Intelligence Summaries are contained in F. S. Regs., Part II. and the Staff Manual respectively. Title pages will be prepared in manuscript.

Place	Date	Hour	Summary of Events and Information	Remarks and references to Appendices
A.16.c.2.3 (Sht 28)	20.8.17		Work on roads continued. Field companies working track from Corps Road East to join up with Corps Road further to the East. Work up to 2nd Supplies Dump day. Work on Tramway continued. Work of doubling the chiltern track from HURST PARK to FERDINAND FARM started by 86 Coy. Lt. J.J.H. BROWN 67 Coy wounded.	
	23.8.17		ditto	
BONDEN CAMP A.30.B.23	24.8.17		Work on communications continues as above. 3 companies of infantry employed nightly. TRAMWAY laid from ADMIRALS ROAD to MINTY FARM with Spur into KEMPTON & MINTY. 2 large dugouts-shelters to 2nd Dressing Station nearly complete. Circuits being placed (at MINTY)	
"	25.8.17		1 section from each Field Coy withdrawn to go to horse lines for a rest.	
"	26.8.17		Work as above continued	
"	27.8.17		Allow coy 32 Bde in PHEASANT TRENCH. 2 sections of 67 Coy to stand by for continuation of strong point unable to go forward & returned to camp about 1 a.m. (1.30?)	
"	28.8.17		Work on chiltern track & promenade track continues. Lt. Col. FAN WHITE left for England on leave.	SMB

Army Form C. 2118.

WAR DIARY
or
INTELLIGENCE SUMMARY.
(Erase heading not required.)

CRE 11' Div

Place	Date	Hour	Summary of Events and Information	Remarks and references to Appendices
X CAMP	29.8.17		11: Div Recce HQrs moved back to X Corps: 3 Field Coys ord 51st Div: 67th & 88 Field Coy Accompanied. CAMMBANK 68 Field Co in Bivouac at ISLY FARM. 6 = East York withdrawn to Bivouac as A 30 colors for rest.	
"	30.8.17		67 Field Coy engaged on KEMPTON PARK - GOUDNIER FARM ROAD. 68 Field Co	
"	31.8. "		engaged on HURST PARK - KITCHEN EN. WOOD Road, working ROCHESTER - HURST PARK. 86 Field Co employed on for KEMMEL - HURST PARK - HURST PARK diversion.	

J.W/Brown/
Captain
T. CRE 11 Div

Army Form C. 2118.

WAR DIARY
or
INTELLIGENCE SUMMARY.
(Erase heading not required.)

CRE 11th DIVISION   Vol 15

Place	Date	Hour	Summary of Events and Information	Remarks and references to Appendices
X Camp A.16. c.2.3. Sheet 27	1.9.17 to 3.9.17		67 Field Co employed in repair of KEMPTON PARK – GROSVENOR FARM Road: 63rd Coy on HURST PARK – KITCHENERS WOOD Road: 86 Field Coy on KEMPTON PARK – PIONEER ROAD.	
"	4.9.17		63rd Coy East gate at rest. (D Reinforcement attached on 2nd for instruction & not relief (1st Coy on 4th))	
"	5.9.17		Allotment & distribution of work as follows: 67 Field Co to take over from KEMPTON PARK to Rudolph Farm and KEMPTON PARK – MINTY. 63 Coy MINTY FARM via HURST Park – New corner of Kitcheners Wood and a diversion from 50 yards south of MINTY to opposite the looting at HURST PARK, 50 Field to NW corner of KITCHENERS Wood to REGINA CROSS. 6th East yorks. still in rest.	
"	6.9.17		ditto (Major Fairfield returned from leave 8.9.17)	
"	9.9.17		67, 63 & 86 Field Cos relieve by 6 East yorks after work today: Capns moved leave to huts on ELVERDINGHE – POPERINGHE ROAD. 1 section of 67 Field Co sent down to HERZEELE for erection of huts at new D.H.Q. 6th BUNCE exlowly for now with C.R.E. CORPS TROOPS.	
"	10.9.17		Capt CRAMHALL left on leave for England: Major SOMERVILLE & Lt KINGSFORD left on 4 days leave to PARIS. 6th East yorks employed on roads as above, unit except 1 section from MINTY FARM – near HURST PARK which is taken over by A.T. Coy.	E.W.B

Army Form C. 2118.

WAR DIARY
or
INTELLIGENCE SUMMARY.
(Erase heading not required.)

CRE. 11 Div

Place	Date	Hour	Summary of Events and Information	Remarks and references to Appendices
X. Camp	10.9.17		The Company of 6" East yorks returned from the line are employed in clearing & repairing dugouts in KITCHENERS WOOD & old BOSCHE front line.	
"	11.9.17		ditto.	
"	12.9.17		Lt. Col. F.A.K. WHITE returned from England. Lt. WESTCOTT reports for attachment. Lt RUNCIMAN left 68 Coy for attachment to 59 Bde RFA. Major PRATT reports to 86 Field Co.	
"	13.9.17		Work on repairs dugouts continued. Lt. WESTCOTT went to 2nd Army HQ.	
"	14.9.17		"	
"	15.9.17		" Lt. O'Kelly left for England (leave).	
"	16.9.17		"	
"	17.9.17		"	
"	18.9.17		" Capt J.R. HOBSON left for England (leave).	
POPERINGHE	19.9.17		R.E. HQrs moved to POPERINGHE. Work as above continued.	
"	20.9.17		"	
"	21.9.17		Presentation of M.C. & M.M. ribbons by G.O.C.: regimental sports: work as above continued by 6 East yorks.	EWS

Army Form C. 2118.

WAR DIARY
or
INTELLIGENCE SUMMARY.
(Erase heading not required.)

C R E 11th Div

Place	Date	Hour	Summary of Events and Information	Remarks and references to Appendices
POPERINGHE	22-9-17		Pioneer Coy continue work on aircraft cleaning dugouts: 86 Field Coy at work on horse standings for 3 Tunnelling Companies on the line: 1 Coy of Pioneers on construction of horse standings for Pioneer Battalion ditto	files
"	23-9-17		ditto	
"	24-9-17		3 Field Companies took over work from 3 Field Coys of 61st Div. & moved to billets in CANAL BANK.	
BORDER CAMP	25-9-17 to 30 "		Div Hd Qrs moved to BORDER CAMP: 86 Field Coy on right sector. 67 Field Coy in mid sector. 68 Field Coy on right sector, work in huts repairing & relaying duckboard tracks: repairing dugouts: widening & repairing tramway. Field Coy & Pioneer Battalion on Canal front. Canadian 12 D.R.	

WAR DIARY or **INTELLIGENCE SUMMARY**

Army Form C. 2118.

OCTOBER 1917
CRE 11 DIVISION

Place	Date	Hour	Summary of Events and Information	Remarks and references to Appendices
BORDER CAMP.	1.10.17 to		Work on roads, duckboard tracks, etc. of divisional sector of front continues & provision siding at AUSTERLITZ and big canteens	
"	3.10.17		Advance D.HQ. in CANAL BANK	
"	4.10.17		Division attacked at 6 am. & return of 26 Field Coy. allotted for constant extensive repairing party of above post in right Bde rear, more forward 10-30 am and forward then repairs track before dark, casualties slight. 2 section of 68 Field Coy detailed for similar work in eff. Bry and section did not move forward till 7 pm.	
"	5-10-17 to		Work on roads, duckboard tracks, diggers and stables at AUSTERLITZ continues & Field Conference of Divisional Pioneers Brig.	
"	8-10-17		On LEKKERBOTERBEEK completed	
"	9-10-17		Division attacked at 5-20 a.m. One of the failure to reach its final objective, Another details of consolidation of shing trench were not sent forward. Work on roads, tramways etc. continued	
"	10-10-17		Field Coy's relieved by 18 Division	

Army Form C. 2118.

WAR DIARY
or
INTELLIGENCE SUMMARY.

(Erase heading not required.)

C.R.E. 11th Div.

Instructions regarding War Diaries and Intelligence Summaries are contained in F.S. Regs., Part II. and the Staff Manual respectively. Title pages will be prepared in manuscript.

Place	Date	Hour	Summary of Events and Information	Remarks and references to Appendices
POPERINGHE	11-10-17		R.E. Hd.Qrs. moved to POPERINGHE. Div. Hd.Qrs. to EPERLECQUES. Field Cos. & Pioneers employed on roads & shelters at AUSTERLITZ and GHENT Cuttings.	
"	12-10-17		Capt. BUDDLE A&F. proceeded to U.K. on 30 days leave.	
"	13-10-17		Major SOMERVILLE proceeded on 10 days leave. Lieut. E.R. CANHAM joined 68th Field Co.	
"	14-10-17		Work on roads and shelters continued.	
EPERLECQUES	15-10-17		R.E. Head Quarters rejoined 11th Div. at EPERLECQUES. Field Cos. moved as follows:- 67th to BLEUE MAISON, 68th to WESTROVE + 86th to MOULLE. Work carried on by S.R.E. for Pioneers who continue work under orders of C.E. XIII Corps.	
"	17-10-17		68th Field Co. moved to MATRINGHEM.	
NORRENT FONTES	18-10-17		Moved to NORRENT-FONTES. 86th Field Co. moved to ECQUEDECQUES.	
"	19-10-17		86th Field Co. moved to BULLY GRENAY.	
"	20-10-17		86th Field Co. taking over work from 509th Field Co. and 2 sections moved to advanced billets at ST PIERRE. 67th Field Co. moved to ECQUEDECQUES.	

Army Form C. 2118.

C.R.E. 11th Div.

WAR DIARY
or
INTELLIGENCE SUMMARY.
(Erase heading not required.)

Place	Date	Hour	Summary of Events and Information	Remarks and references to Appendices
NORRENT FONTES	21-10-17		Advanced parties of 67th & 68th Field Cos. taking over work from 459th and 12th Field Co. respectively. (Capt. O'HANHALL, 68th Field Co. left to take over command of 406th Fd Co. 45th Division.	
"	22-10-17		67th Field Co. moved to LES BREBIS.	
BRAQUEMONT	23-10-17		Moved to BRAQUEMONT and took over from CRE. 6th Div. – Lt H. W. OBSON. Joined 58th Field Co. 5th East Yorks Pioneers around BETHUNE from XIII Corps.	
"	24-10-17		83rd Field Co. working on Trenches & 7/9th line forward & on shelters at MAZINGARBE and LESBREBIS. 67th Field Co. (in reserve) nothing on.	
"	25-10-17		Dugouts, dressing stations and shelters. 68th Field Co. moved from MATTRINGHAM to LES BREBIS. 2 Officers & 100 O.Rs. of infantry attached to each Field Co. for work. One Coy. 6th E. Yorks (Pioneers) moved to MATTRINGHAM. In work on 1st Army trench system.	
"	26-10-17		Major SOMERVILLE returned from leave. Work continued as in 24th inst.	
"	27-10-17		67th Field Co. (in reserve) working on Communication Trenches, dugouts, dressing stations & by side from standing. 58th " " " " in reserve. General Communication trenches, pipeline repairs & by 10th River standing. 83rd " " " " " Large dugout near BOIS DE H.Q. and " " "	

Army Form C. 2118.

C.R.E. 11th Div.

WAR DIARY
or
INTELLIGENCE SUMMARY.
(Erase heading not required.)

Instructions regarding War Diaries and Intelligence Summaries are contained in F.S. Regs., Part II. and the Staff Manual respectively. Title pages will be prepared in manuscript.

Place	Date	Hour	Summary of Events and Information	Remarks and references to Appendices
BRAQUEMONT	28-10-17		Work continued as on 27th.	
"	29-10-17		" " " "	
"	30-10-17		67th Field Co. relieved by 68th Field Co. The latter going into Reserve.	
"	31-10-17.		Work continued.	

C.H.Kingsford.
Capt. & Adjt.
For C.R.E. 11 Div.

WAR DIARY or INTELLIGENCE SUMMARY

Army Form C. 2118.

Nov. 1917. C.R.E. 11 Div.

Vol 17

Place	Date	Hour	Summary of Events and Information	Remarks and references to Appendices
BRAQUEMONT	1/11/17		5th S. Yorks Pioneers kon on Coy. moved to MAROC for work on Communication Trenches.	
"	2/11/17		67th Field Co. working on Communication Trenches + Brigade Head Quarters + Bn. Hors Standings.	
			68th " " (in quarries) working on Communication Trench stations + Bn. Hors Standings.	
			86th " " " " " + Bn. Hors standings.	
			5th S. Yorks (P.) Kon on Coy " " tack communication from Edon.	
"	3/11/17		Work continued as on 2nd.	
"	4/11/17		" " " "	
"	5/11/17		" " " "	
"	6/11/17		Work continued as on 2nd. Major R.E.B. PRATT proceeded on 30 days leave, commencing from 7th inst. 11 Lt. HEBUNCE proceeded to Camouflage Course.	
"	7/11/17		Work continued as on 2nd. 11 2/Lt. PIMINGTON proceeded on 10 days leave. Q.M.S. M. WHITE proceeded on duty.	
"	8/11/17		88th Field Co. returned to 85th Field Co. for labor from its Coy's.	
"	9/11/17		67th Field Co. working on communication trenches + one sect. on Bn. Hors standings.	
"			" " " " + advance line, support for Bn. Hd. Qrs + 1 sect. on Bn. Hors standings.	
"			" " " " " + dugouts + Bn. Hors Standings + shelter for M.Vckrs.	
			11 Lt. BUNCE returned from Camouflage Course.	

Army Form C. 2118.

WAR DIARY
or
INTELLIGENCE SUMMARY.
(Erase heading not required.)

Instructions regarding War Diaries and Intelligence Summaries are contained in F. S. Regs., Part II. and the Staff Manual respectively. Title pages will be prepared in manuscript.

Place	Date	Hour	Summary of Events and Information	Remarks and references to Appendices
BRAQUEMONT	10/11/17		Raid on enemy front line trench at 9.a.m. Party of 67th Field Co. attached to Nor'mp. Buckshire was made to carry out Programme owing to failure to eject enemy bombers from weak. 68th Field Co. attached for working "Dummies" on flanks. Casualties to 67th Co., one killed & 3 wounded.	
"	11/11/17		Work carried on as on 9th. 2/Lt. R. LOCKHART proceeds on 2nd course of Instruction.	
"	12/11/17		"	
"	13/11/17		"	
"	14/11/17		" 2/Lt. D.P. O'KELLY proceeded on Veterinary Course.	
"	15/11/17		" Capt. G.A. BUDDLE returns from leave.	
"	16/11/17		"	
"	17/11/17		" Lt. Jones proceeds on Bridging course.	
"	18/11/17		" Capt. G.N. KINGSFORD left for England on leave.	
"	19/11/17		"	
"	20/11/17		"	
"	21/11/17		"	
"	22/11/17		"	

Army Form C. 2118.

WAR DIARY
or
INTELLIGENCE SUMMARY.
(Erase heading not required.)

CRE 11th Div

Place	Date	Hour	Summary of Events and Information	Remarks and references to Appendices
BRAYMONT	23.11.17 to 26.11.17		Work continued as above. Employ. 96 Eastyorks (Pioneers) who has been detailed for work under C.E.: Every returned today	
"	27.11.17		6): Field Coy tents over from 46 Field Coy of 46 Div) on HILL 70 sector on left of Divisional front. Chief work repair & improvement to C.T.s. (3 Brigade in in line) One section of said Field Coy has been continuously in reserve employed in repair to stables & horse standings & erection of huts at Transport lines of affiliated Brigade.	
"	28.11.17		Tramway from EDDY SPUR (N.7.a.27) towards CITE ST EMILE in hand	
"	29.11.17		" " " & work on above	
"	30.11.17		Capt J.R. HOSSON (86 Field Co) evacuated sick	Bro?????? ??? company for ??? CRE 1 Div

Army Form C. 2118.

WAR DIARY
or
INTELLIGENCE SUMMARY
(Erase heading not required.)

CRE 11th Division   VM/8

Place	Date	Hour	Summary of Events and Information	Remarks and references to Appendices
BRAQUEMONT	1.12.17		67, 68 & 86 Field Coys in line with 3 sections + HQ prs forward. 1 section at Transport-lines working on horse lines & section of huts etc. 68 Coy in right s.s.B (ST AUGUSTE SECTR) and 67 Coy on left (HILL 70 SECTOR) in centre. STEENWERK SECTR. Chief work is being done on communication trenches, revetting & placing cavalry and other work in construction B.O.Ps, maintenance of 2" pipes water supply and construction of Tramway (9th Divisionals) from about N.7.a.27 to N.7.a.20" light railway up to ST EMILE from N.7.a.8 being done by 6th East Yorks PIONEERS. Surveys of track round to date.	
"	2.12.17 to 4.12.17		Work as above.	
"	4.12.17		Capt G.N. KINGSFORD returns from leave.	
"	7.12.17		Capt. J.R. HODSON arrives from hospital.	
"	8.12.17		Capt A.F. REID left for R.E School of Instruction. Major REID PRATT returned from leave. Lieut ANTHONY joined 86 Field Coy	
"	9.12.17		Work as usual	
"	10.12.17		Continued erection of 8 NISSEN HUTS at LES BOEUFS for rows. Take away 71 Hopton NISSEN & return to two them for march.	

Army Form C. 2118.

WAR DIARY
or
INTELLIGENCE SUMMARY.
(Erase heading not required.)

Instructions regarding War Diaries and Intelligence Summaries are contained in F. S. Regs., Part II. and the Staff Manual respectively. Title pages will be prepared in manuscript.

C R E 11th Division

Place	Date	Hour	Summary of Events and Information	Remarks and references to Appendices
BRAQUEMONT	14-12-17		Work as above continued	
"	14-12-17		Dismantles NISSEN hut in BRAQUEMONT for removal to MAZINGARBE	
"	15-12-17		Work as above	
"	16-12-17		1 Section 86th Field Coy moves from BRAQUEMONT for erection of NISSEN huts & work at R.E. mass lines	
"	17-12-17		Work continued as above.	
"	18-12-17		Representation of Field Cos. of 3rd Canadian Division arrived to go round work preparatory to taking over.	
"	19-12-17		Major P.E.B. PRATT left to assume duties of C.R.E. 42nd Div. Capt. G.A. BUDDLE to be O.C. 86th Field Co. — Capt. C.G.N. KINGSFORD to be Adjt. Major BUDDLE to be Acting C.R.E.	
"	20-12-17		Lt. Col. F.A.K. WHITE returned on 30 days leave. 67th Field Co. handed over to 8th Can. Field Co. & moved to DROUVIN.	
"	21-12-17		57th Field Co. moved to BUSNES. 85th Field Co. handed over to 8th & 9th Can. Field Co. and moved to VERQUIN.	
"	22-12-17		68th Field Co. handed over to 9th Can. Field Co. & moved to VERQUIN. 85th Field Co. moved to HURIONVILLE.	

T2134. Wt. W708—776. 500000. 4/15. Sir J. C. & B.

Army Form C. 2118.

WAR DIARY
or
INTELLIGENCE SUMMARY.
(Erase heading not required.)

C.R.E. 11th Division.

Place	Date	Hour	Summary of Events and Information	Remarks and references to Appendices
LABEUVRIERE.	23-12-17		Handed over to C.R.E. 3rd Canadian Division & moved to LABEUVRIERE.	
"	24-12-17		Location of Field Cos. 67th at BUSNES. 58th at VERQUIN. 86th at HURIONVILLE. Field Cos. training & supervising erection of shelters for Brigade units.	
"	25-12-17		Cos. employed as above.	
"	26-12-17		" " "	
"	27-12-17		" " "	
"	28-12-17		68th Field Co. moved to LABOURSE and 2 sections to LE PREOL for work under R.E. 1st Corps.	
"	29-12-17		67th & 86th Field Cos. training & supervising erection of Brigade shelters.	
"	30-12-17		Work as above.	
"	31-12-17		" " "	

Captain & Adjutant, R.E.
11th Division.

Army Form C. 2118.

WAR DIARY
or
INTELLIGENCE SUMMARY.
(Erase heading not required.)

C.R.E. 11th Division

Instructions regarding War Diaries and Intelligence Summaries are contained in F. S. Regs., Part II. and the Staff Manual respectively. Title pages will be prepared in manuscript.

Place	Date	Hour	Summary of Events and Information	Remarks and references to Appendices
LABOURSE	1/1/18		67th & 85th Field Cos. Training & improving and building of Division Shelters.	JM/19
			68th Field Co. at LABOURSE wiring ANNEQUIN Line under orders of C.E. 1st Corps	
"	2/1/18		Work continued as above.	
	15/1/18		Orders for relief of 45th Div. on 18/1/18 received. Capt. HOBSON (85th Fd Co) wounded with 67th & 85th Field Co. Training & improving and building of shelters.	
	16/1/18		68th Field Co. working under orders of C.E. 1st Corps.	
"	18/1/18		Lt. Col. F.A.E. WHITE D.S.O. returned from special leave.	
"	19/1/18		Major BUDDLE returned to 85th Field Co.	
"	20/1/18		Work continued as above.	
"	21/1/18		86th Field Co. moved to BETHUNE.	
"	22/1/18		85th Field Co. moved to NOYELLES and took over from 465 Field Co.	
"			67th Field Co. moved to BETHUNE.	
SAILLY-LABOURSE	23/1/18		Hd. Qrs. moved to SAILLY-LABOURSE and relieved 46th Division.	
"	24/1/18		67th Field Co. moved to ANNEQUIN & took over from 438 Field Co. Major FEARFIELD	
			68th " " " MAZINGARBE " " " 465 " (68 Fd Co Engineer	
"	25/1/18		Field Co. reorganise to establ. Field Co. engaged in constructing Railway dugouts	
			67th Field Co. engaged in constructing Railway dugouts	

WAR DIARY
or
INTELLIGENCE SUMMARY
(Erase heading not required.)

Army Form C. 2118.

Place	Date	Hour	Summary of Events and Information	Remarks and references to Appendices
SAILLY LABOURSE	26/1/18		68th Field Co. on repairs & construction of trenches and dugouts.	
"	26/1/18		85th " " " to trenches & construction of dugouts, T.M. & M.G. emplacements	
"	27 31/1/18		Work carried on as above.	
"	"		Work carried on as above.	

G.W.Kingford
Captain & Adjutant, R.E.
11th Division.

WAR DIARY
or
INTELLIGENCE SUMMARY.
(Erase heading not required.)

Army Form C. 2118.

HQ RE 11
C.R.E. 11 Dn
SA 266

Place	Date	Hour	Summary of Events and Information	Remarks and references to Appendices
SAILLY-LABOURSE	1/2/18		Field Coy. + Parties working in trenches. Work + T.M. + M.G. emplacements.	
"	2/2/18		Major SOMERVILLE, 57th Field Cy arrived on 10 days leave.	
"	3/2/18		Nothing extra.	
"	4/2/18		Lieut. JONES N. proceeded on 14 days leave. Capt. POUND R.T.	
"	5/2/18		Joined 58th Field Cy. vice Capt. HOBSON relinquished such.	
"	6/2/18		Work carried out as before.	
"	7/2/18		Capt. WHITE C.D.C. proceeded to BLENDECQUES to 208th Company. Lt. A.L. JONES 58 F	
"	8/2/18, 9/2/18		Field Cy. proceeded on 14 days leave. Lieut. E.D. KNIGHT, 57th Field Cy. proceeded 14 days leave.—	
"			Lt. H. WHITE returned. Work continued as before.	
"	12/2/18		Capt. G.A. MARSHALL R.M.C. relieves Capt. D. MEEK R.A.M.C. who proceeds to 58 Dn H.Q.	
"	13/2/18		57th Field Cy. working on trenches, more dugouts T. 2 Coal H.Qrs. Fordros + MUNSTER O.P.	
"			Army Gas Store & issuing Sapper near A SAP REDOUBT.	
"			58 " " " " Sapper Sn T. M. Cally	
"			85 " " " M.G. emplacement & Alleys at S.H.1 + maintenance of the Rabbit	
"			2/5 Welsh Pioneers " "	

Army Form C. 2118.

WAR DIARY
or
INTELLIGENCE SUMMARY.
(Erase heading not required.)

Instructions regarding War Diaries and Intelligence Summaries are contained in F.S. Regs., Part II. and the Staff Manual respectively. Title pages will be prepared in manuscript.

Place	Date	Hour	Summary of Events and Information	Remarks and references to Appendices
SAILLY-LABOURSE	14/2/18		Work continued as on 13/2.	
"	20/2/18		" " "	
"	21/2/18		Lt. O'KELLY 86th Field Co. Proceeded on 30 days leave with effect from 22/2/18.	
"	22/2/18-24/2/18		" " as above.	
VERQUIN	20/2/18		Div. Hd. Qrs. moved to VERQUIN. Lt. JOBSON 68th Field Co.	
"			Proceeded on 14 days leave with effect from 25/2/18.	
"	25/2/18		Work continued as above.	
"	28/2/18		Lt. Col. C.J. BRADLEY attached to 85th Field Co. for Fortnight from 28/2/18.	

CR Humphreys

Captain & Adjutant, R.E.
11th Division.

Vol 21

Sirhit

WAR DIARIES
for Month of March 1918
of H.Q., R.E., 61st, 68th,
and 86th Field Coys. R.E.

WAR DIARY

Army Form C. 2118.

C.R.E. 11th Division

Place	Date	Hour	Summary of Events and Information	Remarks and references to Appendices
VERQUIN	1/3/18		67th Field Co. working on repairs to Trenches, deep dugout to right Dugt. Head Quarters, Clouard's Post, constructing Cubi Gardens to Tumulus + Dugouts, Elephant Shelters in 59th R.F.A. Head Quarters and Wiring in BARTS Alley.	
			68th Field Co. working on repairs to Trenches, M.G. Emplacements, Firing Cubi Gardens, repairing Dugout + erecting Screen.	
			86th Field Co. working on repairs to Trenches, constructing new Shaft in tunnel, clearing Dugouts, fixing Cubi Gardens, erecting Elephant Shelters + repairing Hutts at NOYELLES and repairs to BREWERY Chateau at VERMELLES.	
			S.R.E. Works Division working on repairs to Trenches, constructing Saps to two M.G. Emplacements, maintenance of Light Railway, wiring in Shiny Champagne, dugouts, deep dugout as a 1st.	
"	2/3/18		Work continued as on 1st.	
"	3/3/18		" " " " 1st Lt. 6 D.L. HUNTER joined 67th Field Co.	
"	4/3/18		" " " " 1st except Lt. 67th Field Co. who were relieved in CAMBRIN Sectn by 465th Field Co. 46 Div. Head Quarters of 67 Co. moved to MAZINGARBE and two Sections to NOYELLES.	

Army Form C. 2118.

WAR DIARY
or
INTELLIGENCE SUMMARY.
(Erase heading not required.)

C.R.E. 11th Division.

Place	Date	Hour	Summary of Events and Information	Remarks and references to Appendices
VERQUIN	5/3/18.		Work continued as before. CAMBRIN Sector handed over to 46th Division.	
"	6/3/18.		57th Field Co. constructing Elephant Gun Shelters in 10th Avenue. Sec. Engr. workshop and cleaning & stacking cellars in PHILOSOPHE.	
			68th Field Co. fixing Anti-gas doors, driving gallery for M.G. Emplacement, constructing Shelters & reconstructing Divisional Hut at MAZINGARBE.	
			86th Field Co. repairing cellars in NOYELLES & constructing Shelters and Shelter making 10 Shelters in CROSS WAY and moved support for advanced Batt. Head Qrs.	
			1st E. Yorks Pioneers maintaining Trenches, constructing Gun Emp. & revetting Shelters in 10th AVENUE, M.G. dugouts & emplacements and maintenance of Roads & Railways.	
"	7/3/18.		Work continued as above.	
"	8/3/18.		" " "	
"	9/3/18.		" " "	2nd Lieut. A.C. SOAR joined 68th Field Co.
"	10/3/18		" " "	2nd Lieut. T. ET. DAVIES, 57th Field Co. proceeded on 14 days leave. Summary Shot Gunner into force.
"	11/3/18.		" " "	Lieut. A.L. JONES, 68th Field Co. proceeded to No. 1 Army Co.
			57th Field Co. moved to NOYELLES & took over new cantin. Original Sects.	
			68th Field Co. moved afternoon Hand Grenades from LONE TRENCH to PHILOSOPHE.	

Army Form C. 2118.

WAR DIARY
or
INTELLIGENCE SUMMARY.
(Erase heading not required.)

Instructions regarding War Diaries and Intelligence Summaries are contained in F. S. Regs., Part II. and the Staff Manual respectively. Title pages will be prepared in manuscript.

Place	Date	Hour	Summary of Events and Information	Remarks and references to Appendices
VERQUIN	12/3/18		38th Field Co. Hors. Emers. moved from SAILLY LABOURSE to VERQUIGNEUL. Staff fell in SAILLY R.E. dump carrying following essentials for attached men: 1 Sapper, 1 Pick, 1 Shovel, 2 Sandbags, 1 B.C. Pulls Carriers #1 Ref. Pkt. Pr. carried.	
	15/3/18		March continued as on 11th inst. Lt. Col. G.R. BRADLEY reported for attachment to HQ. 2nd Lt. T.W.E. DUNKLEY reported for attachment (Staff course) on 15th. 81 Field Co. Hors. Emers. moved from NOYELLES to VERQUIGNEUL. 1st Lt. L.H. PARTRIDGE, 87th Field Co. reported for attachment in addition to two officers on 15th inst.	
"	16/3/18 to 17/3/18		69th Field Co. Constructing deep dug outs in GERMAN SWITCH LINE, elephant shelters in VILLAGE LINE, Bomb proof shelters round Bye Rose Lines. 65th Field Co. Sigon'rs M.G.E. on 10th AVENUE (NEW SWITCH), Gas doors, digging FOREST TRENCH, repairing BOYAU 65, S.A.A. at LABOURSE, SCREEN on LE RUTOIRE PLAIN. 8th Field Co. dugouts in HULLUCH ALLEY & CROSSWAY, elephant shelters in CROSSWAY. Gas doors. Repairing trenches A-framing revetting CROSSWAY TRENCH. 6th E. Yorks. Regt (P) Constructing dugouts in 10th AVENUE, CURZON STREET, LE RUTOIRE ALLEY (G6a Y3) & JUNCTION KEEP (for 2nd H.A.) M.G.E. in POSEN ALLEY and MANNING TUNNEL. Splinter proof shelters in GRENAY-VERMELLES LINE.	

Army Form C. 2118.

WAR DIARY
or
INTELLIGENCE SUMMARY.
(Erase heading not required.)

Instructions regarding War Diaries and Intelligence Summaries are contained in F.S. Regs., Part II. and the Staff Manual respectively. Title pages will be prepared in manuscript.

Place	Date	Hour	Summary of Events and Information	Remarks and references to Appendices
VERQUIN	17/3/18		Attachment of Lt. T.W.E. DUNKLEY ceased.	
"	18/3/18		Work continued as before. Fire broke out at SAILLY R.E. DUMP by enemy shelling. Fires being huts and one ablution shed burnt out. 11.45 P.M.	
"	19/3/18		Capt. G.N. KINGSFORD, Adjutant R.E. proceeded on 14 days leave. Work continued as before. Additional by 87th Field Co. Repairing dressing station at VERMELLES. 68th Field Co. M.G.E. in SEVENTH AVENUE.	
"	20/3/18		Work continued as on 19th inst.	
"	21/3/18		Work continued as on 19th inst. Additional, 86th Field Co. constructing shelter for visual signalling post.	
"	22/3/18 or 23/3/18		Work continued as on 21st inst.	
"	24/3/18		Capt. R.D DUFF, 68th Field Coy proceeded on leave with effect from 23rd inst. 87th Field Coy continuing dugouts in GERMAN SWITCH at G.17.d.55.15 and G.17.d.70.80. Strengthening elephant shelters at G.16.c central, M.G. dugout at G.16 & 93. 32 Bob R.B. Repairing toy horse lines pickets along tracks, tree roots	

WAR DIARY or INTELLIGENCE SUMMARY
Army Form C. 2118.

Place	Date	Hour	Summary of Events and Information	Remarks and references to Appendices
VERQUIN	24/3/18		68th Field Co. R.E. Constructing dugouts at G.25 d 38 in VILLAGE LINE. Two Coys on 10TH AVENUE SWITCH. M.G. dugout in SEVENTH AVENUE. Repairing trenches. Fitting gasdoors. Wiring GUN TRENCH. Constructing shelters G.23 d 15. 88th Field Co. Constructing deep dugouts on HULLUCH ALLEY, FOSSE WAY and CROSSWAY. Fitting gasdoors. Repairing trenches & horse lines. Continuing Signal Station LE RUTOIRE FARM.	
"	25/3/18		Work continued as on 24th inst.	
"	26/3/18		Work continued as on 24th inst.	
"	27/3/18		Work continued as on 24th inst. CAMBRIN SECTOR taken over from 46TH DIVISION.	
"	28/3/18		67th Field R.E. Work as before and shelters at G.2 a y 2. 63rd Field C.R.E. Work as before. 86th Field G. R.E. Work as before.	
"	29/3/18		67th Field Co. R.E. Dugouts at G.9 a 67, G.3 c 38. Shelters at G.2 d y 2, repairing dugout at G.4 d 43. Gas doors. Pipe line, maintenance of Trenches. 68th Field G. R.E. Dugouts at G.23 d 18, G.23 d 36, C.30 & 53, G.18 d 25 60 and C.17 d 78. Expected gasdoors, maintenance of trenches & screens.	

WAR DIARY
or
INTELLIGENCE SUMMARY.
(Erase heading not required.)

Army Form C. 2118.

Place	Date	Hour	Summary of Events and Information	Remarks and references to Appendices
VERQUIN	29/3/18		86th Field Coy. R.E. Reports on FOSSE WAY, HULLUCH ALLEY and CROSSWAY, work station at COMMAND POST, maintenance of trenches, loose wires	
"	30/3/18		Work continued as before	
"	31/3/18		Work continued as before by Field boys horse lines removed to SAILLY - LABOURSE ROAD at F 20 d 2 3	

E. Wilson Kerr
Lieut. & Adjutant
Captain & Adjutant, R.E.
11th Division.

11th Divisional Engineers

C. R. E.

11th DIVISION.

APRIL 1918.

WAR DIARY

INTELLIGENCE SUMMARY.

Army Form C. 2118.

C.R.E. 11th Division.

VA 22

Place	Date	Hour	Summary of Events and Information	Remarks and references to Appendices
VERQUIN	1/4/18		68th Field Coys horse lines removed to F.20.d.2.3 on SAILLY – BEUVRY ROAD.	
"	"		57th Field Coy. Constructing dugout at BART'S POST and R.B. H.Q'rs	
"	"		Elephant shelters at WINDY CORNER. Mission Hut at ANNEQUIN FOSSE. Maintaining trenches, repairs to horse lines. Repairing gas doors.	
"	"		68th Field Coy. Constructing dugouts in 9th AVENUE, 10th AVENUE + VILLAGE LINE. Hung JOHN'S WAY trench. Water patrol. Screens on plain. Gas doors.	
"	"		86th Field Coy. Constructing dugouts in CROSSWAY, FOSSEWAY + HULLUCH ALLEY. Gas doors. Splinter proof sentry boxes in O.B.1.	
"	"		6th B.Q Yorks Regt (P). Dugouts in CURZON STREET, 10th AVENUE + JUNCTION KEEP, M.G. dugout in GRENAY–NOYELLES LINE at L.12.c. 35.45. M.G.E in POSEN ALLEY and MANNING TUNNEL. Repairing trenches	
"	2/4/18		Work continued as above.	
"	3/4/18		" " " " "	Major G.M.KINGSFORD returned from leave and took over from Lt E.P. CANHAM (Offg. Adjt.).
"	4/4/18		" " " " "	
"	5/4/18		" " " " "	Lt. E.P. CANHAM rejoined 58th Field Co.

WAR DIARY
or
INTELLIGENCE SUMMARY.
(Erase heading not required.)

Army Form C. 2118.

Place	Date	Hour	Summary of Events and Information	Remarks and references to Appendices
VERQUIN	5/4/18.		67th Field Co. constructing deep dugouts, repairing high lines, making gas alarm & wire work.	
"			68th " " " " " " " "	
"			85th " " " " Fixing gas alarms, making trenches boards & wire work.	
"			5th E. Yorks Pioneers " " " shaft for T.M. Emps. & "	
"			" " " " " " M.G. emplacements.	
"	7 & 8/4/18.		Work continued as above.	
"	9/4/18.		As a result of heavy enemy gas shelling the officers and casualties were reported:- 57th Field Co. 43 O.Rs. 7 58th Field Co. 6 O.Rs.	
"	10/4/18.		Further gas casualties as follows:- 67th Field Co. 13 O.Rs, 85th Co. 1 Off. + 11 O.Rs, 81st Field Co. 4 O.Rs. Lt. Col. BRADLEY proceeded to BRUAY on completion of attachment. 57th Field Co. in Coy Reserves handed over to 23rd Field Co. 1st Div.	
"	11/4/18.		1 O.R. gas casualty in 57th Field Co. 2 Lt. SUTER H. Riding Regt. attached for operations in transmission tips to Field Co. Orders of the Brigade Received (HOHENZOLLERN Sect) to proceed of 1st Div. casualties. 57th Field Co. relieved 22nd Field Co. 1st Div. Div. O.C. Sumps at SAVY - LIBOURSE and FOSSE 12 handed over to O.Rs 12th Div. Tok. are Reduit LES BREBIS from E.O.C. 45th Div.	

GM/P

WAR DIARY or INTELLIGENCE SUMMARY

Army Form C. 2118.

Place	Date	Hour	Summary of Events and Information	Remarks and references to Appendices
VERQUIN	12/4/18.		67th Field Co. working in deep dugouts at BARTS Cor. & O.B.N. H.Qrs, NOYELLES Nymn. & gun cover.	
			18th " " 3 " " M.G. emplacement & misc. work.	
			83rd " " 2 " " T.M.O. " " emplacement of trenches, tramic, gas alarms & misc. work.	
			S.L.E. Hydro Section working on 3 deep dugouts & divisional communication trench at Comm't Col PHILOSOPHE.	
"	13 & 14/4/18.		Work continued as above.	
BRACQUEMONT	15/4/18.		Div. Headquarters moved to BRACQUEMONT. Work continued as above.	
"	16 - 19/4/18.		Work continued as above.	
"	20/4/18.		" " " 11th Lt. J.O'HAGAN joined 28th Field Co. vice 11th Lt. E. PIMINGTON wounded gunshot & evacuated on 10th inst.	
"	21 - 22/4/18.		" " "	
"	23/4/18.		" " " Capt. DUFF, 18th Field Co. returned from leave on c.ccalk.	
"	24/4/18.		" " " 11th Lt. H. SHOPLAND joined 68th Field Co. vice 11th Lt. BLAKE 9th O.O.R. reinforcements arrived for No. 3 Field Co. to replace gas casualties dc.	
"	25/4/18.		32nd O.I. Rly. returned to HOHENZOLLERN taken over by Bde. F/12 Div. 87th Field Co. Handed over to 23rd Field Co.	

G.M.R.

WAR DIARY
or
INTELLIGENCE SUMMARY.
(Erase heading not required.)

Army Form C. 2118.

Place	Date	Hour	Summary of Events and Information	Remarks and references to Appendices
BRAQUEMONT	26/4/18.		67th Field Co. working on 2 Inf. and 2 M.G. dugouts.	
			68th " " " 4 Inf. dugouts, firing Gas doors & misc. works.	
			83rd " " " 3 " and 1 R.E.O. Dugout + misc. works.	
			6th E. Yorks Pioneers working on 3 Inf. & 1 M.G. dugout.	
			2nd Lt. JOBSON returned as sick.	
			2nd Lt. PARTRIDGE as Gas Officer.	
"	27/4/18.		Work continued as above.	
"	28–30/4/18.		Work continued as on 26th. One working section of each Co. attached to Hon. Inns. Resting out of 85th Field Co. constructing dugout for Div. Head quarters at BRAQUEMONT.	

E.M. Pengord.
Captain & Adjutant, R.E.
11th Division.

Army Form C. 2118.

WAR DIARY
or
INTELLIGENCE SUMMARY.
(Erase heading not required.)

C.R.E. 11th Division.

Instructions regarding War Diaries and Intelligence Summaries are contained in F. S. Regs., Part II. and the Staff Manual respectively. Title pages will be prepared in manuscript.

Place	Date	Hour	Summary of Events and Information	Remarks and references to Appendices
BRAQUEMONT	1/5/18		87th Field Co. working on 2 M.G. dugouts + chambers for Bn. H.Q. dugout, repairs to trenches + misc. work.	
			68th Field Co. working on 4 Inf. dugouts, digging + repairing trenches, fixing gas horn + wire work.	
			85th " " " 3 Inf. + 1 R.A.P. dugout + fixing gas horn.	
			" " " 3 Inf. + 2 M.G. + on Bde. H.Q. dugout	
			G.S.E. Yorks Pioneers working on 3 Inf. + 2 M.G. + Bde. H.Q. dugout = 67th + 85th at NOYELLES, 68th at MAZINGARBE. Oh.	
			Field Co. Guide as follows := 67th + 85th at NOYELLES, 68th at MAZINGARBE. Oh. Horse lines and one working section from each Field Co. at BRAQUEMONT.	
"	2/5/18		Work continued as above.	
"	3/5/18		" " " " " 34th Inf. Bde. relieved 32nd Bde. in the HULLUCH Sector.	
			" " " Field Co. continue work in their present sectors. One Coy. section of 87th + 85th Field Co. working on Inf. Bde. H.Q. dugout + tunnel at BRAQUEMONT. Lt. BLAKE rejoined 68th Field Co. from Hospital.	
"	4/5/18		Work as above. Capt. C. KINGSTON R.A.M.C. reported for duty as M.O. i/c C.E. Works area. Capt. E.G. MARSHALL R.A.M.C. to 35th Field Amb.	
"	5-8/5/18		Work continued as above.	
"	9/5/18		" " " " Major T.P. DALTON R.E. reported for one months dissolvement - Proceed G 57th Field Co.	

G.H.R.

WAR DIARY
INTELLIGENCE SUMMARY

Army Form C. 2118.

Place	Date	Hour	Summary of Events and Information	Remarks and references to Appendices
BRAQUEMONT	10/5/15.		57th Field Co. working on 2 Inf. and 2 M.G. Dugouts.	
			68th " " " 2 Inf. Dugouts and Dugout for R.E. Headquarters at PHILOSOPHE.	
			83rd " " " R.A.P. Explained width.	
			Castg. Sections of 57th & 83rd Field Co. constructing dugout at Bn. Headquarters.	
"	11/5/18.		5th E. Yorks Pioneer working on Inf. and on M.G. Dugout.	
"	12/5/18.		Work continued as above. 83rd Inf. relieved the 22nd Inf. Bde. in the EYE Sectn.	
"	13/5/18.		LES BREBIS Dump Limits added last night. 1 O.C. N.C.O. Gallipoli + 3 men attached.	
"	14-15/5/18.		Work continued as above.	
"	16-18/5/18.		" " "	
"	19/5/18.		" " " 22nd Inf. Bde. relieved the 34th Inf. Bde. in the HULLUCH Sectn.	
"	20-22/5/18.		" " "	
"	23/5/18.		" " " Lieut. L. J. BLAKE, 68th Field Co. Evacuated on 14 days special leave with effect from 24/5/18. 11 Lt. SUTEP proceeded attached as Assumedi.	

Army Form C. 2118.

WAR DIARY
of
INTELLIGENCE SUMMARY.
(Erase heading not required.)

Instructions regarding War Diaries and Intelligence Summaries are contained in F. S. Regs., Part II. and the Staff Manual respectively. Title pages will be prepared in manuscript.

Place	Date	Hour	Summary of Events and Information	Remarks and references to Appendices
BRAQUEMONT	24/5/18		57 Field Co. working on 2 Inf. on M.G. and 3 Tret Rev Dugouts.	
			68 " " 2 " Dugouts + on dugout for R.E. H.Q. at PHILOSOPHE.	
			83 " " 2 " and on M.G. Dugouts.	
			S.R.E. Yorks (Pioneers) working 4 Inf. + one M.G. Dugouts. Also on dugouts for Bde. H.Q. at PHILOSOPHE and 2 Tret Rev.	
			Details fatigues of 67th + 86th Field Co. coro trenching tramroad from Bde. H.Q. to Div. H.Q. at BRAQUEMONT.	
25-26/5/18			Work continued as above.—	
"	27/5/18		" " " " " — 343rd Inf. Bn. relieved 33rd Inf. Bn. in the STELLE Sector.	
"	28-30/5/18		" " " " "	
"	31/5/18		Work continued as above.— Lt. E.R. CANHAM relieved Lt. W. JOBSON as Staff Officer attached to C.R.E.	

A.M.Rumford
Captain & Adjutant. R.E.
11th Division.

C.R.E.
11TH DIVISION.

(6339) W. W160/M3016 1,500,000 10/17 McA & W Ltd (E1898) Forms W3091. Army Form W.3091.

Cover for Documents.

Nature of Enclosures.

War Diaries
C R E
~~67, 68, 86 Field Coys R.E.~~
June 1918

Notes, or Letters written.

Army Form C. 2118.

WAR DIARY

INTELLIGENCE SUMMARY.
(Erase heading not required.)

C.R.E. 11th Division.

Instructions regarding War Diaries and Intelligence Summaries are contained in F. S. Regs., Part II. and the Staff Manual respectively. Title pages will be prepared in manuscript.

Place	Date	Hour	Summary of Events and Information	Remarks and references to Appendices
BRAQUEMONT	1/6/18		67th Field Co. working on 2 Inf. Dugouts, On. H.Q. Coy. up + Test Bn. Dugout.	
"	"		68th " " " " 3 Inf. Dugouts + On. Dugout for O.S. H.Q. PHILOSOPHE.	
"	"		83rd " " " " 2 Inf. + On. M.G. Dugout.	
"	"		5th E. Yorks. (Pioneers) working on + Infy. On M.G. + On. H.Q. Dugout. PHILOSOPHE.	
"	2-3/6/18		Work continued as above.	
"	4/6/18		" " " 33rd Inf. Bde. relieved 32nd Inf. Bde. in the HULLUCH sector.	
"	5-6/6/18		" " " 83rd Field Co. commenced work on two circular L.G. emplacements.	
"	7/6/18		" " " Capt. G.T. POUND, 83rd Field Co., proceeded on 14 days leave with effect from 8/6/18.	
"	8/6/18		Work continued as above.	
"	9-11/6/18		" " "	
"	12/6/18		" " " 32nd Inf. Bde. relieved 34th Inf. Bde. in the ST. ELIE sector.	
"	13/6/18		Work continued as above. 2/Lt. D.H. LEVINKIND joining 83rd Field Co. on proceeding on 14 days leave with effect from 13/6/18.	
			2/Lt. H.C. ANTHONY returned to such (25/5/18).	
"	14/6/18		Work continued as above.	G.M.R.

T2134. Wt. W708—776. 500000. 4/15. Sir J. C. & S.

WAR DIARY
or
INTELLIGENCE SUMMARY.
(Erase heading not required.)

Army Form C. 2118.

Place	Date	Hour	Summary of Events and Information	Remarks and references to Appendices
BRAQUEMONT	15/8/18.		The following work is in hand :-	
			67th Field Co. - Dugouts at CROSSWAY, NOYELLES Defences, STANSFIELD Road, LIMBER Trench. VERLODS M.G. and STANSFIELD Road R.E.-dp. Costing water on Delousing Chamber at D.H.Q. + misc. works.	
			68th Field Co. - Dugouts in RESERVE Trench (Joy), N Sap Redoubt + REDO PHILOSOPHE. Costing works or repairs to CUCIGNY Hqrs + misc. work. M.G.	
			83rd Field Co. - Dugouts in LIMBER TRENCH and MUCHEAP. Two L.G. screens implements. Pushing action knocking chambers in D.H.Q Tunnel and making Carden Huts at BOIS DU FROISSART.	
			5th E. York (Pioneers) - Dugouts at Col. H.Q. PHILOPHE, VICTORIA Redt. VENDIN Alley. JOHNS WAY dummy station and TRIANGLE - Repairs to trenches. One Co. in rest. One Co. at work at HERSIN.	
	16/8/18.		67th Field Co. commenced Dugout in LIMBER TRENCH. 68th Field Co. commenced dugout No. 34 in Reserve Trench.	
	17/8/18.		Work continued as above	
	18/8/18.		5th Field Co. completed Dugout in STANSFIELD Road. 6th 2 Vista completed Dugouts in Triangle + Village Ave. Major J.P. DALTON R.E. completed attachment to 67th Field Co. + returned to U.K.	

Army Form C. 2118.

WAR DIARY
or
INTELLIGENCE SUMMARY.
(Erase heading not required.)

Instructions regarding War Diaries and Intelligence Summaries are contained in F.S. Regs., Part II. and the Staff Manual respectively. Title pages will be prepared in manuscript.

Place	Date	Hour	Summary of Events and Information	Remarks and references to Appendices
BRAQUEMONT	19/6/18		Work continued.	
"	20/6/18		" - 34th R.F. Bn. relieved 32nd Bn. in the HULLUCH sector.	
"	21/6/18		" - Major G.A. BUDDLE, 83rd Field Coy. proceeded on 14 days leave with effect from 22/6/18.	
"	22/6/18		Work continued. 6 - 2 Yorks Pioneers completed enlargement to VENDIN ALLEY Dugout.	
"	23-25/6/18		Capt. BENTLEY, 9th W.Yorks attached for instruction. 83rd Field C. completed L.G.P.M Posts in STANSFIELD Trench and CHAPEL Alley.	
"	26/6/18		" - 6.2 Field C. completed Delousing Chamber at MAZINGARBE ABBATOIR.	
			† commenced work on new chamber at NOYELLES.	
"	27/6/18		83rd Field C. commenced work on Sentries Chambers at NOYELLES. Work continued. 85th Field C. commenced work on L.G.P.M Posts in OUTZOY Street.	
"	28/6/18		Work continued. 33rd R.F. Bn. relieved 32nd R.F. Bn. in the ST.ELIE sector. 6 - 2 Yorks Pioneers commenced working E.P.I. Shelters in BREWERY Trench.	
"	29/6/18		Work continued. Fire line of Six Horse Shoe at COUPIGNY.	
"	30/6/18		Work continued. Second Coy. of Six Horse Shoe. 3 day Tour: finished. Army Divisional Sappers of relief finished at 60 Horse Trench. An isolation Camp has been formed to accommodate 35 cases.	

Captain & Adjutant, R.E.
11th DIVISION.

Vol 25

C.R.E.

War Diary
July 1918

Army Form C. 2118.

WAR DIARY
INTELLIGENCE SUMMARY.
(Erase heading not required.)

C.R.E. 11th Division.

Instructions regarding War Diaries and Intelligence Summaries are contained in F. S. Regs., Part II. and the Staff Manual respectively. Title pages will be prepared in manuscript.

Place	Date	Hour	Summary of Events and Information	Remarks and references to Appendices
BRAQUEMONT.	1/7/16.		The following work in hand :-	
			57th Field Co. — Dugouts in LIMBER Trench, NOVELLES Trench & VERLOOS M.G. Emplacement. Resting station and mining Junction Chamber at MAZINGARBE.	
			68th Field Co. — Dugouts in CURZON Trench, Tuckum Sap Redoubt & PHILOSOPHE R.E. H.Q. L.G. Emplt. Oil Res. in CURZON Street. Dressing station in repair to Huts at LOUPIGNY Reinforcement Camp.	
			86th Field Co. — H.Q. Dugout in LIMBER Trench & L.G. Oil Res. in ST. GEORGES Trench and HAY Dump. Dressing Cover over PHILOSOPHE Adv. H.Q. Dugout. [Delivery Chamber at NOVELLES.] Dressing station on Chambers in Div. H.Q. Tunnel.	
			S.R.E. Yards (Mining) — Dugout in JOHNS Alley & E.1. Shelters in Reserve Trench. Return to Trenches.	
"	2-4/7/16.		Work continued as above.	
"	5/7/16.		" " " 68th Field Co. completed Dugouts in N. Sap Redoubt and L.G. Oil Res. in Curzon Trench.	
"	6/7/16.		" " " R.E. Headquarters PHILOSOPHE. Commenced work on 32" x/Work behind 34th Div. in the HULLUCH sector.	
"	7/7/16.		" " " 11th H. SHOPLAND. 68th Field Co. completed report P.W.O.	
"	8/7/16.		" " " 86th Field Co. completed Delivery Chamber at NOVELLES. HERSIN.	
			57th Field Co. mining section commenced " " "	

WAR DIARY or INTELLIGENCE SUMMARY

Army Form C. 2118.

(Erase heading not required.)

Instructions regarding War Diaries and Intelligence Summaries are contained in F. S. Regs., Part II. and the Staff Manual respectively. Title pages will be prepared in manuscript.

Place	Date	Hour	Summary of Events and Information	Remarks and references to Appendices
BRAQUEMONT	9/7/18		Work continued. 5th Field Co. completed Reserving Chambre at MAZINGARBE.	
"	10/7/18		6th E. York (R) commenced Dugout at PHILOSOPHE KEEP. Major A.T. FEARFIELD 58th Field Co, proceeded on sick leave to DEAUVILLE.	
"	11/7/18		6th F.E. Works completed Dugout in JOHN'S WAY.	
"	12/7/18		67th Field Co. completed VERLOOS M.G. Dugout.	
"	13/7/18		Lt. K.H. LOCKHART, 57th Field Co, proceeded to U.K. on appointment.	
"	14/7/18		Indian Owen. at POOL, 5th Devon R. allotted as permanent L.G. garrison + 4 twins. Guns have been issued to each Field Co. in addition to 6 # 1 A.A. Lewis Guns. 34th Inf. Bde. achieved 332nd O.R. in the ST. ELIE Sector.	
"	15/7/18		Work continued. " Lt. J.D. WALKER joined 57th Fd. Co vice Lt. K.H. LOCKHART. Capt. T.P. SNELLING R.A.M.C. relieved Capt. E. KINGSTON R.A.M.C. as O.i/c O.E. Units. Capt. Simpson to i/c V.A.D.M.S. Unit.	
"	16/7/18		Work continued.	
"	17/7/18		" 88th Field Co commenced work on Dugout in VILLAGE Line. 6th E. Yorks " " " " in RESERVE Line.	

WAR DIARY
or
INTELLIGENCE SUMMARY.
(Erase heading not required.)

Army Form C. 2118.

Instructions regarding War Diaries and Intelligence Summaries are contained in F. S. Regs., Part II. and the Staff Manual respectively. Title pages will be prepared in manuscript.

Place	Date	Hour	Summary of Events and Information	Remarks and references to Appendices
BRAQUEMONT	18/7/18.		Work continued. Lt. TIM VALE returned to Pool as Finds Gun Instructor.	
"	19/7/18.		68th Field Co. completed L.G. Pill Box in CURZON St.	
"	20/7/18.		57th Field Co. positive section completed drainage & dug-outs at CHERSIN.	
"	"		68th Field Co. commenced work on "M.017" Pill Box in VENDIN ALLEY.	
"	21-22/7/18		33rd Inf. Bde. relieved the 32nd Bde. in the HULLUCH Sector.	
"	23/7/18		Work continued. Lt. VALE returned to Unit on completion of M.A.G. Course 23/7/18.	
"	24/7/18.		Major BUDDLE, 86th Field Co. returned from leave 1st return to medical grounds.	
"	25/7/18.		81st Field Co. completed Pill Boxes in ST GEORGES Trench & KAY Number Communications with 2 Pillars at LEPOITRE Farm.	
"	26/7/18.		57th Field Co. commenced work on dugout in O.B.1.	
"	27/7/18.		68th Field Co. completed dugout ("K" Shape) in RESERVE Trench & "M.017" Pill Box in VENDIN ALLEY	
"	28-30/7/18.		Work continued.	
"	31/7/18.		68th Field Co. (Centre Section) completed erection of Hospital Tents Hut at BOIS DU FROISSART Camp.	

Captain & Adjutant. & S.
11th Division

WAR DIARY
INTELLIGENCE SUMMARY

(Erase heading not required.)

Army Form C. 2118.

C.R.E. 11th Division.

Vol 26

Place	Date	Hour	Summary of Events and Information	Remarks and references to Appendices
BRAQUEMONT	1/8/15		The following work is in hand:—	
			67th Field Co. — Dugouts at NOYELLES. Defensive Timber Trench and O.B.1. Repairs to Screen on PUTOIRE Plain. Colliery Cabin overlooking Pit No. 2 at HERSIN.	
			68th Field Co. — Dugout (N–O) in RESERVE Line. New Gun Pit O/O in RESERVE Line. Repairs to gas horn & wire twist rod. Colliery Cabin at COURIGNY Pit.	
			88th Field Co. — Dugout in VILLAGE Line. Gun Em. L.G. Pit O/O at LE PUTOIRE Farm. Overhang Chambers in YERMELLES Tunnel + new work. Railing Lines	
			2nd enquiring Road at COURIGNY Reinforcement Camp.	
			G.H.Q. Units (O) — Dugouts in PHILOSOPHE Pigs and RESERVE Line. Enemy's concrete are Fort 60°. Cartridge & Engine dugboards in HULLUCH Alley, FOSLING Emplacement.	
			In PHILOSOPHE Scheme. Gun Em working & training. 68th Field Co. completed No.1 L.G. Pit O/O in Ourar Line.	
	2/8/15		Work continued as above.	
	3/8/15		" " 1st DRESSES, 2nd Field Co. attached on Staff between Ouver & O.B.1 started.	
	4/8/15		" " 68th Field Co. commenced enlargement of Dugout No.12 in RESERVE Line.	

Army Form C. 2118.

WAR DIARY
or
INTELLIGENCE SUMMARY.
(Erase heading not required.)

Instructions regarding War Diaries and Intelligence Summaries are contained in F.S. Regs., Part II. and the Staff Manual respectively. Title pages will be prepared in manuscript.

Place	Date	Hour	Summary of Events and Information	Remarks and references to Appendices
BRAQUEMONT	5/8/18.		Work continued. 57th Field Co. completed dugout in NOYELLES between Bays SOMERVILLE	
"	6/8/18.		Work continued. 88th Field Co. commenced work on L.G. Pill Box in Reserve Trench.	Received on 4 days' leave (Paris) with effect from 5/5/18.
"	7/8/18.		34th Fd. Ok. returned 331st Bn. in HULLUCH Sector.	Lt. Iveson, Staff Learner Course seconded to 88th Field Co. for 7 days' instruction.
"	8/8/18.		Lt. Cochran, 75cm Officer, Proceeded on leave with effect from 9/8/18. Relieved by 11th. W. JONES, 86th Field Co.	
"	9/8/18.		86th Field Co. commenced work on No. 2 L.G. Pill Box at LE PUTOIRE Farm.	
"	10-11/8/18		Work continued.	
"	12/8/18.		68th Field Co. commenced Dugout at BOYS Post.	
"	13/8/18.		Work continued.	
"	14/8/18.		83rd Field Co. completed Dugout in VILLAGE Trench.	
"	15-16/8/18.		Work continued.	
"	17/8/18.		57th Field Co. completed Dugout in LIMBER Trench.	
"	18/8/18.		57th Field Co. commenced work on Dugout at ST. MARY'S. 68th Field Co. completed dugouts N-O. + enlargement to No. 13 both in Reserve Trench.	

F.M/1/18

Army Form C. 2118.

WAR DIARY
or
INTELLIGENCE SUMMARY.
(Erase heading not required.)

Instructions regarding War Diaries and Intelligence Summaries are contained in F. S. Regs., Part II. and the Staff Manual respectively. Title pages will be prepared in manuscript.

Place	Date	Hour	Summary of Events and Information	Remarks and references to Appendices
BRAQUEMONT	19/8/18		86th Field Co. commenced L.G.O.H.Ocr No. 3 in ST GEORGE'S Trench. Lt. Col. F.A.K. WHITE proceeded on 14 days leave with effect from 20th inst. Major BUDDLE acting C.R.E.	
"	20-21/8/18		Work continued	
"	22/8/18		Work continued	
"	23/8/18		67th Field Co. relieved by 91st Field Co. and moved to AUBIGNY.	
"	24/8/18		68th " " " 73rd " " " " AGNIERES.	
"	25/8/18		88th " " " 74th " " " " HERMIN. 67th Field Co. moved from AUBIGNY to HERMIN. Lt. CANHAM returned from leave.	
HERMIN	26/8/18		11th Div. relieved by 15th Div. Div. H.Q. moved to VILLERS CHATEL. Complete handing over to C.R.E. 15th Div. & moved to HERMIN. 68th Field Co. moved from AGNIERES to HERMIN. Major ROYLE, Manchester Rgt attached for supervision of Fd. Training of Field Cos. 3rd Inf. Bde. moved off as an Independent Force.	
"	27/8/18		Field Co. training.	
"	28/8/18		Co. training. All emphasis laid out to TINQUES.	
ARRAS	29/8/18		C.R.E. joined D.H.Q. at ARRAS. 67th Field Co. moved to BLANGY.	

T2134. Wt. W708-776. 500000. 4/15. Sir J. C. & S.

WAR DIARY
or
INTELLIGENCE SUMMARY.
(Erase heading not required.)

Army Form C. 2118.

Place	Date	Hour	Summary of Events and Information	Remarks and references to Appendices
ARRAS	29/8/18		68th + 85th Field Co. moved to MADAGASCAR Corner. 32nd Inf. Bde. went into the line east of the SCARPE + took over from a mixed force of 45 Div.	
"	30/8/18		68th + 85th Field Co. moved to BLANGY. 33rd Inf. Bde. went into the line on the right of 32nd Inf. Bde. in relief of BRUTINEL'S Force (45 Div.).	
"	31/8/18		67th Field Co. moved to H.34. Cent. (near ORANGE HILL). 68th + 85th Field Co. moved to MONCHY-LE-PREUX. 6th E. Yorks (Pioneers) at BLANGY. Field Co. + Pioneers reconnoitering roads + tramways.	

C.M. Humphrey.
Captain & Adjutant. R.E
11th Division

WAR DIARY of INTELLIGENCE SUMMARY

Army Form C. 2118.

HQ RE 11D SS 27

Place	Date	Hour	Summary of Events and Information	Remarks and references to Appendices
ARRAS	1/9/18		57th Field Co. constructing P.S.W. lines at G.24.a.9.5., reconnoitring main supply & repairing approaches trench tram. from H.28.c. to H.10.d.	
			68th Field Co. Repairing MONCHY – ROEUX road, & bridge at I.25.d.7.5. -	
			85th " " making screens in and S.E. MONCHY & making out light railway at EDITH.	
			1/1st E.York (C) repairing FEUCHY-PELVES road. 2nd R.E. Dump being formed at MONCHY.	
			Capt. LLOYD CHERITON reports for attachment as Staff Learner.	
"	2/9/18		Capt. CHERITON proceeded to 67th Field Co. Lt. MASTERS, 86th Field Co. proceeded on leave to U.K. with effect from 3/9/18. Three Field Cos. & 5 E.York (C) reporting General works & traffic. 2 columns of 85th Field Co. working under 2nd (Canadian) Tramway Co.	
"	3-4/9/18		Work continued.	
"	5/9/18		Lt. Col. F.A.K.WHITE returned from leave, 2 days extension from H.Q.	
"	6/9/18		Work continued as before.	
"	7/9/18		ditto. Lieut G.D.L. HUNTER, 67th Field Coy proceeded on leave to U.K. with effect from 9/9/18	
"	8/10/Sep/18		Work continued. The 456th Field Survey R.E. were attached from 13th inst. & moved into billets at BLANGY. Major ROYLE'S attachment ceased 10th	

ECB

WAR DIARY
or
INTELLIGENCE SUMMARY.
(Erase heading not required.)

Army Form C. 2118.

Place	Date	Hour	Summary of Events and Information	Remarks and references to Appendices
ARRAS	10/9/18		Capt REID, M.C, RE(SR) proceeded on leave with effect from 12th 62LX.	
do	11/9/18		Capt C.L. CHERITON reported from 68th Field Coy. The three field boys & 456 Field Coy working on improved roads stacks (one section of 456 Field Coy working on traffic post & wires at ARRAS). Attachment of Capt. CHERITON ceased. Capt G.N.KINGSFORD, M.C, R.E. proceeded on leave in France with effect from 12th Sept/18.	
do	12/9/18		Work continued on roads, also opening up ways & repairing 3 bridges across SENSEE. Two sections of 456th Field Coy. moved into forward billets at MONCHY. 68th Field Coy. was partially bivouacked - blowing up a solace cement.	
do	13th/14/9/18		Work as before. Attachment of 456 Field Coy. ceased on 14th & they moved out.	
do	15-17/9/18		Work continued. 2nd Lt C.G. STILLMAN proceeded on leave to U.K. on 15th with effect from 19/9/18.	
do	18-19/9/18		Work continued. No 41532 T/Cpl. (A/Cpl) NEWMAN L. 68th Field Coy RE awarded MILITARY MEDAL (dated 11/9/18) in connection with blowing up of sluices across River	

ECB

Army Form C. 2118.

WAR DIARY
or
INTELLIGENCE SUMMARY.
(Erase heading not required.)

Instructions regarding War Diaries and Intelligence Summaries are contained in F. S. Regs, Part II. and the Staff Manual respectively. Title pages will be prepared in manuscript.

Place	Date	Hour	Summary of Events and Information	Remarks and references to Appendices
ARRAS	18/9/18		67th Field Coy were relieved in the line by 9th Field Coy and 67th Field Coy moved from Monchy. over billets at MONCHY.	
			MONCHY to BLANGY.	
do	19/9/18		67th Field Coy moved from BLANGY to FREVILLERS. 88th Field Coy were relieved by 526th Field Coy R.E. 2 Divisions who took over billets at MONCHY. 88th Field Coy moved from MONCHY to FREVILLERS.	
do	20/9/18		68th Field Coy were relieved by 106th Field Coy R.E. 2 Division who took over billets at MONCHY. 68th Field Coy moved from MONCHY to FREVILLERS.	
FREVILLERS	21/9/18		R.E. Headquarters moved from ARRAS to FREVILLERS. C.R.E. 11th Division handed over to C.R.E. 2 Division. 67th 68th & 86th Field Coys training.	
do	22/9/18		Church parade of the 3 companies under S.P.P.E. 86th Coy bought NRTFACREAVES joined 85 F.C. officiated. Per Lt KING S.C.F. C of E. 11th Division Capt G.N. KINGSFORD M.C. R.E. returned from leave in France. Lieut W.E.A. MASTERS M.C. R.E. 86 Field Coy R.E. returned from leave in U.K.	

P.R.B.

Army Form C. 2118.

WAR DIARY
or
INTELLIGENCE SUMMARY.
(Erase heading not required.)

Instructions regarding War Diaries and Intelligence Summaries are contained in F. S. Regs., Part II. and the Staff Manual respectively. Title pages will be prepared in manuscript.

Place	Date	Hour	Summary of Events and Information	Remarks and references to Appendices
FREVILLERS	23/9/18		Co. training & refitting. Capt. A.T. POUND 286th Fd Co. transferred to 547th Field Co.	
"	24/9/18		Transport of this Field Co. moved to BERNEVILLE with 248 Inf. Bde. Group.	
"	25/9/18		Field Co. & transport moved to OCEAN WORK near VIS-EN-ARTOIS	
VIS-EN-ARTOIS	26/9/18		R.E. H.Q. moved to ADEN HILL near VIS-EN-ARTOIS. This Field Co. moved after dark to neighbourhood of CAGNICOURT.	
ARRAS-CAMBRAI ROAD	27/9/18		R.E. H.Q. moved to main ARRAS-CAMBRAI Road north of VILLERS-LES-CAGNICOURT (K.B. central). Zero hour of attack 5.20 a.m. Field Co. were employed as follows:- 67th Field Co. - Haut Sombon bridge on Arras-Cambrai Road & main ARRAS - CAMBRAI Road. - Portion & trestle bridge for infantry about 200 yds. east of main road. Reconnaissance of roads through MARQUION to be ETINDY. 686 Field Co. - supply of bridging material to 67th Field Co. Constructed two cork float bridges over Canal du nord. SAINS-LEZ-MARQUION. Reconnoitred bridge on AGACHE RIVER & found intact.	

D. D. & L., London, E.C.
(A10266) W_t W₅30/P713 750,000 2/16 **Sch. 82** Forms/C2118/16

WAR DIARY
INTELLIGENCE SUMMARY

Army Form C. 2118.

Place	Date	Hour	Summary of Events and Information	Remarks and references to Appendices
ARRAS-CAMBRAI Road.	28/9/18		85th Field Co. - Medium Pontoon Bridge at main road crossing completed 4.30 p.m. Trestle Bridge + 18 ft. girder span on main road 3.30 p.m. W.T. Road Completed 3.30 p.m. S.R.E. Hutts (R.) - 1 Coy on road opposite W.T. Cries on night 28/29. ½ Coy each attached to this Field Co. - 42 all ranks arriving Div. Engr. to git. gun teams. (Summary of work attached.) Major H.T. SOMERVILLE, O.C. 87th Field Co, and 8 O.Rs wounded. 67 Field Co. moved to MARQUION, and 88th + 85th Field Cos. to south of BARALLE. 67th Co. reconnoitering. 88th Co. on repair to Pontoon bridge + improving MARQUION Water supply. 85th Co. dealing with green cross on main ARRAS-CAMBRAI Road. S.E.Hutto (R.) on forward road repairs.	
BARALLE.	29/9/18		C.R.E. + xxx R.E. H.Q. moved to BARALLE. Field Co. reconnoitering, dugouts + water supply. S.R.E. Hutto (R.) on road repairs.	
"	30/9/18		Work as above. 11/A.R.SAF. proceeded on leave roll effect from 1/10/18	

Captain & Adjutant, R.E.

Summary of work carried out by R.E. and Pioneers 11th Division on 27th September 1918 near MARQUION during the attack over the CANAL DU NORD.

A copy of C.R.E's Order No.10 is attached.

J.A.K White

Lieut.Colonel, R.E.
C.R.E. 11th Division.

30. 9. '18.

War diary

The detail of the work carried out by the various units is as follows:-

68th Field Company, R.E.

½ Company with ½ Company Pioneers with 4 pontoon wagons loaded with cork floats reached BUISSY about 8-30 a.m. Reconnaissance party pushed forward and selected sites for footbridges and sent back for wagons and remainder of party.
When within about 150 to 200 yards of canal bank the wagons came under heavy M.G. fire, several horses and 4 drivers being wounded, the teams were therefore unhooked and sent back and the wagons were pushed down by hand reaching bank about 10 a.m. Footbridge near G.crossing was repaired and two other footbridges across the swampy bottom of canal about 60 ft.wide were also thrown across successfully enabling the Infantry to cross without any difficulty.

The footbridge at W.20.b.8.0. was afterwards converted to take pack transport and was in use for the M.G.Battalion pack transport by 12 noon.

Reconnaissance party pushed forward into MARQUION and sent back report at 1 p.m. that the main road culvert over AGACHE was intact and no sign of being mined.
They later made further reconnaissance of MARQUION. As the culvert was not broken the remainder of the 68th Field Company were held in reserve.

86th Field Company, R.E.

The first task was to construct a Weldon trestle bridge for horse transport alongside the demolished culvert at W.9.c.7.6. and to replace culvert with an iron girder bridge 18ft. span to take one way lorry traffic.

½ 86th Field Company with ½ Company Pioneers and trestle wagon, tool cart and 3 lorries with girder bridge pushed up to W.1.d.0.1. by 9 a.m..
Reconnaissance parties were pushed forward but were unable to reach the site of the work owing to heavy shelling and M.G. fire before 1, a.m.
At 11.55 a.m. the working parties and material were ordered forward, and work was commenced at 12.55 p.m. the attacking parties not having left this culvert until 12.20 p.m.
The trestle bridge (one trestle and 2 bays superstructure) was constructed on the S. side of the road and the bridge and deviations to it were completed by 2.5 p.m.

Meanwhile work on the iron girder bridge 18ft. span 10ft roadway for lorry traffic was in hand on the Southern half of the main road and was completed by 3.25 p.m. A second bridge of the same type was constructed alongside the first on the following morning (complete by 11.30 a.m.) to provide 2 way lorry traffic.
At 2.5 p.m. as soon as trestle bridge was complete, the remaining ½ Company (less reconnaissance party) were pushed forward with the pontoons to the canal bank and work was commenced on a medium pontoon bridge for horse transport on the S. side of the main road and about 15 yards from the site of the old bridge. Considerable work had to be done on the approaches and a way cut through a broad belt of wire but bridge and approaches were complete and open for traffic at 4.50 p.m.
The length of the pontoon bridge was 120ft.

A reconnaissance party pushed forward in rear of the
34th Brigade attack on OISY LE VERGER and sent back
excellent information on the condition of roads etc.
Summary of reconnaissance report is attached.

67th Field Company, R.E.

The chief task of the 67th Field Company (plus
½ Company Pioneers) was to construct a D.type pontoon
bridge for lorry traffic near the demolished main road
bridge.
24 pontoons with special superstructure were pushed
forward by motor transport and crossed the lorry bridge
over the culvert at 3.30 p.m. Work on the approaches
had been commenced at 1.40 p.m. and work on the bridge
itself was started as soon as pontoons arrived.
The bridge was 120ft.long and the approaches were carried
back a distance of nearly 100 yards on the W. bank in
order to clear the main road for the construction of the
Inglis Bridge.
The construction of the bridge was most excellently
carried out and the bridge and approaches were available
for lorry traffic by 7.30 p.m.
A trestle and pontoon bridge for horse transport
(H.crossing) was to be constructed at W.15.a.9.8. The
bridge consisting of 2 pontoons and 3 trestles 90ft.span
was constructed and made an excellent Infantry crossing
but there was no road or track on the East bank possible
for wheeled transport.
A reconnaissance party followed the 32nd Brigade attack
on EPINOY and sent back reports which are included in
the summary.
Carried out the following work on Y-Z night. The 6th
East Yorks Pioneers repaired the main road from W.8.a.5.4.
to W.9.c.7.6. including work on crater at W.8.b.6.1
and removed some trees across the road.

Cleared the road through BARALLE to W.9.c.7.6..
On the 27th September 1½ Companies were employed on bridging work with Field Companies constructing approaches etc.
½ Company worked with the R.A. clearing roads and assisting the batteries to move into forward positions.
1 Company which had worked the previous night and ½ Company after completing infantry crossings with 68th Field Company worked on repairs and clearing obstructions including barricades on the road through MARQUION W.9.d.2.4 to W.16.b.6.4. and W.16.b.6.4. to W.5.d.8.8.
These roads were cleared and open to lorry traffic on the evening of the 27th inst.

Army Form C. 2118.

WAR DIARY
INTELLIGENCE SUMMARY.
(Erase heading not required.)

C.R.E. 11th Division.

Vol 28

Instructions regarding War Diaries and Intelligence Summaries are contained in F. S. Regs., Part II. and the Staff Manual respectively. Title pages will be prepared in manuscript.

Place	Date	Hour	Summary of Events and Information	Remarks and references to Appendices
BARALLE	1/10/18		Field Coys. reconnoitering dugouts, roads & SENSÉE Canal crossings. 6th E. Yorks (P) on forward work repair. Lt. BUNCE, 83rd Field Coy. proceeded on leave with effect from 2/10/18.	
"	2/10/18		67th & 83rd Field Coys. consolidating main line of resistance under Bde. Admin. 68th Field Co. on main defences of bridges over Canal du Nord. 6th E. Yorks (P) in Div. Reserve.	
"	3/10/18		Work continued as above. Capt. A.F. REID, 67 Field Co., returned from short leave. Having obtained an extension.	
"	4/10/18		Work continued as above. Capt. G.N. KINGSFORD, M.C. R.E. relinquished position of Adjutant on being appointed Commanding Officer 83rd Field Company. Lieut. E.R. CANHAM, 68th Field Coy. acting adjutant vice Capt. G.N. KINGSFORD.	
"	5/10/18		67th Field Coy. consolidating main line of resistance under Bde. orders. 68th Field Coy. maintaining bridges over Canal du Nord. 86th Field Coy. cleaning streets in MARQUION. 6th E. Yorks (P) work by other	
"	6/10/18		by Field Coy. repairing road by BARALLE WOOD. Work by other companies as on 5/10/18.	F.C.B

WAR DIARY
or
INTELLIGENCE SUMMARY.
(Erase heading not required.)

Army Form C. 2118.

Place	Date	Hour	Summary of Events and Information	Remarks and references to Appendices
BARALLE	7/10/18		Work continued as before. Lieut E D L HUNTER by "Field Coy" proceeded to Training Course at ROUEN. 2/Lt H. W. ADLER joined 68th Field Company from Base. 2/Lt C. G. STILLMAN by "Field Coy" returned from leave to UK having received an extension.	
do	8/10/18		Work continued. 2/Lt E D KNIGHT by "Field Coy" & 2/Lt H. SHOPLAND 68th Field Coy, and 2/Lt W. JONES 85th Field Coy returned from Training Course at ROUEN. Lieut (A/Captain) D.E. CLERK reported from 572nd Field Coy (56th Division) for duty with 85th Field Coy. D. E. CLERK. 2/Lt F.A. GREAVES left 86th Field Coy - transferred to 572nd Field Coy vice Capt. D.E. CLERK. Lieut E.T. DAVIES by "Field Coy" R.E. went on leave to UK with effect from 11th instant.	
do	9/10/18		85th Field Company moved from MARQUION to SANCOURT. Other companies held in readiness to move at tomorrow's notice. Reconnaissance of route through SANCOURT & BLECOURT into through ABANCOURT by 68th Coy.	

EPC

Army Form C. 2118.

WAR DIARY
or
INTELLIGENCE SUMMARY.
(Erase heading not required.)

Instructions regarding War Diaries and Intelligence Summaries are contained in F.S. Regs., Part II. and the Staff Manual respectively. Title pages will be prepared in manuscript.

Place	Date	Hour	Summary of Events and Information	Remarks and references to Appendices
BARALLE	10/10/18		67th Field Coy moved to SANCOURT Lentrue at S.8.c.8.0 68th Field Coy. ditto location S.5.c.5.2 6th B. Yorks (P.g.T.P) moved to same area at S.8.d.2.6. All three Field Companies reconnoitring roads and wells 6th B. Yorks (P.g.T.P) working on roads at SANCOURT	
do	11/10/18		67th 68th Field Companies reconnoitring roads tangents, and searching for booby traps. 81st Field Coy. reconnoitring bridge sites. Erecting trestle bridge across CANAL DE L'ESCAUT at T.8.a.3.3. for H.T. Pioneers working on roads at SANCOURT, BLECOURT, BANTIGNY and CUVILLERS	
do	12/10/18		67th Field Coy building bridge across CANAL DE L'ESCAUT at Lock N 3A to 17. — passable for field guns. 68th Field Coy clearing repairing roads BLECOURT area 81st Field Coy. repairing and decking two bridges over CANAL DE L'ESCAUT at Lock T.2.d.8.6. THUN LEVEQUE. Repairing wells at SANCOURT. Pioneers working on roads SANCOURT, BANTIGNY & CUVILLERS	

Army Form C. 2118.

WAR DIARY
or
INTELLIGENCE SUMMARY.
(Erase heading not required.)

Instructions regarding War Diaries and Intelligence Summaries are contained in F. S. Regs., Part II. and the Staff Manual respectively. Title pages will be prepared in manuscript.

Place	Date	Hour	Summary of Events and Information	Remarks and references to Appendices
BARALLE	13/10/18		Division relieved during night 12/13th by 2nd Canadian Division. CRE 11th Div. handing over to O.C. 2nd Brigade Canadian Engineers.	
do	14/10/18		Field companies moved down to MARQUION. 6th E. Yorks Regt. (P) moved to INCHY. Field companies improving billets by 2nd Coy. fitting up baths at SAILLY. 86th Coy improving billets. 62nd E. Yorks Regt. (P) moved to Rear CAMBRAI (57B A8 & 64) forward onwards under Chief Engineer.	
do	15/10/18		Companies bathing the equipping unnecessary. 86th Coy working on baths at SAILLY. Lieut E.D.KNIGHT proceeded on leave.	
do	16/10/18		As 15/10/18. 2/Lt A.C.SOAR returned from short leave to U.K. on 19/10/18	
do	17/10/18		As 16/10/18	
do	18/10/18		64th Coy. working on B.L.I. at BOIS DE BOUCHE. 86th Coy moving to NEUVILLE ST REMY. Lieut. H.E.BUNCE returned from short leave to U.K. 2/Lt. W.JONES 86th Field Coy proceeded on 14 days leave to U.K. with effect from 20th inst.	
do	19/10/18		64th Coy. working on B.L.I. at BOIS DE BOUCHE. 68th Coy training & equipping. 86th Coy. working on Reception Camp at NEUVILLE ST. REMY.	

WAR DIARY
or
INTELLIGENCE SUMMARY

Army Form C. 2118.

Place	Date	Hour	Summary of Events and Information	Remarks and references to Appendices
BARALLE	19/10/18		Cherry Farm. Preparing for trek.R.E. 67th & 68th Field Companies inspected by Major General T.R. DAVIES. C.B. commanding 11th Division congratulated by him upon their bridging and other work during the recent operations from 27th September to 12th October 1918. (86th Field Coy. being at NEUVILLE ST REMY were not inspected by G.O.C. 11th Division)	
do	20/10/18		67th Field Coy. moved to THUN ST. MARTIN with 32nd Brigade. 68th Field Coy. moved to ESCADOEUVRES with 33rd Brigade. 86th Field Coy. clearing repairing routes at NEUVILLE ST. REMY. 6th Q. Yorks Regt (P) moved to THUN ST MARTIN for work on roads under C.E. XXII Corps. Working on ESCAUDOEUVRES - IWUY ROAD. 86th Field Coy placed at disposal of C.E. XXII Corps for making up girder bridges in TILLOY DUMP.	
NAVES	21/10/18		C.R.E's Headquarters moved from BARALLE to NAVES with 67th & 68th Field Companies repairing bridges D.H.Q. 86th Field Coy making bridges at TILLOY DUMP. 6th Q Yorks Regt(P) working on roads.	
NAVES	22/10/18		as for 21/10/18	

E.R.C.

Army Form C. 2118.

WAR DIARY
or
INTELLIGENCE SUMMARY.
(Erase heading not required.)

Place	Date	Hour	Summary of Events and Information	Remarks and references to Appendices
NAVES	23/10/18		Work as on 22/10/18. 68th Field Coy. reconnoitring for bridge sites over CANAL DE L'ESCAUT south of DENAIN. 88th Field Company R.E. inspected by Major General H.R DAVIES, C.B. commanding 11th Division & congratulated by him upon their bridging and other work during operations from 27th September to 12th October 1918. Division placed under two hours notice to move to IIIrd Corps from 0800 24th Inst. Lieut. D.P.O. KELLY 86th Coy. returned from short leave to U.K.	
do	24/10/18		Work continued.	
do	25/10/18		Work continued as before by 86th Coy & Pioneers. 68th Field Coy. moved from ESCADOEUVRES to VILLERS en CAUCHIES 67th Field Coy. moved from THUN ST MARTIN to HASPRES, 67th Field Coy. clearing road of debris for demolished bridge or P. 13. a. 55	
do	26/10/18		in HASPRES. Repairing HASPRES – DENAIN ROAD. 68th Field Coy. Repairing & improving billets. 88th Field Coy. making up bridges in TILLOY R.E. DUMP. 68th Yorks Regt. (Pnrs) moving to SAULZOIR and working on SAULZOIR – VERCHAIN and VERCHAIN – MONCHAUX ROADS under Chief Engineer XXII Corps. 68th Field Coy. repairing road to level crossing	
do	27/10/18		Work continued at SAULZOIR STATION	E.C.

Army Form C. 2118.

WAR DIARY
or
INTELLIGENCE SUMMARY.
(Erase heading not required.)

Place	Date	Hour	Summary of Events and Information	Remarks and references to Appendices
NAVES	28/10/18		Work continued as before by 37 Field Company constructing trestle bridge over SELLE RIVER in HASPRES (P.13.c.0.4y)	
do	29/10/18		Work continued	
do	30/10/18		87th Field Company constructing girder bridge over SELLE RIVER in HASPRES (P.13.c.0.4)	
do	31/10/18		68th Field Company improving billets and training. Spanning battn. 86th Field Company working on bridges at TILLOY DUMP. 6th E. Yorks Regt (P.) working on roads under Chief Engineer.	

E.R.Bankier
Lt Col RE
11 Div.

Army Form C. 2118.

WAR DIARY
or
INTELLIGENCE SUMMARY.
(Erase heading not required.)

C.R.E. 11th Division

Place	Date	Hour	Summary of Events and Information	Remarks and references to Appendices
NAVES	1/11/18		67th Field Coy. constructing heavy girder bridge over SELLE River at HASPRES (P.13.c.04) 68th Field Coy. standing by. 86th Field Coy. moving from NEUVILLE ST REMY to NAVES. 6th E. Yorks Regt. tacking. 67th 68th & 86th Field Companies and 6th E. Yorks Regt.(P) moved to VERCHAIN.	
do	2/11/18		C.R.E. moved to HASPRES and took over from C.R.E. 4th Div. 67th & 68th Field Companies and two companies Pioneers moved from VERCHAIN to ARTRES. 67th & 68th Coys reconnoitering roads in VERCHAIN, QUERENAING, ARTRES, PRESEAU and CURGIES. 86th Field Compy. making plank roadway P.10.B.9.4.	
HASPRES	3/11/18		C.R.E. moved from HASPRES to QUERENAING and then to PRESEAU. 67th & 68th Field Coys moved from ARTRES to CURGIES. Reconnoitering roads. bridges. searching for mines at JENLAIN and TRIEZ.	
PRESEAU	4/11/18		Repairing roads in ARTRES	E.R.C.

Army Form C. 2118.

WAR DIARY
or
INTELLIGENCE SUMMARY.
(Erase heading not required.)

Instructions regarding War Diaries and Intelligence Summaries are contained in F. S. Regs., Part II. and the Staff Manual respectively. Title pages will be prepared in manuscript.

Place	Date	Hour	Summary of Events and Information	Remarks and references to Appendices
PRESEAU	4/11/18		86th Field Coy. moved from VERCHAIN to QUERENAING. Maintaining bridges at ARTRES. 6th E Yorks headquarters & remaining company moved from VERCHAIN to QUERENAING. Pioneers working on roads ARTRES, PRESEAU, JENLAIN - SAULTAIN.	
do	5/11/18		86th Field Coy. reconnoitring roads & bridges & working party by troops at SEBOURG, ROISIN. 68th Field Coy. ditto at ROISIN, 5TH and CURGIES and ANGREAU. 86th Field Coy. moved from QUERENAING to ARTRES. Maintaining heavy bridges over RHONELLE RIVER. Reconnoitring two Weldon trestle bridges. 6th E Yorks Regt (P) moved two companies to CURGIES and their HQ remaining company to FORT CURGIES. Working on roads. 67th Coy. erected pontoon bridge at A 26 c 3 y (SEBOURG) 68th Coy. repairing forward roads 68th Coy. building trestle bridge at A 26 c 3 y. Reconnoitring roads round filling craters.	
do	6/11/18		68th Coy. clearing roads filling sheekholes CURGIES - SEBOURG.	

WAR DIARY
or
INTELLIGENCE SUMMARY.
(Erase heading not required.)

Army Form C. 2118.

Place	Date	Hour	Summary of Events and Information	Remarks and references to Appendices
PRESEAU	6/11/18		6th E Yorks Regt (78) working on roads CURGIES - LE TRIEZ - SEBOURG - ROISIN. 2/Lt D.H. LEVINKIND proceeded on short leave to U.K. 67th Field Coy. building heavy girder bridge for tanks at A26 & 37. Suitable for traffic at 1700 hours. Reconnoitring roads ROISIN - BETTRECHIES, and bridges over RIVER HONNELLE. 68th Field Coy. building trestle bridge at PRÉ BÉLÈNE, B26 a 1.9. Reconnoitring bridges over R. HONNELLE at PRÉ BÉLÈNE and CUSSIGNIES, and roads ROISIN to AUTREPPE. Filling craters and shell holes through ROISIN. Clearing road mines.	
do	7/11/18		85th Field Coy moved to LE TRIEZ. 6th E Yorks Regt (P) (One company moved to LE TRIEZ). Working on roads PRESEAU - CURGIES - LE TRIEZ - ROISIN, SEBOURG - ROISIN. E.T. DAVIES, by 3rd Field Coy RE was awarded a Bar to the Military Cross. 2/Lt W.H. LEVINKIND 86th Field Coy was awarded the Military Cross.	

Army Form C. 2118.

WAR DIARY
or
INTELLIGENCE SUMMARY.
(Erase heading not required.)

Place	Date	Hour	Summary of Events and Information	Remarks and references to Appendices
PRESEAU	7/11/18	(1a)	Sergt W. TAGGART, 67/ Field Coy and Cpl H.E. RIXON, 68th Field Coy were awarded the D.C.M.	
			6/RE moving with 9th Div to CURGIES.	
	8/11/18		67 & 68th field companies moved to ROISIN. H.Q. of 6th B. Yorks plus two companies moved to ROISIN. 67/ & 68th Field Companies finishing heavy gunner bridge at PRE BELENE, B 26 a 19. 68th Coy also clearing crater at B 25 a 20. 68th Coy also clearing debris from under railway at B 20 a 5 0, which was made passable at 1800 hours and reconnoitring roads AUTREPPE to GUSSIGNIES. Pioneers working on roads ROISIN - ANGREAU, ROISIN - MEAURAIN, craters at railway at B 27 c 27.	
ROISIN	9/11/18		8th Field Coy moved to PRE BELENE. 6/RE moved with 9th Div to ROISIN. 67/ 68th field Coys (mostly) working on heavy bridge B 26 a 19. 67th Coy reconnoitring bridges at I 4 c 10 and H 5 a 20 85, and roads through HERGIES - HON HERGIES - HON HERGIES - BUTIAU - 68th Coy reconnoitring roads through EUGNIES - BUTIAU - LE CAMP PERDU - AULNOIS.	

WAR DIARY
or
INTELLIGENCE SUMMARY.
(Erase heading not required.)

Army Form C. 2118.

Place	Date	Hour	Summary of Events and Information	Remarks and references to Appendices
ROISIN	9/11/18 (6a)		6th E Yorks Regt. (P) working on roads ROISIN - AUTREPPS, and main BAVAY - NONTIGNIES ROAD, and to EUGNIES.	
AULNOIS	10/11/18		CRE moved with HQ from ROISIN to AULNOIS. 86th Field Coy. moved from PRE BELENE to NOIRE FEMME FARM. The Pioneers moved to EUGNIES - HERGIES AREA. 468th Field Coys. building heavy bridge at PRE BELENE, consisting of three girder spans and one timber span, total about 65 feet, completed for traffic at 1400 hours. 6th E Yorks Regt (P.) Working on roads filling craters at B 30 a 3.9, B 22 a 1.6, C 25 a, C 25 d, C 26 c, C 29 d 9.6, C 24 c 7.9.	
do	11/11/18		468th Field Companies moved from ROISIN to AULNOIS by orders of the CRE given on 9 inst. Notice was received from Division that hostilities would cease at 1100 hours this day. Reconnaissance by 86th Field Coy. of roads for craters mines in BLAREGNIES - AULNOIS - QUEVY LE GRAND, HAVAY and COEGNIES - CHAUSSEE	

Army Form C. 2118.

WAR DIARY
or
INTELLIGENCE SUMMARY.
(Erase heading not required.)

Instructions regarding War Diaries and Intelligence Summaries are contained in F. S. Regs, Part II. and the Staff Manual respectively. Title pages will be prepared in manuscript.

Place	Date	Hour	Summary of Events and Information	Remarks and references to Appendices
AULNOIS	11/11/18		6th & Yorks Regt (?) repairing culvert at C.25 d 9.5. Working on roads and filling craters at C.26 c 2.4, C.29 c 7.9, C.29 d 9.5, C.29 d 8.1, C.28 c 5.7, B.30 a 3.9, I.2 b 2.6, I.3 a 2.3, I.3 a 3.3, I.3 a 4.2.	
do	12/11/18		69th Field Coy. reconnoitring road QUEVY LE GRAND — COEGNIES CHAUSSEES. Filling craters at D.30 a 1.9. E.13 a 6.8, E.13 a 4.9.	
			68th Field Coy. Repairing road AULNOIS – BLAREGNIES. Repairing culvert at D.15 b 4.8. Removing mines.	
			86th Field Coy. Filling craters at I.6 b 5.8, J.1 c 6.9, G.29 d 9.7, G.29 c 8.9, G.23 d 8.2.	
			6th & Yorks (?) Working on craters I.3 a 9.3, C.23 d 8.1, C.27 d 7.9, C.27 b 6. in addition to those stated yesterday. Constructing trestle bridge at E.8 b 1.7'. Filling crater at D.30 a 1.9.	
do	13/11/18		68th Field Coy. repairing roads: building culverts at D.21 b 5.7 and D.15 b 4.8.	
			86th Field Coy. working on craters as 12/11/18	

Army Form C. 2118.

WAR DIARY
or
INTELLIGENCE SUMMARY.
(Erase heading not required.)

Place	Date	Hour	Summary of Events and Information	Remarks and references to Appendices
AULNOIS	14/11/18		by 2 Field Coy. erecting timber trestle bridge at E 8 b 1.7. 68th do including culverts at D 21 b 5 Y. D 15 c 3.6 and D 15 b 4.8. 86th Field by 62nd E. Yorks Regt (?) continuing work on crating. Major G.N. KINGSFORD M.C. R.E. proceeded on one months leave to U.K. with effect from 18/11/18.	
do	15/11/18		Work as on 14/11/18.	
do	16/11/18		Work as on 15/11/18. 86th Coy. filling crater at E 4 a 8.8. 68th Coy. filling crater at D 25 d 2.2	
do	17/11/18 to		by 2 Coy. completing bridge at E 8 b 1.7. To take all traffic except tanks. Filling up divisional batt's. Carting timber from Boche dump to R.E. Dump at AULNOIS.	
	22/11/18		18th Coy. Removing trees from road D 9 c 2.1 - D 25 d 3.1. Repairing crater at D 9 c 2.1. Building culvert at D 21 c 5 Y. Filling in installing road at B 26 a 1.9 and bringing Hatton trestle bridge dismantling material to AULNOIS.	
(etr over)			86th Coy. laying dug sleepers over craters at C 29 c 8.9 + C 29 d 8 Y.	

Army Form C. 2118.

WAR DIARY
or
INTELLIGENCE SUMMARY.
(Erase heading not required.)

Place	Date	Hour	Summary of Events and Information	Remarks and references to Appendices
AULNOIS	19/11/18		86th Coy (att) Securing crater at J.1.c.6.9. filling in and hard staff, relaying sleepers for one way lorry traffic. 8/9 Yorks Regt (T.P.) working on roads improving billets. MAJOR C. J. FEARFIELD M.C., RE returned from short leave to U.K. on 19/11/18. 2/Lieut SHOPLAND R.E. proceeded on short leave to U.K. on 18/11/18 with effect from 21/11/18.	
do	22/11/18		All the companies engaged in recreational training.	
do	23/11/18		Companies bathing training.	
do	24/11/18 & 25/11/18		Ditto.	
do	26/11/18		C.R.E. moved his headquarters from AULNOIS to HASNON. 67th Field Coy moved his 32 Bde to AULNOY. 68th Field Coy moved with 33 Bde to OMNAING. 86th Field Coy moved with 34th Bde to MAING.	
HASNON	29/11/18		67th Field Coy moved with 32 Bde to EUGNIES. 68th Field Coy moved with 33 Bde to DOUR. 86th Field Coy moved with 34th Bde to ROISIN.	

Army Form C. 2118.

WAR DIARY
or
INTELLIGENCE SUMMARY.
(Erase heading not required.)

Place	Date	Hour	Summary of Events and Information	Remarks and references to Appendices
HASNON	27/11/18		68th E Yorks Regt (79) moved from EUGNIES to ANZIN district arriving 28th inst.	
do	28/11/18		67th Field Coy moved from AULNOY to LES GLODENNES (HASNON)	
			68th Field Coy moved from OMNAING to HASNON.	
			85th Field Coy moved from MAING to LES FAUX (HASNON)	
do	29/11/18 to 30/11/18		Companies improving billets; recreation. Assisting farmers with horses.	
			68th Coy repairing roads	

E.P.Burton
Lt. Col. RE
11th Division

Army Form C. 2118.

WAR DIARY
or
INTELLIGENCE SUMMARY.
(Erase heading not required.)

C.R.E. 11th A. Division

Place	Date	Hour	Summary of Events and Information	Remarks and references to Appendices
HASNON	1/12/18		Companies improving billets, forming educational recreation rooms, building tables, attaching benches to trestles. Practising farmers with lorries.	
	2/12/18		14 PARTRIDGE arrived to take the rank with Lieut. Jeng 2/12/18 three reduced one from each company. Lieut. Command of Capt. CLERK	
	3/12/18		86th Field Coy. R.E. moved to ST. AMAND to met workshops at 8th Corps R.E. Yard.	
	4/12/18		Work continued as above.	
	5/12/18		85th Field Coy. erected temporary trestle bridge at O.26 d.13 (sheet 74).	
			Other work continued as before	
	8/12/18		86th Field Coy. making loopholes for MT's 11 Division at RAISMES.	
	9/12/18		Fitting up balcony at 32 Bde. at WALLERS. Work continued by other companies as before.	
			Work at WALLERS	
	10/12/18		Work continued. 85th Field Coy. working on permanent concrete bridge at O.28 d.13 sheet 74.	
	16/12/18		68th Field Coy. building dam at DAISY MILL, DENAIN	
			2/Lt H.G.F. FEASEY joined 68th Field Company for duty.	
	16/12/18		Work as before 2/Lt C.G. STILLMAN R.E. proceeds to England to buy soda water factory for 11 Division.	
	17/12/18			
	18/12/18		Work continued. Lt Col SPECKWHITE D.S.O. C.R.E. 11 Division proceeds one months spent leave 21st with effect from 19/12/18 Major G.A. BUDDLE, M.C. R.E. assumed duties of C.R.E.	

Major G.A. BUDDLE, M.C. R.E.

Army Form C. 2118.

WAR DIARY
or
INTELLIGENCE SUMMARY.

(Erase heading not required.)

Instructions regarding War Diaries and Intelligence Summaries are contained in F. S. Regs., Part II. and the Staff Manual respectively. Title pages will be prepared in manuscript.

Place	Date	Hour	Summary of Events and Information	Remarks and references to Appendices
HASNON	19/12/18 to 23/12/18		Work continued at ST AMAND, WALLERS, RAIMES, DENAIN & O.28.d.13. Major G.N. KINGSFORD M.C. returned from leave to U.K. on 20/12/18.	
do	24/12/18		H.X.H. PARTRIDGE M.C. R.E. returned from leave to U.K. on 21/12/18. All sections returned from detachment for Xmas. 2/Lt H. SHORLAND proceeded on special leave to U.K. with effect from 19/12/18.	
do	25/12/18 to 26/12/18		Holiday.	
	27/12/18		Three sections one from each company under command of Capt REID. M.C. R.E. moved to SOMAIN forward on 8th Corps Concentration Camp. Major J.R. BUDDLE M.C. R.E. proceeded on special leave to U.K. for 30 days to U.K. with effect from 28/12/18. Major C.J. FEARFIELD M.C. R.E. assumed duties of C.R.E. 11th Division.	
do	28/12/18 to 31/12/18		Work continued on dam at DENAIN. Baths Delousing chamber at DENAIN. Baths & Delousing chamber at WALLERS. Delousing chamber at CONDÉ. Concrete Bridge at O.28.d.13. & Stabling at RAISMES. 2/Lt WALLER & one section of 69 Field Coy proceeded to ST AMAND for work on 8th Corps workshops on 28/12/18. Capt. T.R. SNELLING R.A.M.C. M.O. R.E. & L.J. MASTERS R.E. proceeded on short leave to U.K.	
	31/12/18		Lt L.H. PARTRIDGE by Field Coy R.E. awarded M.C.	

G.R. Bareham
Major 94th Fld Coy R.E.
11th Divn.

Army Form C. 2118.

WAR DIARY
or
INTELLIGENCE SUMMARY.
(Erase heading not required.)

C.R.E, 11th DIVISION.

Instructions regarding War Diaries and Intelligence Summaries are contained in F. S. Regs., Part II. and the Staff Manual respectively. Title pages will be prepared in manuscript.

Place	Date	Hour	Summary of Events and Information	Remarks and references to Appendices
HASNON.	1.1.19 to 4.1.19.		Three Sections, one from each Company, under the command of CAPT. REID. M.E.,R.E, on work at VIIIth Corps Concentration Camp SOMAIN. 67th Field Company making loose boxes for D.A.D.V.S, 11th Div. at RAIMES, erecting Delousing Chamber at WALLERS. 68th Field Coy working on improvements to Theatre HASNON. 86th Field Coy working on permanent bridge at 0.28 d 1.3. (Sheet 44)	
	4.1.19.		Major G.A.BUDDLE M.C, R.E, 86th Field Coy awarded D.S.O. and mention	
	5.1.19. to 11.1.19.		Lieut G.O.HUNTER R.E, 67th Field Coy proceeded on short leave to U.K. 67th Field Coy completed work for D.A.D.V.S, at RAIMES	
	11.1.19.		Work continued as above	
	11.1.19.		iiLt.J.D.WALKER and Section returned from ST.AMAND.	
	11.1.19. to 16.1.19.		67th Field Coy - Delousing Chamber completed at WALLERS, work continued as above	
	16.1.19.		Lt.MASTERS M.C, 86th Field Coy, returned to Coy from short leave to U.K. 67th Field Coy, one section proceeded to SOMAIN for work under CAPT. REID.	
	18.1.19.		iiLieut WALKER proceeded to SOMAIN for duty with CAPT REID.	
	19.1.19.		CAPT&DUFF M.C,R.E, relieved Capt Reid M.C,R.E, at SOMAIN.	
	20.1.19.		Lieut Col.F.A.K.WHITE D.S.O,C.R.E, rejoined leave from U.K.	
	20.1.19. to		Work continued as above.	
	24.1.19.		67th Field Coy, Capt Reid M.C.R.E. proceeded on 30 days special leave to U.K.	
			Sections on detachment at SOMAIN rejoined their respective Companies	
	25.1.19.		Lieut,Masters M.C,R.E, proceeded to ROUEN R.E. Training School.	

Army Form C. 2118.

WAR DIARY
or
INTELLIGENCE SUMMARY.
(Erase heading not required.)

Instructions regarding War Diaries and Intelligence Summaries are contained in F. S. Regs., Part II. and the Staff Manual respectively. Title pages will be prepared in manuscript.

Place	Date	Hour	Summary of Events and Information	Remarks and references to Appendices
HASNON.	27/1/19.		General Parade of 11th Div.R.E. and presentation of Medals ribbons by G.O.C. Division.	
	28/1/19.		Major G.A. BUDDLE D.S.O, M.C. rejoined 86th Coy after 30 days leave	
	31/1/19.		Major G.M. KINGSFORD proceeded to U.K. for demobilization, Command of 67th Field Coy handed over to Lieut E.T. DAVIES M.C, R.E,. Lieut.STILLMAN M.M. R.E, rejoined 67th Field Coy from U.K.	

E.Knight.
Lieut & /Adjutant R.E.
For C.R.E. 11th Division.

11 Division

Herewith copy
of War Diary for
month of Feb 1919.

D O'Kelly
Lt. / Col.
for CRE 11th Division

C.R.E.
11th DIVISION
No. 53/486
Date

Army Form C. 2118.

WAR DIARY
of
INTELLIGENCE SUMMARY.

HEADQUARTERS.
11TH DIVISIONAL ROYAL ENGINEERS.

(Erase heading not required.)

Instructions regarding War Diaries and Intelligence Summaries are contained in F. S. Regs. Part II. and the Staff Manual respectively. Title pages will be prepared in manuscript.

Place	Date	Hour	Summary of Events and Information	Remarks and references to Appendices
HASNON	1/2/19		Major G.A.Buddle, D.S.O., M.C., R.E. to be C.R.E., 11th Division, and Acting Lieut-Colonel whilst so employed. Lieutenant D.P.O'Kelly M.C. takes over Command of 86th Field Coy. 67th Coy work on repairs to damaged billets 68th Field Coy on repairs to damaged billets 86th Field Coy, construction of concrete bridge at O.28.d.1.3. Sheet 44.	
	2/2/19		Church Parade - No work.	
	3/2/19		Parade of Divisional Engineers. Lt.-Col. White bids farewell on leaving Division to take up appointment as C.E., IVth Corps. Captain J.B.Cowper reports for duty from 87th Field Coy., R.E., and takes over Command of 86th Field Company.	
	4/2/19 5/2/19		Work continued as above. Sections detached for work at SOMAIN Concentration Camp rejoin their respective Units. Captain D.E.Clerk proceeds on 1 months leave to U.K.	
	6/2/19 to 8/2/19		Work continued as above. Lieut. F.C.Willis rejoins from leave to U.K. Captain R.D.Duff proceeds to Corps Demobilisation Camp.	
	9/2/19		Church parade - No work.	
	10/2/19 to 16/2/19		Lt. W.Jones proceeds to England for demobilisation. 2/Lieut. F.C.Cocks is attached to VIIIth Corps Signal Company for duty. Lieut. A.D.Sinclair returns from leave to U.K.. Work continued as above.	
	17/2/19		Major C.J.Fearfield and Captain A.O.T.Webb proceed on leave to U.K.	
	18/2/19 to 24/2/19		2/Lieut. H.M.Keeble is attached to 1st Army Signal Company for duty. Work continued as above.	

Army Form C. 2118.

WAR DIARY
or
INTELLIGENCE SUMMARY.

H.Q.R.E., 11th Division.

(Erase heading not required.)

Instructions regarding War Diaries and Intelligence Summaries are contained in F.S. Regs., Part II. and the Staff Manual respectively. Title pages will be prepared in manuscript.

Place	Date	Hour	Summary of Events and Information	Remarks and references to Appendices
Hasnon	25/2/19 and 26/2/19		Captain A.F.Reid rejoins from leave, and takes over command of 67th Field Company from Lieutenant E.T.Davies.	
	27/2/19		Work continued as above. R.E.Hqrs and Three Field Companies moved to CITE MARTIN, DENAIN.	
Denain.	28/2/19		Field Companies employed on clearing and repairing billets. Lieutenant W.Jobson proceeds to U.K. on short leave.	

D.O'Kelly

Lieut. & A/Adjutant, R.E.,
11th Division.

Army Form C.2118.

WAR DIARY
or
INTELLIGENCE SUMMARY.
(Erase heading not required.)

Instructions regarding War Diaries and Intelligence Summaries are contained in F. S. Regs. Part II. and the Staff Manual respectively. Title pages will be prepared in manuscript.

Place	Date	Hour	Summary of Events and Information	Remarks and references to Appendices
DENAIN.	1/3/19.		All Field Coys, employed on cleaning and repairing billets at CITE MARTIN. Major R.L.Roseveare 11th Div:Sig.Coy. granted leave to U.K. 1st March to 10th.	
"	2/3/19.		Work as above.	
"	3/3/19.		Work as above.	
"	4/3/19.		Work as usual. Capt. A.O.T.Webb.M.C. rejoined from leave and takes over command of 11th Div.Sig.Coy. Lt.D.P.O'KELLY,M.C.R.E. transferred from 86th Field Coy.R.E. to Hd Qtrs to be Adjutant, 11th Divisional Engineers.	
"	5/3/19.		Lieut.L.H.PARTRIDGE.M.C.R.E.,granted 14 days Special Leave to U.K. 4th to 18th March.	
"	6/3/19.		Capt.A.O.T.WEBB. proceeded to 8th Div:Sig.Coy.R.E. as Officer Commanding. Lieut.SINCLAIR.A.W.(M.C.) assumes command of the 11th Div.Sig.Coy.R.E.	
"	6/3/19		Field Coys Billets inspected by G.O.C.,11th Division.	
"	7/3/19		Work as above. Lieut.C.R.SARGENT. granted leave to U.K. 7th to 21st March.	
"	8/3/19.		Draft of 28 O.Rs of 11th Div:Sig.Coy.proceeded to 2nd Army Sig.Coy. for duty.	
"	to 18/3/19.		Lieut.E.T.DAVIS.M.C. proceeded on short leave to U.K. Field Coys employed on cleaning and packing harness and equipment.	
"	19/3/19.		Major W.L.Roseveare returns from leave & takes over command of 11th Div.Sig.Coy.R.E. Major J.B.F.COWPER. 86th Field Coy.R.E. granted leave to U.K. 2nd Lt E.H.LEVINKIND.M.C. takes over command of 86th Field Coy.R.E. Lieut.C.G.STILLMAN 67th Field Coy.R.E. proceeded to 457 Field Coy R.E. 62nd Division.	
"	20/3/19		Work as above.	
"	21/3/19		Lieut.W.JOBSON.M.C.,rejoins 68th Field Coy.R.E.,from leave.	
20/3/19 to 22/3/19	22/3/19.		R.E. Band visit to DENAIN.	
"	23/3/19.		Major.FEARFIELD.M.C.R.E., proceeded from 68th Field Coy.R.E. to 22nd Field Coy.R.E., to take over command. Lt.L.J.BLAKE takes over command of 68th Field Coy.R.E.	
"	24/3/19			
"	25/3/19 to 26/3/19		Work as usual.	
"	27/3/19.		Lieut.W.JOBSON.M.C.,proceeded to U.K. for Demobilization.	
"	28/3/19.		Work as usual.	
"	29/3/19		Lieut.E.T.DAVIS.M.C. rejoins Unit from leave.	
"	30/3/19			
"	31/3/19		Work as above:	

O.Kelly
Lt.& Adjutant.R.E.
11th Div:R.E.Brigade Group.

6/4/19

Army Form C. 2118.

WAR DIARY
or
INTELLIGENCE SUMMARY.
(Erase heading not required.)

HQ RE
11th DIVISION

No 34

Place	Date	Hour	Summary of Events and Information	Remarks and references to Appendices
Rue de St Amand	March 17/3/19		Administration of Divisional RE. Col C.A. Bell D.S.O. M.C. R.E. who was appointed O/CRE 11 Division to proceed to V/K ENGINEER no CRE V/K ENG MNES SIR AREA	
DENAIN	20/19		to other moveable line	

D Dunn
Capt & Adjutant. R.E.

C.R.E.
11TH DIVISION
No. 53/505
Date

Army Form C. 2118.

WAR DIARY
or
INTELLIGENCE SUMMARY.
(Erase heading not required.)

Place	Date	Hour	Summary of Events and Information	Remarks and references to Appendices
DENAIN	1/5/19 to 31/5/19		Companies employed on Camp fatigues cleaning and packing Unit equipment. Work throughout the month as for the 1st. Field Company CADRES reduced from 2 Off.and 50 O.R's. to 2 Off.and 40 O.R's. Capt. A.F.Reid given permission to wear the badges of rank of Major, Lieut.E.T.Davies those of Captain. Demobilization continued. The following units were attached for administration 21/5/19. 216th. A.T. Coy. R.E. 172nd. (T) Coy. R.E. 175th. (T) Coy. R.E. 176th. (T) Coy. R.E. 179th. (T) Coy. R.E. 185th. (T) Coy. R.E. No.1 Siege Coy. R.M. R.E.	

P.O.Kell

Captain. Adjutant.
Hd. Qrs. R.E. 11th. Divnl. Group.

Army Form C. 2118.

WAR DIARY
or
INTELLIGENCE SUMMARY.
(Erase heading not required.)

H.Q. R.E. 11th DIVISION.

JUNE 1919.

Instructions regarding War Diaries and Intelligence Summaries are contained in F. S. Regs., Part II. and the Staff Manual respectively. Title pages will be prepared in manuscript.

Place	Date	Hour	Summary of Events and Information	Remarks and references to Appendices
DENAIN.	7/6/19.		FIELD COYS (CADRES) Despatched to U.K. for DEMOBILIZATION. 67. 68. & 86	
"	14/6/19.		H.Q. Transport, attached for Guard, to 86th Field Coy. R.E. moved to LOURCHES.	
"	17/6/19.		1/6th MINCHINTON transferred to 135% (A.T.) Coy. ANZIN.	
"	26/6/19.		172 (T) Coy. R.E. att'd for administration, despatched to U.K. with Equipment for Dispersal.	
"	27/6/19.		No I Siege Coy. R.M.R.E. att'd for administration moved from ST AMAND to DENAIN.	
"	29/6/19.		185 (T) Coy. R.E. 179 (T) Coy. R.E. 216 (A.T) Coy. R.E. Attached R.E. Coys for Administration, Stores having been handed into Ordnance & Vehicles despatched to O.O. Beaumanoir, Calais, were despatched to Concent. Camp. SOMAIN, for Demobilization.	
	July.			
DENAIN.	1-7-19.		Lorries moved stores etc to Entraining Stage, LOURCHES.	
—	2-7-19.		EQUIPMENT GUARD entrain: at LOURCHES en route via DUNKIRK to ENGLAND for final DISPERSAL.	

P. O. Kelly
Capt & Adjt. R.E.
11th DIVISION GROUP.

G.R.E.
11th DIVISION

Short account of operations carried out by
ROYAL ENGINEERS and PIONEERS

of the 11TH DIVISION from 2ND NOVEMBER 1918.

Reference maps Sheets 51A & 51.

DISPOSITIONS. On 2nd November the 67th, 68th and 86th Field Companies and the 6th East Yorks Regt.(Pioneers) were moved up, under orders of C.R.E. to VERCHAIN.

On the night 2/3rd Novr. the 11th Division relieved the 4th Division in the line East of PRESEAU.

On the 3rd inst. D.H.Q. moved to HASPRES, as also did the C.R.E.

GENERAL PLAN AND NARRATIVE OF OPERATIONS.

Instructions had been issued by D.H.Q. for the 32nd Brigade on right and 33rd Brigade on left to attack, on the 4th inst. a line C.7.b.5.5 - G.1.d.8.0 - along the river AUNELLE and east edge of wood to A.26.c.2.6 - F.29.b.0.4 - F.23.central.

3rd November.

In consequence of enemy's retirement the above instructions for attack were cancelled.

The C.R.E. issued orders to the 67th and 68th Fd.Coys. and two companies of Pioneers to move up to ARTRES and carry out rapid reconnaissance of roads in QUERENAING, ARTRES, PRESEAU, and CURGIES, repairing the worst places to enable horse transport to get forward.

Divisional Headquarters issued fresh instructions later in the day for the pursuit of the enemy to be resumed at 0530 am the 4th inst. the advance to be in bounds to:-
(1) A.27 central - A.21.d.
(2) Ridge east of ROISIN to A.24.central.
(3) Line of the HONELLE.
Final objective - line of BAVAY - MONTIGNIES road.

4th November.

The attack, as ordered, was resumed at 0530 on 4th inst. and both Brigades crossed the river AUNELLE and reached the high ground east of the river, but were counter-attacked and driven back a short distance.

The C.R.E. moved his Headquarters, with D.H.Q. to QUERENAING and later in the day to PRESEAU.

He instructed the 67th and 68th Fd.Coys. to move forward to CURGIES, and carry out immediate reconnaissance of the main roads and bridges and search for mines at JENLAIN, SAULTAIN and LE TRIEZ.

The brick bridge over the AUNELLE at LE TRIEZ A.25.c.3.7 had been demolished by the enemy on his retirement. The material required for a heavy bridge to replace this was telegraphed to Chief Engineer, XXII Corps.

The reconnaissance party of 68th Field Coy. reached the bridge at SEBOURG A.20.c.7.0 before the mine laid there had been fired. The Germans detailed for this duty had apparently been caught in our barrage and were either wound killed or wounded close by. The Officer in charge of the reconnoitring party removed the detonators and cut the mines, rendering the charge harmless, and removed the charge the following day.

The repairing of roads already reconnoitred was continued by all available ranks of the Field Coys. and Pioneers.

The 86th Field Coy. and the remaining Company of Pioneers were brought up to QUERENAING.

Orders were issued by D.H.Q. for the 32nd and 33rd Brigades to resume the attack at 0530 the next morning and capture the ridge East of SEBOURG, and after this had been secured to exploit the line of the second objective, i.e. the ridge east of ROISIN.

5th November.

The 67th Field Coy. erected a pontoon bridge across the River AUNELLE at A.26.c.3.7 for field guns and horse transport. This was completed at 1100 hours.

-2-

The attack by the 32nd and 33rd Brigades at 0530 on that day enabled them to reach a line about 200 yards East of MEAURAINS by 1500, the bulk of the enemy forces having been withdrawn during the previous night.

THE C.R.E. ordered the reconnaissance parties to push forward to SEBOURG, ETH, ROISIN and ANGREAU, and reports were received later showing a considerable number of craters at cross roads.

The 86th Field Coy. moved up to ARTRES to maintain the heavy bridges over the R.HONELLE and the Pioneer Company to FORT CURGIES for work on roads.

Orders were issued by D.H.Q. for 32nd and 33rd Brigades to continue the attack on morning of 6th inst. and sieze the crossings over GRANDE HONNELLE RIVER and advance up to the BAVAY - MONTIGNIES Road.

6th November

The pontoon bridge at A.26.c.3.7 was replaced by 67th Field Company by a Weldon trestle bridge, the pontoon having been damaged by artillery transport during the night and the pontoon holed and sunk. A heavy girder bridge was commenced at site of old brick bridge.

The attacking Battalions of the Infantry Brigades were prevented from getting up to the R.HONELLE by very heavy M.G.fire from far bank of river.

The attack was to be resumed on the 7th.

7th November.

The attack was continued at 0900 with artillery support but very little opposition was met with, and the 32nd and 33rd Brigades reached their onjective, across the river HONELLE with few casualties.

The heavy girder bridge was completed by 67th Field Company at 1700 hours, across the river AUNELLE at LE TRIEZ, capable of carrying tanks.

By this time too, the Field Companies and Pioneers had, by constant work, repaired the main roads up to this point and forward to ROISIN to take lorry traffic.

The 86th Field Coy. and one Company of Pioneers were moved under orders of C.R.E. to LE TRIEZ.

The 67th and 68th Field Coys. examined the bridges over the river HONELLE but found that every one had been demolished including the abutments in most cases. The materials required for a heavy bridge at B.26.a.1.9 were wired to C.E. that night.

Fords, passable for horse transport, were reconnoitred at B.19.a.2.0 and B.27.a.5.0

The 68th Fd.Coy. commenced a Weldon trestle bridge at PRE BELENE but gas shelling by the enemy necessitated a withdrawal for some hours of the working party here.

Roads from ROISIN - AUTHREPPE - BETTRECOMES were reconnoitred by Officers and small parties from each Company and the consequent reports shewed that practically every cross road east of the river HONELLE in the Divisional area had been blown up, leaving huge craters varying from 20 to 40 feet in diameter, ten to fifteen feet deep.

8th November.

Advance began at 0900 by 32nd and 33rd Brigades with final objectives the MONS - AULNOIS Railway. Only slight opposition was encountered until 1400 when general line C.22. central - C.29 cent. had been reached, where they came under considerably increased hostile M.G.fire and shelling. The infantry did not get beyond that line that day.

The 68th Fd.Coy. completed the Weldon trestle bridge at A.26.c. 1.9 early on this way, passable for 18 pounders and horse transport.

The material for heavy lorry bridge was received during the night, and unloaded and carried to the bridge site.

Just beyond this bridge, on the AUTREPPE Road, a large span, (120 feet) brick arch bridge carried the railway over the river HONNELLE and road at B.20.c.4.0. This had been demolished and the debris had blocked the road to a depth of 8-10 feet for a distance of about 100 ft. Two sections of the 68th Fd.Coy. and one company of Pioneers were sent by C.R.E. to work on this blockage, and it was made possible for horse transport by 1800.

The 67th and 68th Field Coys. and two companies of Pioneers were moved forward to ROISIN under orders of C.R.E.

Roads in AUTREPPE and GUSSIGNIES were reconnoitred and work commenced on them.

9th November.
The 67th and 68th Field Coys. commenced the heavy girder bridges at PRE BELENE.

Reconnaissance of forward roads, bridges and mines was continued through HERGIES, HON HERGIES, EUGNIES, BUTIAU, LE CAMP PERDU and AULNOIS. Again it was found that every cross road had been blown up leaving huge craters similar to those already described.

The Pioneers commenced work on ROISIN - AUTREPPE - EUGNIES and main BAVAY - MONTIGNIES roads.

The C.R.E. moved with D.H.Q. to ROISIN, and sent 86th Field Coy. to PRE BELENE for work on roads.

On this day the MONS - MAUBEUGE road was reached by infantry brigades without opposition.

10th November.
The 32nd and 33rd Brigades established themselves without opposition on the high ground east of HAVAY.

Divisional Headquarters with C.R.E. moved to AULNOIS.

The C.R.E. issued orders for the 86th Field Coy. to move to NOIRE FEMME, and the 6th East Yorks Regt.(Pioneers) to EUGNIES and HERGIES for work on roads.

The heavy girder bridge at PRE BELENE B.26.a.1.9 was completed for traffic at 1400 hours on the 10th. This bridge consisted of four spans, a total of nearly 65 feet, to take all traffic except tanks.

11th November.
Information was received that hostilities would cease at 1100 hrs on that date.

67th and 68th Field Coys. moved up to AULNOIS.

Roads through BLAREGNIES - AULNOIS - QUEVY LE GRAND, COEGNIES - CHAUSSEE and HAVAY were reconnoitred by 86th Field Coy. Several mines were cleared. Work on repairing roads was continued.

From 12th to 16th Novr.
Work was concentrated on roads and bridges. Three culverts were rebuilt on AULNOIS - BLAREGNIES Road, and a timber trestle bridge also for lorries erected over river WAMPE at E.8.b.2.8 North east of QUEVY LE GRAND.

GENERAL. The Corps R.E. Dumps from which material was available were situated at -
(1) TILLOY (West of CAMBRAI) and
(2) IWUY - 30 miles distant from AULNOIS as the crow flies.

All heavy bridging and road material had to be drawn from those dumps except, as regards the latter, what could be salved in the district, and the difficulties of transport over the broken roads and bridges were enormous.

By the 16th Novr. all the craters in the Divisional area had been filled in, those on the more main roads metalled and slabbed and capable of taking lorry traffic. Between 400 and 500 tons of metal and brick rubble and several hundred road slabs had been used. East of the River HONNELLE no less than 52 craters had been filled in.

Search parties of the 179th Tunnelling Coy. were attached to the C.R.E. to assist in locating mines. Twenty eight mines were found and removed by these parties, together with fifteen small charges placed along the railways. In addition fifteen mines were removed by the Field Companies plus six small charges from railways.

West (1779?)

11TH DIVISION

D. A. D. O. S.
SEP 1916 - JUN 1919

11TH DIVISION

Army Form C. 2118.

WAR DIARY
or
INTELLIGENCE SUMMARY
(Erase heading not required.)

Sep '16 — June 1916

D.A.D.I.S. XI Division

Vol II

Place	Date	Hour	Summary of Events and Information	Remarks and references to Appendices
Le Cauroy	1/9/16		Usual Routine	
do	2/9/16		Moved Divisional Armourers, Shoemakers & Saddlers Shops to Doullens. 1 W.O. & my clerk moved to Doullens with me.	
Doullens	3/9/16		Moved Divn Tailors Shops & remainder of Ordnance Staff from Le Cauroy to Acheux by W.O. & clerk moved with me to Acheux.	
Acheux	4/9/16		Visited ADOS II Corps in the morning.	
do	5/9/16		Usual routine	
do	6/9/16		Visited DADOS 25' Divn regarding taking over Tents for Dump at Senlis.	
Senlis	7/9/16		Moved Dump from Acheux to Senlis/Hérissart Road. Started 5.30 A.M. Finished 9-0 P.M.	
do	8/9/16		First consignment of Lewis Gun Handcarts received.	
	9/9/16		Usual routine	
	10/9/16		do	
	11/9/16		do	
	12/9/16		do	
	13/9/16		do	
	14/9/16		do	

Army Form C. 2118.

WAR DIARY
or
INTELLIGENCE SUMMARY
(Erase heading not required.)

D.A.D.O.S. XV Division

Instructions regarding War Diaries and Intelligence Summaries are contained in F. S. Regs., Part II. and the Staff Manual respectively. Title Pages will be prepared in manuscript.

Place	Date	Hour	Summary of Events and Information	Remarks and references to Appendices
Senlis	15/9/16 to 21/9/16		Usual Routine	
do	22/9/16		First consignment of P.H.G. Helmets received from Base towards completing Division with 1 P.H.G. & 1 T.H. Helmet per man	
do	23/9/16		Usual Routine	
do	24/9/16		do 8000 pairs of Gumboots received.	
	25/9/16		do	
	26/9/16		do	
	27/9/16		do	
	28/9/16		do	
	29/9/16		do	
	30/9/16		do	

[signature]
D.A.D.O.S XV Div.

Army Form C. 2118.

WAR DIARY
—OF—
INTELLIGENCE SUMMARY

(Erase heading not required.)

D.A.D.O.S. XI Division

Instructions regarding War Diaries and Intelligence Summaries are contained in F. S. Regs., Part II. and the Staff Manual respectively. Title Pages will be prepared in manuscript.

Place	Date	Hour	Summary of Events and Information	Remarks and references to Appendices
Senlis	1/10/16		Moved from Senlis to Acheux. All my Staff went on to Bernaville by road except workshops which went by rail.	
Acheux	2/10/16		Moved from Acheux to Bernaville	
Bernaville	3/10/16		Usual Routine.	
do	11/10/16		Moved from Bernaville to Domart	
do	5/10/16 to 19/10/16		Usual routine	
do	20/10/16		Transferred from II Corps to IV Corps.	
do	21/10/16 to 24/10/16		Usual Routine.	
do	25/10/16 to 31/10/16		Usual Routine. D.A.D.V.S. absent with leave to proceed to England.	

F Webster Lieut
to D.A.D.O.S.
11th Div.

Headquarters,
    11th Division.

     The War Diaries of the undermentioned Units have not been received for the months stated against them. It is requested that they may be forwarded as soon as possible and the attention of the Officers commanding be called to F.S.Regs.para 140 subsection 2 and C.R.140/592 dated 12.12.15 G.R.O. 1598.

Unit	Period
D. A. D. O. S.	July, August. (if possible)
M. V. S.	September, October.

General Headquarters   Sgd. H.Yates Captain
3rd Echelon.   D. A. A. G.
1/12/16.   for   D. A. G.

                    2.

D. A. G.
    3rd Echelon.

        Reference the above.

        The War Diary of M.V.S. for Sept. and October was sent attached to War Diary of A.D.V.S.

        D.A.D.O.S. did not keep a War Diary before Sept.

                        Sgd. G.L.Wright Capt.
                            for Major General
H.Q. 11th Division   Commanding 11th Division.
5th December 1916.

WAR DIARY

D.A.D.O.S. 11th Division.

Octr. & Novr.

Army Form C. 2118.

WAR DIARY
or
INTELLIGENCE SUMMARY

(Erase heading not required.)

A.D.O.S. 11th Division

Place	Date	Hour	Summary of Events and Information	Remarks and references to Appendices
Lulu	1/10/16		Moved from Lulu to Achenc. All my staff on to Beauville by road except workshops which moved by rail.	
Achenc	2/10/16		Moved from Achenc to Beauville.	
Beauville	3/10/16		Usual routine.	
do	4/10/16		Moved from Beauville to Doneart.	
Doneart	5/10/16 to 18/10/16		Usual routine.	
do	19/10/16		Transferred from II Corps to IV Corps.	
do	20/10/16 to 24/10/16		Usual routine	
do	25/10/16 to 31/10/16		Usual routine. A.D.O.S. absent with leave to proceed to England.	

J. Webster
Lieut. Col.
A.D.O.S. 11th Division

Army Form C. 2118.

WAR DIARY
or
INTELLIGENCE SUMMARY

(Erase heading not required.)

Instructions regarding War Diaries and Intelligence Summaries are contained in F. S. Regs., Part II. and the Staff Manual respectively. Title Pages will be prepared in manuscript.

Place	Date	Hour	Summary of Events and Information	Remarks and references to Appendices
Doual	1/11/16 to 4/11/16		Usual routine.	
"	5/11/16	4 pm	Lieut. J. Carbutt arrived as relief for Capt Kennedy admitted to Hospital.	
"	6/11/16		Obtained by L.P. - 2½ rny of Forster Electric + 103 spare batteries for D. Arty. Urgently required supplies from base not forthcoming purchased at asheville.	
"	7/11/16		Usual Routine	
"	9/11/16		Visited D. Arty H.Q. Iron Hall re Establishing lights	
"	10/11/16		Usual routine. Further consignment of Forster refits from Asheville.	
"	11/11/16		Moved from Doual to Yprondene	
Yprondene	12/11/16		Moved Waterlopes to -"-	
"	13/11/16		Usual routine. Corps move ordered. Issues from base for infantry service suspended by Telegrams	
"	14/11/16		H.Q. moved to Cana po lea. Ordnance remained at Yprondene pending further instructions	
"	15/11/16		In Canaple to as R. To Senlis to ass A.D.O.S. II Corps re officer dumps in new area. Two trench stores to be taken over. Lo D.A.D.O.S. II Div came me Rfro.	
Contry	16/11/16		Moved office + part of dumps to Contay. Reported by wire to A.D.O.S. II Corps appointed II + IV Corps.	

2449 Wt. W14957/M90 750,000 1/16 J.B.C. & A. Forms/C.2118/12.

Army Form C. 2118.

WAR DIARY
or
INTELLIGENCE SUMMARY

(Erase heading not required.)

Instructions regarding War Diaries and Intelligence Summaries are contained in F. S. Regs., Part II. and the Staff Manual respectively. Title Pages will be prepared in manuscript.

Place	Date	Hour	Summary of Events and Information	Remarks and references to Appendices
Hedauville	17/11/16		Moved from Contay to Hedauville. Notified A.D.O.S. II Corps.	
	18/11/16		Moved workshops from Forceville to Hedauville. 2nd Div. Artillery Sub-parks to II Div. for Ordnance services. Loads purchased in Amiens of Stores etc.	
	19/11/16		Usual routine	
	20/11/16		" "	
	21/11/16		" "	
	22/11/16		Usual routine. Visited Salvage dumps at Meaulte & Aveluy & A.D.O.S. II Corps.	
	23/11/16		" Visited Railhead Pull-y-Aire. Commenced transport of Trench Stores to Meaulte from Aveluy. 18th Div. dumps.	
	24/11/16		" Visited salvage Trench & Gun dumps. Visited A.D.O.S.	
	25/11/16		" Local purchases of cloths for Divl signs at Doullens. Sgt-major arrived from attached to work 2nd Div. Artry.	
	26/11/16		" "	
	27/11/16		Moved to Forceville.	
Forceville	28/11/16		Usual routine. Visited Railhead, Aveluy & Meaulte	
	29/11/16		To D.H.Q. & Amiens for local purchase of Artizan's Park saddlery	
	30/11/16		Usual routine.	

J. Cuthbertson Lieut
D.A.D.O.S.
11th Division

2449 Wt. W14957/M90 750,000 1/16 J.B.C. & A. Forms/C.2118/12.

WAR DIARY
or
INTELLIGENCE SUMMARY

Army Form C. 2118.

DANOS XI Corps Vol 1

Place	Date	Hour	Summary of Events and Information	Remarks and references to Appendices
Forceville	1/12/16	Usual Routine	Transferred from I to XI Corps.	
	4/12/16	"	2nd Divisional Artillery moved from 11th Div. to 2nd Div.	
	5/12/16	"	Conference of D.D.O.s at A.D.O.S. Office re Boot-Prevention.	
	6/12/16	"	5th & 266th Field Cos. and 10th D.C.L.I. (Pioneers) moved to 11th Div.	
	9/12/16	"	Commence to gather Boot Prevention Reserve of Stores. Visited IX Army Office Depot	
	12/12/16	"	100 airs 17th Emergency Ammunition Carriers returned for re-delivery by E.R.P.	
	13/12/16	"	Weekly conference at A.D.O.S. IV Corps Office.	
	15/12/16	"	Reported Box Iredell first consignment received	
	16/12/16	"	Transferred 263 Field Coy to 31st Division	
	18/12/16	"	Supply conformer - not present - not available	
	19/12/16	"	Douellens for L.P.	
	20/12/16	"	Transferred 11th D.C.L.I. (Pioneers) to 2nd Division. Athenian?	
	21/12/16	"	Transferred 5th Field Coy to 2nd Div.	
	23/12/16	"	Albanite for L.P.	
	24/12/16	"	219th Coy R.E. transferred from 33rd Div to 11th Div.	
	27/12/16	"	Ammo for L.P. Body Shields ordered 250 each received	
	28/12/16	"	IX Army Officers Clothing depot got stores.	
	30/12/16	"		
	31/12/16	"		

F Chibota Lieut
D.A.D.O.S.
11th Army

WAR DIARY or INTELLIGENCE SUMMARY

Army Form C. 2118.

Copy.   OADOS   11 Division   Vol 8

Instructions regarding War Diaries and Intelligence Summaries are contained in F.S. Regs., Part II. and the Staff Manual respectively. Title Pages will be prepared in manuscript.

(Erase heading not required.)

Place	Date	Hour	Summary of Events and Information	Remarks and references to Appendices
Toronville	1/1/17		Usual Routine. A.D.O.S. Conference. 2nd Army Chiefs medallists from XIII Corps.	
"	2/1/17		63rd Div. Artillery Transferred to 11th Div.	
"	3/1/17		L. Corporal - Officers Clothing Depot for Stores.	
"	4/1/17		Staff visitor for 63rd Div. arrived.	
"	5/1/17		63rd D.A.C. arrived. Advance party.	
"	6/1/17		11th D.A.C. move to rear area. S.A.A. return ammn. Lorries to D.A.C. employed	
"	9/1/17		Transferred 219th Field Co. R.E. to 32nd Division. Visited D.A.D.O.S. 63rd Div.	
"			to arrange to exchange.	
"	13/1/17		Visited Contrenville to British Billets.	
"	15/1/17		Visited A.D.O.S. weekly conference. Division to Cartigny Pasrehase - so fields for workshops up.	
"	16/1/17		Informal issue from Reserve with representations of 11th Div. Divn. to British I Army Clothing Depot for Stores	
"	17/1/17		Informal issues from Reserve.	
"			Communications much. Stores ammn at being handed over to Contrenville. D.A.D.O.S.	
"	18/1/17		Visited H.Q. of 63rd Div. arrive.	
"			Visited various dumps in this area to extent in surplus items were accumulated with	
"	20/1/17		transferred 63rd Divnl. Artillery. 11th Div. Field Coys, Pioneer Battn. Reserve Co. to 63rd Div.	
"	21/1/17		Moved office to Contrenville. Office to Marcoins.	
"	22/1/17		" Office to Contrenville. all to Tourneville	
"	23/1/17 to 31/1/17		" all to Contrenville. special office 10 am.	
			Refitting of Division	

F.W. Webster Capt.
A.D.O.S.
11th Div.

WAR DIARY for month of February, 1917.

D.A.D.O.S.

Army Form C. 2118

WAR DIARY
or
INTELLIGENCE SUMMARY
(Erase heading not required.)

Instructions regarding War Diaries and Intelligence Summaries are contained in F. S. Regs., Part II. and the Staff Manual respectively. Title Pages will be prepared in manuscript.

Place	Date	Hour	Summary of Events and Information	Remarks and references to Appendices
YPRENCH	1-2-17		Inspects the animals of 60th F.A.B.	
"	2-2-17		Ordinary duties. Visits M.V.S.	
"	3-2-17		Lecture to officers other than R.A. at 33rd Inf. Bde H. Qrs. On Cleanness.	
"	4-2-17		Inspects animals for evacuation at M.V.S.	
"	5-2-17		Inspects animals of 33rd Inf. Bde Group.	
"	6-2-17		Inspects animals of 34th Inf. Bde Group.	
"	7-2-17		Lecture to R.A. officers.	
"	8-2-17		Inspects animals of 33rd Inf. Bde Group.	
"	9-2-17		Inspects animals of Div. Sig. Co. + Div. H. Qrs.	

1875 Wt. W593/826 1,000,000 4/15 J.B.C.&A. A.D.S.S./Forms/C. 2118.

WAR DIARY or INTELLIGENCE SUMMARY

Army Form C. 2118.

Place	Date	Hour	Summary of Events and Information	Remarks and references to Appendices
Contay	1/2/17		Normal Routine.	
"	2/2/17		24 Lewis Guns received to complete battalions to 14 guns each.	
"	5/2/17		G.E. Lorries (Peerless) 67, 68 + 86 Field Co. moved from 63rd Div. to 17th Div.	
"	10/2/17		Moved from III Corps to XIII Corps. Visited A.D.O.S. at Doullens.	
"	11/2/17		Chief Butler, D.A.D.O.S. proceeded on leave to Scotland.	
"	19/2/17		Three Precautions enforced. Leaves from Base suspended.	
"	21/2/17		Moved from Contayville to Cramplen.	
"	22/2/17			
Cramplen	24/2/17		Sent lorries out to Raitchial Pulls Églises to obtain stores to store tent. O.a.D.S. arrived from leave.	
"	25/2/17		Moved to Raincheval. Offices + part stores	
Raincheval	26/2/17		Lorries not allowed to run on roads. Urgent issues made from Raincheval. Instructed by A.D.O.S. I Corps, 2 limbers only available moved stores from Raincheval to stores. Leaves from Base resumed.	
"	27/2/17		Much remaining stores by trains from Cramplen.	
"	28/2/17		A.D.O.S. I Corps visited to inspect office stores workshops laundry & exchanges.	

F. Webster Capt.
D.A.D.O.S.
17th Div.

Copy.

Army Form C. 2118.

WAR DIARY
or
INTELLIGENCE SUMMARY

(Erase heading not required.)

Instructions regarding War Diaries and Intelligence Summaries are contained in F. S. Regs., Part II. and the Staff Manual respectively. Title Pages will be prepared in manuscript.

Place	Date	Hour	Summary of Events and Information	Remarks and references to Appendices
Reninghelst	1/3/17		Usual routine	
"	9/3/17		Chinese Coy per battalion received to complete to 16 per battalion	
"	10/3/17		Leave ditto	
"	13/3/17		Permission given to run an Army between Richard & Abeele Transferred Divisional School to Abeele for Ordnance services	
"	15/3/17		Visited Brigade dumps. Visited A.D.O.S re return of certain articles of winter scale — No authority under orders are published	
"	16/3/17		Reported that insufficient number of P.U. tents were being returned.	
"	17/3/17		Reported accumulation of Ordnance stores in Brigade dumps contrary to Regulations	
"	19/3/17		Arrange for local purchase to Armentry.	
"	22/3/17		Transferred L. + L. T.M. Batteries to 2nd Canadian Division for Ordnance.	
"	23/3/17		Conference at A.D.O.S. office re issue of stores insufficient where	
"	24/3/17		Low supply of ordnance men. Requested that copies be sent to Ordnance.	
"	25/3/17		Ordered vans from Rouen	
"	27/3/17		Unfortetisioners from above.	
"	28/3/17		Asked Ordnance 3rd Div. to accept stores for 11th Div. Arty. to avoid transfer	
"	31/3/17		then Carpenter. Remade wagon from Rouen above.	

F.C. Webster Capt.
D.A.D.O.S.
11th Div.

WAR DIARY.

April 1917.

D.A.D.O.S.

WAR DIARY
—or—
INTELLIGENCE SUMMARY

(Erase heading not required.)

Army Form C. 2118.

Place	Date	Hour	Summary of Events and Information	Remarks and references to Appendices
Reinchevel	1/4/17		Arranged to supply 11th D.A. by lorry unless found impracticable	
"	2/4/17		to D.A.D.O.S. 3rd Div. re above and to M.R. Artillery. One lorry of stores delivered including horse shoes obtained from I.C.T.	
"	3/4/17		to Amiens. L.P. of material for Emergency park saddles. All men in Workshops put on making these saddles.	
"	6/4/17.		Transferred 11th D.A. to 3rd Div. Asked Rouen to send one truck only of urgent stores. Amiens re L.P. for Emergency park saddles.	
"	7/4/17		Move indefinite. Stores rejoined. Received issues from Base.	
"	8/4/17		Let lorry with stores to 11th D.A.	
"	9/4/17		To I Corps A.D.O.S. re possible moves arrangements, also re return of Irishmen to Base etc. Offered staff of 3 to 3rd Div. to run the necessary work of the Divn Arty. Received 2 Artzluvis guns from Salvage. Rails for infantry.	
"	10/4/17		3rd Army Ordnance dispatcheors lending staff to 3rd Div. Arrangement cancelled. To Amiens. L.P. for Battn standard nails. Flags, bunches etc. Workshops re Lewis Gun ship	
"	11/4/17		Division commenced moving. Received orders Move to Rethune 12/4/17	
"	13/4/17		Move of Ordnance to Rethune suspended.	
"	14/4/17		Asked 3rd Div. to Transfer 11th D.A. back to me. Transferred accordingly	
"	15/4/17		to A.D.O.S. V Corps. Instructed to wait for Railhead Stores Rect. Wire Telling to Stores. Sent two lorries with stores to Artillery down from 3rd Div. on 16th by lorries	
"	16/4/17		to M.R. Rennes. To D.D.O.S. I Army re move. To A.D.O.S. 1st Anzacs re move. to D.A.D.O.S.	
"	17/4/17		5th Australian Division re Talbois and Dump. to Amiens Road Rubslane.	

WAR DIARY
INTELLIGENCE SUMMARY

(Erase heading not required.)

Army Form C. 2118.

Place	Date	Hour	Summary of Events and Information	Remarks and references to Appendices
Rainsval	18/4/17		Reconnoitred Two trucks to Bapaume Railhead.	
"	19/4/17		Detail of move of 11th D.A. from 3rd Div received. Wired for information of Y & Z. T. M. Bo. who were with 3rd Canadians. Sent 2 lorry loads of stores to clear dump also W.O. & storemen & 3 fatigue men to remain with me lorry to clear Railhead and issue to Artillery. Sent lorry with detail stores & pomp up from Beaucourt to Artillery. 200 lorris Bon slings now finished. Board of Survey held on Contains, fatauis Leather, & 2nd Cartridges.	
"	20/4/17		Sent stores to res dump. Wires from D.D.O.S. Fifth Army re movement of Two 1Pdrs. Replied.	
"	21/4/17		Mount Office & remainder of stores from D.A.D.O.S. N ₄t Sheet 57.5. Opened office. Lock ups & store tents from D.A.D.O.S. 5th Australians. Commenced issues.	
N 4/14	22/4/17		Arranging camps. Stove tents on loan from V Corps. Expect to winter clothing.	
"	23/4/17		Now esk for defect suggested. Visited D.A.D.O.S. Bretencourt to Australian re Salvage stores. came to out camp. Visited D.A.D.O.S. Arras Park to Bere.	
"	24/4/17		March to new Cartridge stores etc.	
"	25/4/17 26/4/17		Moved office & staff also Workshops to picture camp. Lorry to Rainsval - Bretencourt and party of Laundry to H.30.a.1.2.	
H.30.a.1.2.	27/4/17		Visited A.D.O.S., ANZAC Corps. Obtained Auth from 0.0. ANZAC CT. Albertz.	
	28/4/17 to 30/4/17		General working & arranging. Arranged to remove future kit at Rainsval. Winter clothing being received in parts of Brakes to Rainsval. Salvage dump arranged with Laundry W of Atamain camp.	
			of Survey sanctioned.	

F. C. Roberts Capt,
D.A.D.O.S,
11th Div.

WAR DIARY.
May 1917.

D.A.D.O.S.,11th.Divn.

*****

Army Form C. 2118.

WAR DIARY
~~INTELLIGENCE SUMMARY~~
(Erase heading not required.)

Instructions regarding War Diaries and Intelligence Summaries are contained in F. S. Regs., Part II. and the Staff Manual respectively. Title Pages will be prepared in manuscript.

Place	Date	Hour	Summary of Events and Information	Remarks and references to Appendices
H.30.a.1.2.	1.5.17		Took charge temporarily of Laundry. Sent lorries to Reinchevent. Cleared for Paris etc. Rushed. Inspected pumps. Damaged 2 Vickers Guns, 1 Lewis Gun, several rifles etc in process of limits. Reported verbally to "A". Further reports to be submitted. Drift Army instructs Laundry at Abbeville to discontinue, permits Arranged to transfer Laundry arrangements. Cavalry 1 am 3/5/17. elsk.	
	2.5.17		General Routine. Amp/2/5/17 reported to Divisional depot 9pm duty.	
	3.5.17		General "	
	4.5.17		Do - do - Posted Copy "Report" Questions re formation work there.	
	5.5.17		X, Z, T.M.B₂ in Area. Wired 19th Div. to Transfer Rfly. not J.C.T. Wired I.C.T	
	6.5.17		to Transfer at once	
7.5.17 to 11.5.17		Y, Z Transferred from J.C.T. to 115 Div. General Routine.	
	13.5.17		Suspended issue from Havre & Rouen. Suspended Laundry issue from Abbeville. Extra Laboured wagons P.S. received in replacement of Lewis Gun Side Cars.	
	14.5.17		Stop issue of transport intends from Havre to Calais Base	
	16.5.17		Moved from Fienvinus? to Albert	
	17.5.17		" Albert to Meteren	
	18.5.17		" Meteren to St Omer Capigal; Reinclessum from Calais	
	19.5.17		Resumed issue from Abbeville Laundry	

Army Form C. 2118.

WAR DIARY
INTELLIGENCE SUMMARY

(Erase heading not required.)

Instructions regarding War Diaries and Intelligence Summaries are contained in F. S. Regs., Part II. and the Staff Manual respectively. Title Pages will be prepared in manuscript.

Place	Date	Hour	Summary of Events and Information	Remarks and references to Appendices
St Pol Cappel	20.5.17		Wired location to D.D.O.S. II Army	
	21/5		Arranging postage. 770 tents at Tournai R. 36 = 7.0.	
	24/5		150 yoken Rules received from Corps	
			100 " " " Base	
			200 sets of Packsaddling received, 100 sets held in reserve at O.R. 13th C.T.	
	25/5		Sorted Positions. Visited D.D.O.S. Army re 2 Th.	
	30/5		Received 7 - 17pdr MK II wagons ammunition + 2 limber wagons to replace MK I.	
	31.		To Corps re General question. General Routine	

Webster Capt A.O.D.
D.A.D.O.S.
11th Div

2449 Wt. W14957/M90 750,000 1/16 J.B.C. & A. Forms/C.2118/12.

D.A.D.O.S. 11th Division.

Army Form C. 2118.

WAR DIARY
INTELLIGENCE SUMMARY

(Erase heading not required.)

Instructions regarding War Diaries and Intelligence Summaries are contained in F. S. Regs., Part II. and the Staff Manual respectively. Title Pages will be prepared in manuscript.

Place	Date	Hour	Summary of Events and Information	Remarks and references to Appendices
St from April.	1/6/17		General Routine. Arrange that D.A.D.O.S. 36th Division will advise on types after Ordnance staff during leave. Joint Onyken Salvage Officer will supervise the Divisional interests. Visited Base Depot & Yukon Packs & special stores.	
	2/6/17		D.A.D.O.S. on leave from 12/6/17. Yukon packs (100) being altered, one per sample from IX Corps. Emergency articles being completed.	
	3/6/17		150 Yukon Packs from Third Army R.E. Workshops – total now 403.	
	5/6/17		100 nls Pack saddlery recd. from IX Corps Troops Ordnance Officer.	
	6/6/17		10 Barrels Vickers R.S. and 20 Thermometers recd. from O.O. IX C.T.	
	7/6/17		10 prints Vry 1"s recd via O.O. IX C.T. from Base. 60 Petrol M-Grn from IX C.	
	8/6/17		60 assistant pattern Grenade carriers from Base.	
	9/6/17		Moved to M.36 c.18. 7 Grenade Carrier R.R. recd from IX Corps for trial	
Oosthoek	12/6/17		66 Special Water Fans received from IX Corps for trial — " — " — report.	
	16/6/17		22 Belt drums for M. Guns " "	
	18/6/17		Suspended reins from Base	
	19/6/17		Transferred Divnl. artillery and M.I. coy. Train to 36th Div. not except 20.P.S. first Blanket Turnout to Railhead. Moved to Morris. Workshops left at Oosthoek	
Morris	20/6/17			
Proven	22/6/17		Moved to Proven. divnl Base & reserve issues	
Eperlecques	24/6/17		Moved to Eperlecques. Workshops moved from Oosthoek to Eperlecques.	

Army Form C. 2118.

WAR DIARY
INTELLIGENCE SUMMARY
(Erase heading not required.)

Instructions regarding War Diaries and Intelligence Summaries are contained in F. S. Regs., Part II. and the Staff Manual respectively. Title Pages will be prepared in manuscript.

Place	Date	Hour	Summary of Events and Information	Remarks and references to Appendices
Ecoivres	26/6/17		191 Vigilant Series copies received from Base.	
"	28/6/17	1500	Armr. Refrigerators handed over in IX Corps area. Packanything, preliminaries Bells 76. S. & Yukon Packs (500 & 100 rd. Tins each) returned to IX Corps.	
	29/6/17		Visited 32nd Bde. in completing equipment.	
	30/6/17		Issued Routine.	

F. Webster, Capt. A. O. D.
D. A. D. O. S.
11th Division
1/7/17.

WAR DIARY.

July, 1917.

D.A.D.O.S. 11th Division.

Army Form C. 2118.

WAR DIARY
or
INTELLIGENCE SUMMARY
(Erase heading not required.)

Place	Date	Hour	Summary of Events and Information	Remarks and references to Appendices
Eperlecques	1/7/17		Visited A.D.O.S. XVIII Corps re supply of German Machine Guns. Available only from Base. 32nd Bde. H.R. Ord. Advanced Dumps. M. Larko. Artillery Dumps & D.A.C. & 5th Bde. R.F.A.	
	2/7/17		Confirmed move from 36th Div. to 11th Div. of 11th Arty & No. 1 Coy. Train. March Artillery Advance Dumps to St James Expt. Visited Base Depot Calais re German M. Guns. First available was 24 Army none available & S intends on Gun Park med.	
	3/7/17		Artillery Dumps removed to Eperlecques. Inspection of 32nd & 34th Bde. Transport by I.O.M. 5th Army Heavy Workshop. Wires intends for vehicles entrenched. Guns from Gun Park - 21, 18 feet and 34 - 4.5 How. Emergency Ammunition carries — delivered to Artillery.	
	4/7/17		295 sets Packsaddlery G.S. received from Base. Visited all units of 33rd Bde.	
	5/7/17		Visited at Lines. Dailies & 11th Manchester re general equipment	
	6/7/17		Dumps formed with Artillery. (A.25 d. 3.8) Visited Dv. Arty re Guns equipment 32nd M.S.C. & Bde H.R. and Bde. W. M. at Dumps. Inspected Subcamp dumps.	
	7/7/17		Received 150 Yukon Packs from Base. (Completing Division to 250)	
	8/7/17		Fifth Army Gun Park opened. L. Dunkirk for Kertek for Staining Tents.	
	9/7/17		Inspected Divnl. Dumps at Wattin.	

Army Form C. 2118.

WAR DIARY
or
INTELLIGENCE SUMMARY

(Erase heading not required.)

Instructions regarding War Diaries and Intelligence Summaries are contained in F. S. Regs., Part II. and the Staff Manual respectively. Title Pages will be prepared in manuscript.

Place	Date	Hour	Summary of Events and Information	Remarks and references to Appendices
Eperlecques	11/7/17		A.D.O.S. XIII Corps inspected Dumps & Office Records. Visited Dorati re equipment.	
	12/7/17		Visited 32nd Bde & withdrew Ordnance W.O. & stores to Eperlecques. D. Entry H.R. re equipments. Inspected Dumps & P.T.O. recoats. Visited D.A.Z. & Salenya. To A.D.O.S. XIII Corps re special issues for the Offensive.	
	13/7/17		To St Omer re Sewing Machine for Tailors Shop. Price too high.	
	15/7/17		12 Clinometers recd from Base for M.G. Corps.	
	16/7/17		To Calais re a/s indents & Sewing Machine. I Army intends having priority for coming Offensive. 32nd Bde Dumps formed with artillery Dumps. 5 German M.Guns for instructional purposes recd.	
	17/7/17		Received 60 arti Packsaddlery I.S. from Base (completing Division to 360)	
	18/7/17		Visited D. Artillery also preparing for cloth for flags etc.	
	20/7/17		To Railhead. Reconsigned Carts Water tanks to Artillery. To 32nd Bde units re equipment. To Calais re Gas appliances.	
	21/7/17		Conference at A.D.O.S. office XVIII Corps. Lt Armingh re Bleach. Visited Adv. dumps.	

Army Form C. 2118.

WAR DIARY
or
INTELLIGENCE SUMMARY
(Erase heading not required.)

Instructions regarding War Diaries and Intelligence Summaries are contained in F. S. Regs., Part II. and the Staff Manual respectively. Title Pages will be prepared in manuscript.

Place	Date	Hour	Summary of Events and Information	Remarks and references to Appendices
Fantleopes	22/7/17		Recd 10 Slings for Lewis Guns from Base for Trench.	
Wormhoudt	23/7/17		Moved Stores & office to Poperinghe (L.M.b.1.8.) Self to Wormhoudt with M.R.	
	24/7/17		To Railhead re Trucks. Gentleopes re return of Rortage. Offices re lorries for Railhead. Master Gunner dumps to main dump. Leave in town to 51st Div. 30 Yukon Packs. March from Wormhoudt to	
Poperinghe	25/7/17		196 tents returned to XVIII Corps - at Peselhoek. Poperinghe.	
	26/7/17		Drew from O.O. XVIII C.T. Special stores for the Offensive - Hot Food Containers 4	
	27/7/17		Cliff Cutters 7. Water bottles with strings 4,900. Kujaraska 200. Cutters wire - lug 300. Short 300. From Ord. 39th Div. Special carriers for Amm, Bulls/Bombs 150. From 51st Div. 200 Bulls amm. '303 M.Gun.	
	28/7/17		Issued Wire Cutters 600 to C.R.E. Drew 3 Anti-aircraft first mountings for Lewis Guns from XVIII Corps. Sent lorries to Base for tents two waterproof in anticipation of exchanges received for 32nd Bde. Drew Emergency Amm. Carriers from Bomb Park 15 Prs. 4.5 How. issued to D.A.E. Drew forage for Reserve Corps. M.N.Y. + Z.	
	29/7/17		A.D.O.S. visited Dumps.	
	30/7/17 31/7/17		Drew 574 sets Packsaddlery G.S. (issued) to D.A.E. Lintope for lipercamps 160 + 50 = 210. F.C.Webster D.A.D.O.S. 11th Div.	

WAR DIARY AUGT. 1917.

D.A.D.O.S. 11th Div.

Army Form C. 2118.

WAR DIARY
INTELLIGENCE SUMMARY
(Erase heading not required.)

Instructions regarding War Diaries and Intelligence Summaries are contained in F.S. Regs., Part II. and the Staff Manual respectively. Title Pages will be prepared in manuscript.

Place	Date	Hour	Summary of Events and Information	Remarks and references to Appendices
Poperinghe L.11.b.1.8	1/8/17		General Routine. Visited Railhead.	
	2/8/17		Visited 32nd Bde. H.Q. & all units also 3rd Bde. H.Q.	
	3/8/17		Recd 10 Cradles carrying from Base.	
	4/8/17		Corps conference 10 a.m. Submitted tabulated statement of Service Dress to H.R. showing excess wear. Recd 6 Cradles carrying from Base.	
	5/8/17		Reported to D.D.O.S. X Army that 542 Pistols Webley outstanding.	
	7/8/17		Purchased 65 hurricane lamps for A.P.M. Recd 19 cradles carrying completing to 125.	
	8/8/17		Moved Office stores to A.22 d.6.5. Sheet 27.	
	9/8/17		Applied for special authority for Sugar stores & Tea stores for Adv. Training Camps.	
	10/8/17		Visited 33rd Bde. H.R. & Transport lines & R.Ms.	
	11/8/17		Corps Conference. Visited Magazines B.59 + D.59 B.59 + D.57 Bdys R.F.A. Car failed during Operations. Submitted double indent.	
	13/8/17		Cancelled indents for Rupture Trusses. Brotenk Pricematic Compasses. Sent lorry to Calais for Stores. Recd 80 Conforvan Hypites. No car available.	
	14/8/17		Visited 33rd Bde & all units. Recd 2 T.M.S from X Corps School.	
	15/8/17		Purchased ropes for Yukon Packs.	
	16/8/17		Visited 32nd Bde H.R. & C.Os of Units. Arranged conference of R.Ms. No car available	
	17/8/17		Conference at R.Ms of 32nd Bde at Bde H.R. Gave Lists of equipment to be completed & returned all indents. All arms of 32nd Bde inspected & reported by Armourer	
	18/8/17		Conference of C.O. of Units. C.Os of Units re equipment at Corps. 10 am. To 34th Bde. 13:5., Staff Capt.	
	19/8/17		Conference of R. Ms. at 34th Bde H.R. Large deficiencies notified. Visited Salvage Co. & Vermat Camp. Arrange for intents to be submitted immediately. Mr. Jenkin re Smart Coats.	

2449 Wt. W14957/M90 750,000 1/16 J.B.C. & A. Forms/C.2118/12.

Army Form C. 2118.

WAR DIARY
or
INTELLIGENCE SUMMARY

(Erase heading not required.)

Instructions regarding War Diaries and Intelligence Summaries are contained in F. S. Regs., Part II. and the Staff Manual respectively. Title Pages will be prepared in manuscript.

Place	Date	Hour	Summary of Events and Information	Remarks and references to Appendices
Dept HQ Peperinghe A.22 d.6.5 Sheet 28.	20/8		Sent to Calais for Ford Cab: for Mr. Yorke. (returned to Salonge in arrow by air). General Routine. No car available.	
	24/8		General Routine: No Car available.	
	25/8		Corps Conference.	
	26/8		Conference of R the 33rd Bde. Visited 34th Bde. and B.F. commanding. Salvage section.	
	27/8		Revised bicycles in replacement of horses. No car available.	
	28/8		To Calais. Visited Base Supplies re outstanding indents. Arranged to send back items for deficiencies of battle equipment if necessary.	
	29/8 30/8		General Routine. No car available.	
	31.		3 New Ford T. M's drawn from Base Park. To Baillend a Corps 2 p.m. returns.	

H. Webster Capt. D.A.D.S.T. 8th Div.

Vol 16

CONFIDENTIAL.

WAR DIARY OF

D.A.D.O.S. 11TH DIVISION.

FROM SEPT. 1ST TO SEPT. 30TH 1917.

Army Form C. 2118.

WAR DIARY
or
INTELLIGENCE SUMMARY

(Erase heading not required.)

Instructions regarding War Diaries and Intelligence Summaries are contained in F. S. Regs., Part II. and the Staff Manual respectively. Title Pages will be prepared in manuscript.

Place	Date	Hour	Summary of Events and Information	Remarks and references to Appendices
A.22 d.6.5" Sheet 28	1/9/17		Conference at A.D.O.S. Office XVIII Corps. No car available afternoon.	
	2nd 3rd 4th		Routine. No car available.	
	5/9/17		Buckland. 11th Div. Div. Training Camp. Stores. H.Q. 32nd Bde. Salvage Officer Briston.	
	6/9/17		Routine. No car.	
		13.0	Pistols from Base. Visited RO, Coppa Wapps. W. Riding stores. T.L. Stores, 33rd Bde H.R.	
			34th Bde H.R. Lincolns stores. Manchester stores. D.H.R.	
	7/9/17		To W. Ridings, 5th Army. D.D.O.S. 33rd Bde Borders, Staffords, & Sherwood Foresters	
			to Salvage Briston. Pts, T.M.S at Briston. T.L stores & O.T.C.	
	8-12/9		Routine – no car available.	
	13/9/17			
	14/9/17		To 33rd Bde mit units. 34th Bde & all units.	
	15/9/17		To 33rd Bde all units – D.H.R me. A.num of Ordnance. Inspected for blankets Browning.	
	16/9/17		No car.	
	17/9/17		D.A.D.O.S. granted 10 days leave. It Morris acting during interval.	
		12 – 2" T.M.s	returned by R.T.I.Z. All 1/2 instruts for 2" T.M. Stores cancelled. Visit from A.D.O.S.	
	18/9/17	23.00	Blankets + 1920 Horse Rugs received. Blankets to 32nd Bde.	
	19/9/17	35.00	Blankets 22 90 Horse Rugs received. Blankets to 33rd Bde.	
	20/9/17	18.00	Blankets rec'd. to 32nd Bde.	
	21/9/17	6.800	Blankets rec'd returned to 34th Bde 1 Bty. Visit from A.D.O.S.	
	24/9/17	5 1st	D.A. moved to 11th Div. for Ordnance. Visit from A.D.O.S.	

Army Form C. 2118.

WAR DIARY
or
INTELLIGENCE SUMMARY

(Erase heading not required.)

Instructions regarding War Diaries and Intelligence Summaries are contained in F. S. Regs., Part II. and the Staff Manual respectively. Title Pages will be prepared in manuscript.

Place	Date	Hour	Summary of Events and Information	Remarks and references to Appendices
A 22 d.6.5. Shot 28.	26/9/17	10.0	Blankets not issued	
	27/9/17		D.A.D.O.S. returned from leave.	
	27 & 30		Issued Rations.	

J. Coutts Webster Capt. M.O.D.
D.A.D.O.S.
11th Div.
1/10/17.

CONFIDENTIAL.

WAR DIARY OF

D.A.D.O.S. 11TH DIVISION.

FROM OCTOBER 1ST TO OCTOBER 31ST 1917.

WAR DIARY or INTELLIGENCE SUMMARY

Army Form C. 2118.

Instructions regarding War Diaries and Intelligence Summaries are contained in F. S. Regs., Part II. and the Staff Manual respectively. Title Pages will be prepared in manuscript.

(Erase heading not required.)

Place	Date	Hour	Summary of Events and Information	Remarks and references to Appendices
A.2.2, A.C.S	1/10/17		Conference at A.D.O.S. Office.	
	2/10/17		Reported Bulk demands by D.R.L.S. matter of Telegram unsatisfactory	
	4/10/17		Move - from 9th Division to 11th Division - 9th Seaforth Highlanders (Pioneers)	
	5/10/17		Conference at A.D.O.S. Office	
	8/10/17		Move 51st Div'l Artillery to 17th Division, 9th Seaforth Highlanders (Pioneers) to 9th Division	
Eperlecques	10/10/17		Commenced moving stores to Eperlecques	
	12/10/17		To A.D.O.S. XIII Corps. To D.D.O.S. Dept. Army. Moved Office stores to Eperlecques. A.D.O.S. XIX Corps asked to give any assistance required	
"	13/10/17		Visited D.D.O.S. First Army + A.D.O.S. I Corps for instructions. Reported sinus.	
"	14/10/17		Wired Calais. various issues	
"	15/10/17		To Calais to inspect all possible stores returning deficiencies along of Base. Instruction to Gun Park to draw 2.3 Lewis Guns and possible stores to remedy deficiency	
	16/10/17		Visited Brigades re-unit & re deficiencies. Officers for Sewing Machines which Calais Shop issues Transfer arms sent to Base. Accepted timber in 2 ft.	
	17/10/17		Fatigue from Employment Coy. returned - replaced by 5 from Left Battalion. Visited Mermont Forth. O.D.O.S. 1st Corps for instruction. 1st Army Gun Park for vehicle same. Cancelled all 1st Hitch on Gun Park	
Mermont Forth	19/10/17		Moved to Mermont Forth. Reported location to First Army + 1st Corps.	

Army Form C. 2118.

WAR DIARY
INTELLIGENCE SUMMARY
(Erase heading not required.)

Place	Date	Hour	Summary of Events and Information	Remarks and references to Appendices
Arras Forts	19/10/17		Visited D.A.D.O.S. 6th Div. re takeing over with Lee Officer + Camp Commandant	
"	20/10/17		Lt Artillery Arty, HQ D.A.C., A.D.O.S. At Corps + DADOS 6th Div. with Lee Officer + A.Q.V.S.	
"	21/10/17		General Routine.	
Boisleux	23/10		Moved office & stores to Boisleux.	
	24/10		Stores - from 6th Div. to 11th Div. No 7 C.C.S., 232 Army Coys Dep. H.Q. 14th A.F.A. Bde C.R.E. Bdy R.E. 8th Bdy R.F.A. 11th Divl R.E. Colm. B Special Coy R.E.	
	25/10		Recd. 40 W.T Fort Guitarmen, Varieties Off Clothing Depot Batterie.	
	26/10		Move - from lst Army Troops to 11th Div. - A/14 A.F.A.B. from 11th Div to lst Army Troops - A/53 Bdy R.F.A. 5 P.B. were arrived to Infuse 5"A" class men of A.O.C. Wired Base for 1200 features for Infantry Personnel. Visited Lewis Parks + No 1 Mobile Workshops.	
	27/10		Visited units of 57th Bde R.F.A. + H.R. E Lewis Personnel.	
	28/10		Lt la Buhu - W Locker, Lewis Insider. T.M. Brigade. Lt 32nd Bde A. R. 1883 Lewis Received	
	29/10		Sent to 11th Div Arty for Rail Supplies for 11th Div Artillery. Horses. 11th Div. M X C.T. Received	
	30/10		14 Army F.A.B.A. + Am Ct.	
	31/10		Visited Artillery units of 59th Bde Table re refitting. RXH C.T. To 11th Div Move. from V.C.T. to 11th Div. H.R. 5th Cav. Div. Arty 5th Cav D.A.C. M.T. Ammn. Sub. Park	
			409 Bergmen recd from Bases re detailers to forward Relien. 50.90 features red " "	

Contributor Capt ACR
D.A.D.O.S. 11th Div. 1/11/17

CONFIDENTIAL.

WAR DIARY

OF

D.A.D.O.S 11th DIV.

DATE. FROM NOVEMBER 1st 1917
TO NOVEMBER 30th 1917

Army Form C. 2118.

WAR DIARY
or
INTELLIGENCE SUMMARY

(Erase heading not required.)

Instructions regarding War Diaries and Intelligence Summaries are contained in F. S. Regs., Part II. and the Staff Manual respectively. Title Pages will be prepared in manuscript.

Place	Date	Hour	Summary of Events and Information	Remarks and references to Appendices
Boulogne and	1/11/17		12 – 2" T.M's. from 5th Cav. Div. Arty. to Base.	
	2/11/17		To Fifth Army – Conference at D.D.O.S. Office. 100 Jackson Packs and 12,000 N.G. containers recd.	
	3/11/17		To Corps and to 33rd Bde + Railhead. Visit from D.D.O.S. First Army to inspect Stores + Syst. Forms. Move – From I Corps Troops to 11th Divn. units. Heads 51st 52nd 53rd 55th 5th 60th 61st + 66 Battns, 5th Canadian Bn Library, M1 Coy 5th Can Divn Train	
	4/11/17		49TD (3rd) Blankets received. Visited R.As., also 33rd Bde units.	
	5/11/17		Visited Gun Park for Artillery stores.	32nd Bde M.R. Waits S.C.R.A. 5 Gun Parks to empth station in sight. etc.
	6/11/17		L. 1. O.H. M1 Shops conv., A.D.O.S. Corps, Reinforcement Camps Stores + D/DAff.o. Reported Artillery parties on funerals.	
	7/11/17		Railhead – 1.O.M. M1 Shops.	
	8/11/17		Visited Rams Shove Room to check interchange in connection of advance from Cassel	
	9/11/17		3500 Pullovers received 10/11/17 distributed	
	10/11/17		50 Jumpers received	
	12/11/17		Gent Army approved to act temporarily during absence of D.A.D.O.S. at instructional course in Amenitair. Visited I.O.M. M1 Workshop.	
	13/11/17		Return – Visited R.A. M.R. – Gun Park + 46 Division re stores etc.	
	14/11/17		D.A.D.O.S. left for course. Visit from /A.D.O.S. 1st Corps.	
	15/11/17			

Army Form C. 2118.

WAR DIARY
or
INTELLIGENCE SUMMARY
(Erase heading not required.)

Instructions regarding War Diaries and Intelligence Summaries are contained in F. S. Regs., Part II. and the Staff Manual respectively. Title Pages will be prepared in manuscript.

Place	Date	Hour	Summary of Events and Information	Remarks and references to Appendices
(Arrangement)	16/11/17		O.O. Corps Troops dismount 17 persons for medical unit leaving immediately for "after hunt"	
"	17/11/17		89th Relief lot moved in from 59th Divn	
"	18/11/17		Visited Battrn in several of mine areas	
"	19/10/17		232 Army troops Co R.E. moved to 3rd Corps troops	
"	20/11/17		Purchased 6 tarns, 2 whistles, and 24 torches for night operations 33rd Brigade.	
"	21/11/17		150 sets of parachuting put in order	
"	23/11/17		Visited Reinforcement camp at Allonagne, explained bulk system of indenting submitted patterns of apron & coat for covering artillerymen's lorries.	
"	24/11/17		250 L machine gun Co: (passed 11th Divn on H.K. m & Co)	
"	30/11/17		Employment Co: moved in to this Divn and 822 nd Corps (Area)	

M. Furman
Lieut A.O.D
acting DA. & OS
11th Divn

CONFIDENTIAL.

WAR DIARY OF

D.A.D.O.S., 11TH DIVISION.

FROM DECR. 1ST TO DECR. 31ST 1917.

Army Form C. 2118.

WAR DIARY
or
INTELLIGENCE SUMMARY
(Erase heading not required.)

Instructions regarding War Diaries and Intelligence Summaries are contained in F. S. Regs., Part II. and the Staff Manual respectively. Title Pages will be prepared in manuscript.

Place	Date	Hour	Summary of Events and Information	Remarks and references to Appendices
Bruyport	1.12.17		Collected as Conveying stops for various M.T. from 1st Corps troops. Capt J. Coates W.O.M.S. returned from Commutation Course resumed duty.	
	2.12.17		Move - MT Supply Col to 20st Division. Lieut. Saunidge departed. Visited T. MSp.	
	3.12.17		M. Tractor Artillery #2.	
	4.12.17		Visited Train - 150 tr. M.T. E.	
	5.12.17		Inspector of Armourers visited Skips. gave instructions re fitting dismounting stops etc.	
	6.12.17		Obtained Glycerine from Sun Park for M.T. Co. in view of frost. Purchased Sewing Machine for Tailors Skp.	
	7.12.17		Second day withdrawn. Rickbot not closed in time for distribution of stores to units. All stores therefor delivered day following their arrival. Visited, O.M. N.1, Reinforcement Camp, R. McCrea, A.O.D. (Officer in charge of Field Workshop Stores) arrived from 2nd army	
	8.12.17 to 11.12.17		Captain Graham arrived from 2nd army for instruction in Divisional work with a view to the elimination of operation in intents of traveller vans of units sufficiencies. Visited MSkips, & the Stores, Artillery, I.O.M. Skips, Sun Park, heavy mobile Skps. A.D.O.S. Corps Colonel Divisional Salvage, Bootts. Jn. during this period. Capt Graham departed 11/12/17.	
	13.12.17		Visited Corps. W.Rdup, JL. MWks, West Jpbo, 33. B.H.R. atmo Rette, T.M. Field Coy	
	14.12.17		Visited Reinforcement Camps a 34K Bde - all units.	
	15.12.17		More B Special Cry R.E. to G.H.R. Troops	
	16.12.17		Amerette man of B Special Coy. Received wire from Army. Rear changed Name to Tebbi for all units attached to the Division.	

WAR DIARY
or
INTELLIGENCE SUMMARY

Army Form C. 2118.

Instructions regarding War Diaries and Intelligence Summaries are contained in F. S. Regs., Part II. and the Staff Manual respectively. Title Pages will be prepared in manuscript.

(Erase heading not required.)

Place	Date	Hour	Summary of Events and Information	Remarks and references to Appendices
Engagement	17.12.17		Programme of Bulk orders to be as in Sched. A. Supplies required 60 per Bde. Proceed with manufacture in Shops.	
	19.12.17		to new area. No stores offrs. and had to	
	20.12.17		Move. B Special Coy R.E. to 3rd Army Corps. Command moving stores to new area. Bourlonfork evacuated — withdrawn. Lorries returned for many.	
	21.12.17		Ditto. Ditto continued moving stores to nodepo. Move. 5th E.D.A. and 8th attached units to 3rd Canadian Division. D.A.D.O.S. 3rd Can. Div. arrived to take over all our stores in Peronne.	
	22.12.17		Moved office stores to Beauvière. Visited Railhead at Tilloloy.	
Beauvière	23.12.17		Moved to Beauvière. Visited 34th Bde units. Visited 30th Bde units to medically for early admission & demands for stores to replace deficiencies.	
	24.12.17		Visited Artillery. Arranged delivery of stores to reference points.	
	25.12.17		Delivered Artillery stores.	
	26.12.17		Xmas precautions. Renew-in-way Railhead closed.	
	27.12.17		To Clair re entire supplies of clothing to meet elements immediately. Arranged for a reissue of the automatic pants.	
	28.12.17		Capt & Qmts. White A.P.D. O.S.D.O.S. proceeded to England on 14 days leave. Lieut. Savage A.O.D. arrived to act during absence of D.A.D.O.S.	
	29.12.17 to 31.12.17		General Routine. Command consist of Keen stores taken from on 31/12/17.	

J. Coutts Webster Capt. A.D.P.
D.A.D.O.S. 11th Div.

CONFIDENTIAL.

WAR DIARY
OF
D.A.D.O.S. 11TH DIVISION

FOR PERIOD JAN. 1ST TO 31ST 1918

WAR DIARY

INTELLIGENCE SUMMARY

Army Form C. 2118.

Place	Date	Hour	Summary of Events and Information	Remarks and references to Appendices
ABBEVILLE	1/1/18		Reports receipt of 600 Khaki Line number 2030-3161	
	2/1/18		Received kit for 3rd Bn from O.O. Corps Yps. Rives Ret. Nr 2750 and one truck of stores received.	
	3/1/18		Surplus 4.5 Howitzer handed over to 15 D/59 to 48 Kr Baty C.O.O.	
	4/1/18		Yeo trucks of stores received.	
	5/1/18		Usual routine. 6 Rnds for 4.5 How received from Dunkirk.	
	6/1/18		5-18pdr Guns and 3 18pdr Carriages arrived at Rail Head. R.G. notified.	
	7,8/1/18		Usual routine.	
	9/1/18		One truck of stores received.	
	10/1/18		One truck of stores received. One a. Kirk, 2/Lt. reported for return to unit. 1 F.S.D.C. details & [illegible] since 10.1.18 off sick. any weakness amount of [illegible] & [illegible] to report absent in about to be again on [illegible] sheet [illegible].	
	11/1/18		Usual routine. [illegible] in little rain to be [illegible]	

Army Form C. 2118.

WAR DIARY
or
INTELLIGENCE SUMMARY

(Erase heading not required.)

Instructions regarding War Diaries and Intelligence Summaries are contained in F. S. Regs., Part II. and the Staff Manual respectively. Title Pages will be prepared in manuscript.

Place	Date	Hour	Summary of Events and Information	Remarks and references to Appendices
Bonsecourt	12/1/19.		Capt. J. Smith WO to retirement from here. New precautions on. Arranged with R.T.O. sent 2 F.L. wagon to Railhead to remove stores to Temporary dump, also supply turned	
	13/1/19.		Railhead. Cleared Truck. Took precautions remainder. Petrie closely stores at my dump. to D.D.O. 5th Army Corps Subms to Pot Corps A.D.O.S. re moving tomorrow of 5th Div. Inspected lorries with stores to Le Bourse re taking over from units.	
	14/1/19		Dump Railhead. made necessary arrangements.	
	15/1/19		Le Railhead morning. Sent W.O. Railhead report a reference to Le Bourse with Name consists to commence taking over. New Railhead transferred to Le Bourse with More consists. New precautions on at trains tomorrow. Railhead remains at Sillers. Arranged F.S. wagons to chop stores.	
	16/1/19		Le Railhead. Took spare stores + trucks vehicles. Cleared stores excepting whole transports with following trays. In AP1 Workshops / F.D. Ambz + part. Vickers are from Le Bourse. Ambitious left as empty. Railhead of Le Bourse from 18k. Received no stores.	
	17/1/19		Le Railhead. Ent to 4k Canadian Division forwards return begs to st any Moor. mobile slips for stops transport for lathes runs. Arranged to have Shot M.G. Corps from and to shop on 18th for transit of stops. Summary of was exchanged in Division via the Ourne workshops and to R.T. together with normal units. Arranged for F.S. wagon to clear vehicles at Le Bourse.	
	18/1/19		Sat Railhead party to Le Bourse.	
	19/1/19		Cleared Railhead at Le Bourse. Dumped in Temporary store.	
	20/1/19		Attended conference at A.D.O.S. 1st Corps. Details of landing in of stores from units being disbanded. Forthis details to follow. Visited 3rd Bdl H.Q. re units of Bdl. also FS B Hdl.	

2449 Wt. W14957/M90 750,000 1/16 J.B.C. & A. Forms/C.2118/12.

Army Form C. 2118.

WAR DIARY
or
INTELLIGENCE SUMMARY
(Erase heading not required.)

Instructions regarding War Diaries and Intelligence Summaries are contained in F.S. Regs., Part II. and the Staff Manual respectively. Title Pages will be prepared in manuscript.

Place	Date	Hour	Summary of Events and Information	Remarks and references to Appendices
Le Beuvrière	21/1/18		Office Routine. Certain Workshops. Arranged to move stores 22nd if passes granted by Army for lorries to run.	
	22/1/18		Pass for five lorries. Stores & Bell Office to Le Beuvrière. Visited new camps & arranged accommodation. Staff Captain R.A. called. Arranged to ascertain revised intake of stores required.	
Le Beuvrière	23/1/18		Moved Office only to Le Beuvrière. Moved part of Office. Paravanes & Lamps	
	24/1/18		Details received from Artillery. Adjusted demands on Gun Park & Base. Visited Gun Park & drew all available stores. Visited Reinforcement Camps Etaples & Allotted at Le Beuvrière. Leave on Armoured Store Tent to A.D.O.S. 46th Div. Lorries returning empty. Reserves of all Gun Appliances from Ammunition Shops, at Etaples available. A.D.O.S. inspected stores etc. Remainder to be sent on arrival from Base.	
	25/1/18		Visited Staff Captain R.A. re Gun Stores & Water Cart. Reported numbers of civil nights etc required to A.D.O.S. at Corps. Visited Train companies. Move from 46th Div to 11th Div 110 Cavalry Coy - 172 Army Exp. Coy - 91 Labour Coy- 3 Quarter, 4 Park- 6 Building Coys, 5 Tun, Coys, Area Commandant at Corps & Park. General Routine arranging Dumps, Rations, covers etc.	
	26/1/18		Lt. I.O.M. re Stores for repairs in Etaples. 2 Lorries for 0/157.	
	27/1/18		General Routine. A.D.O.S. called & from Padre for Instruction of M.T.R. Davis in aim of Relief Fund. Received notification of disbanding of 6th Bastion, 1st Canning Fusiliers & 7th W.Riding. Saw R.N.f of London, Manchester, & Durham. Referred A.A. Armourers for Instructions.	
	29/1/18		Lt. J.C.R.A. re Bell supply. Canvas compound D.A. drew up Watts Gut for K/58.	
	30/1/18		A.D.O.S. at Corps. D.i.D.O.S. at Army, and Major Moore AFD from Cairo inspected this depôt.	
	31/1/18		Made aircraft arrangements for receiving returning stores from disbanded battalions	

J. Coutts Webster Capt. A.O.D.
R.A.D.O.S. 11th Div.

D.A.D.O.S
11th DIV

WA 21

Army Form C. 2118.

WAR DIARY
or
INTELLIGENCE SUMMARY.
(Erase heading not required).

Instructions regarding War Diaries and Intelligence Summaries are contained in F. S. Regs., Part II. and the Staff Manual respectively. Title pages will be prepared in manuscript.

Place	Date	Hour	Summary of Events and Information	Remarks and references to Appendices
Le Rouen	1/2/18	—	Arranged with Quartermaster of 6th Bn. The Border Regt. and with The 9th Bn. The Green Howards re the turning of all stores in charge of those Battalions.	
"	2/2/18	—	Stores being returned by disbanded units.	
"	3/2/18	—	7th Bn. The West Riding Regt commenced handing in stores. Visited this unit to ensure all being in order. 9th Battalion returning 2.3 classes in R.A. mountings for knife drawn. Reported 9th Army battalion emptied & invoiced.	
	4/2/18	—	Saw Quarter Master of 7th Bn. West Riding Regt. Discussed arrangements re return of the stores.	
	5/2/18	—	Routine — Checking returned stores & lists.	
	6/2/18	—	Routine —	
	7/2/18	—	Instructed by A.D.O.S. to receive salved stores from Salvage Officer, to condition same & hand over to R.O.O. for despatch to Base. Arranged with Corps Salvage Officer to enforce present Salvage dumps as Ordnance returned stores dumps.	
	8/2/18	—	Received lists of stores in explanation of the few minor deficiencies from 9th Lancashire Fusiliers.	
	9/2/18.		Received lists do from Lt. Border Regt.	

Army Form C. 2118.

WAR DIARY
or
INTELLIGENCE SUMMARY.
(Erase heading not required.)

Instructions regarding War Diaries and Intelligence Summaries are contained in F. S. Regs., Part II. and the Staff Manual respectively. Title pages will be prepared in manuscript.

Place	Date	Hour	Summary of Events and Information	Remarks and references to Appendices
La Gorgue	10/2/18		Lt 32nd M.G. Coy to ascertain whereabouts of Detachment stores sent by train in part is not revealed to the Co. of Engrs. Lt R.T.O. re timber for the returned stores. C.O. - R.M. of Ox. Bu. West Riding Regt. sends to magazine requisition deficiencies. To be looked in at earliest with implementations. Orders for the completed date.	
	11/2/18		Relative Commons urgently required. Lt Bton to purchase flags. Not available. Commenced to make flags in leather & tailors shop. Will draw to Section Keller modi materials for manufacture.	
	12/2/18		A.D.O.S. called. Inspected dump, reviewed salvage, where Lt. visited Oth M.T. (Rte - Leafield). West Ridings, instructed him as to how Lt could avoid hundred and destroyed. Reported delay to D.A.R. who had and sent.	
	13/2/18		One truck started at Riellet functional stores. Defective tell. Posted O.O. to Corps Troops re their for Allonayes. 1st M. No 13 Extension instal workshops & refused to Water Cart to and Gen. Supply Co. in times quickly. Sent further report to Lt. any up-to-date stores received to MA D.A returned later as overdue.	
	14/2/18		One truck of returned stores sent to Ever.	
	15/2/18		Lt Allonayes- Rd. Training Battalion. to C.O. of West Ridings to hasten completion of deficit the stores returned. Discussed all points fully & gave again detailed instruction re forms.	

Army Form C. 2118.

WAR DIARY
or
INTELLIGENCE SUMMARY.
(Erase heading not required.)

Instructions regarding War Diaries and Intelligence Summaries are contained in F. S. Regs., Part II. and the Staff Manual respectively. Title pages will be prepared in manuscript.

Place	Date	Hour	Summary of Events and Information	Remarks and references to Appendices
Le Bouvre	16/2/18		General Routine – Checking w. Rodrigo stores	
	17/2/18		L.C.O. to Ridinge. Corrected nil list. Asked for a complete return as per instructions. Lewis Guns for A.A. defence. Received distribution.	
	18/2/18		General Routine – Lt. I.O.M. no repairs to vehicles.	
	19/2/18		Lewis Guns for A.A. issued. Reported completion.	
	20/2/18		A.D.O.S. visited to dispose of surplus Lewis Guns. Arranged to visit at 9.30 on 23rd. Above – Artillery Groups to HK Div – 5th Army Field Artillery Brigade comprising S.H.2, 73rd. Bat – D/5th (How) Battery, 5th A.F.A. Ammn Col. and H.Q. 5th A.F.A. Bde. R.F.A. This Brigade arrived today. Inspected the deficient in condition of batteries reference ammunition & vehicles & early.	
	21/2/18		A.D.O.S. visited several R.Wk. stores, completed visit of 33rd. Surplus Lewis Guns sent to O.C. at top troops & 55th Div. reported completion	
	22/2/18		A.D.O.S. completed visit. Called on Col. O. of Artillery. R. Reported deficiencies of stores on Rembroot forwarded, worked for decision auto shapes.	
	23/2/18		In Program re office stores – billets. No recommendation for office purposes.	
	24/2/18		E Interior keeping in surplus stores or reorganisation. Received lists & cheques for stores deficient & constituted units. Priced all, accompanied by	
	25/2/18		D.H.Q. moved to Yerevin. Exchanged during Employment, snuff $2t$. Wired A.D.O.S. for process of Burgen sunfits on recommended suggested for write.	
	26/2/18		No car available. To office re Return.	
	27/2/18		Do. Reported to HK for return. Total amounts payable by 17th 1st Border Regt. (1.18.6) and O.C. 6th Lancashire Fusiliers ($2.1.03$) for deficiencies of Items.	
	28/2/18		No car available, no visit. Reported completion of return in Employed by Pioneers.	

F. Coulter Webster Capt. A.V.C.
L. Lewis, 28/2/18.
D.A.D.O.S.

SECRET

Vol 22

War Diary
of
D.A.D.O.S. 11th Divn
for March, 1918

Army Form C. 2118.

WAR DIARY
or
INTELLIGENCE SUMMARY.
(Erase heading not required.)

Instructions regarding War Diaries and Intelligence Summaries are contained in F. S. Regs., Part II. and the Staff Manual respectively. Title pages will be prepared in manuscript.

Place	Date	Hour	Summary of Events and Information	Remarks and references to Appendices
La Bassée	1/3/18		Reported 4 Gun equipments drawn for Anti Tank defences – to be held as Corps stores.	
	2/3/18		Drew from 1st Army Gun Park, 30 Lewis Guns for distribution to complete scale B.	
	3/3/18		Issued Lewis Guns ammun. (scale B). Arranged with D.A.D.O.S. 43rd Div. to replace 15 Lewis Gun Buckets lost on A/T. return to unit.	
	4/3/18 5/3/18		General Routine. Visit car available from Park for 5 days period.	
	6/3/18		Visited D.A.G. 2nd Inf. Bde. R.A. about afternoon in instruction in Division's Primary work. Commenced making Light Railway from Reuillon to Stores – also lorry on well by Government using Light Railway trucks. Salvage Trucks loaded to times, dispatched to G/Bridge.	
	7/3/18		Light Railway afternoon weight work. Light Railway Stocktaking trucks.	
	8/3/18		Attended stores by lorry. Railway ammun. disposatory. Visited H. Q. M. N3/5 O.C. Div. 270 of 375 m/a at A.D.O.S. at Loges in Baisieux. Mt. 4 M6. 11-11. Change Prisoners Nº 4 MK I to G.S.	
	9/3/18		Reported unusually no important electrical consignment day for Armourer Artificers.	
	10/3/18		General Routine – now considerably approaching "Cartoon Front".	
	11/3/18		Visited W. Later dispatched clothing.	
	12/3/18		General Routine – M.T. O.S.B. with H.M. Armoured Park amalgamated under SDA & M. Division. Mechanical Transport Coy. Nº 3 Armoured Park Limited Specific arrangement with SDA D.A.S.2. Report on certain surplus transport to D.A.R. to arrange return.	
	13/3/18 14/3/18		Visited 43rd Div. 55th Div. 1st D.A.C. to explain action Lt.Col A.D.D.O.S. with A.D.C.S. on light to CRA. Lorry artillery actions. a few sheds, fell into many Rutherford stores.	
	15/3/18		Advance arrangement for moving stores in the event of a move. Battalion I.V.W. to start Ricked moving to Poperinghe. was buffers to be moved to Division Supply gas Section to be started in front of gun dump.	

Army Form C. 2118.

WAR DIARY
or
INTELLIGENCE SUMMARY.
(Erase heading not required.)

Instructions regarding War Diaries and Intelligence Summaries are contained in F.S. Regs., Part II. and the Staff Manual respectively. Title pages will be prepared in manuscript.

Place	Date	Hour	Summary of Events and Information	Remarks and references to Appendices
Le Havre	16/3		March routine in Sig. stores & my camp.	
	17/3		Battalion guns & A.A. defence from two Field	
			programmes came in M.G. & gas instruments not yet started	
	18/3		Sketches issued to each of H Main, 12, 213 Employ. Coy, 15, 212 sec. labour coy. and	
			1st Irish Div. M.T. Coy.	
	19/3		Several Parties. Roulers R.E.(Rosmer) camp. East Park Nº1, Mirrors Camp. Nº 12. 15 m/c & known Soccer	
			Depot Coy. Nº 1.	
	20/3		Same Routine.	
	21/3		Infantry Coy. & Ponols Harvesters. Ahmed Qamber & Frank & M.S. Section.	
	22/3		Same Routine. A.O.D.	
			Rest M.L. Burials attended.	
			Nº 13. Q.H. Kadetts not at army Corps mget.	
	23/3		Marched over attend A.C. games. Reported completion. W.A.A.Cs. Picnic Contingent.	
	24/3		Entrained for Aveth. Interviewed Farm Officer re necessary fully transferred from Branch 116 Rnd Whiny 110F Case Royfronts	
	25/3		Received orders to prepare to parade. Orphor's issues from O.C.H. and A.D.H.C.E. 517 affair	
			Hrs candles 15 per. Received vaccines	
	26/3		81 Reinforcement ready to return. Trained from 5ST D bounce H.K. and B.T.E.D. Return to D.A.C. D.	
	27/3		Same Routine. Rail & A.A. dress of South.	
			PSK Pack A.F.A.B. from 6 A.C.S. Para	
	28-29/30		30, 42, 33 y 34 R Bde. E.O.R. at 14am Reinf. Nº 1 advance party Depot to Toon.	
	30 R			
	31R7			J. Cooks Webster Capt. I.A.C R.A.F.C.

Vol 23

DADOS
War Diary 1st 4/18 – 30th 4/18

Army Form C. 2118.

WAR DIARY
or
INTELLIGENCE SUMMARY.
(Erase heading not required.)

Instructions regarding War Diaries and Intelligence Summaries are contained in F. S. Regs., Part II. and the Staff Manual respectively. Title pages will be prepared in manuscript.

Place	Date	Hour	Summary of Events and Information	Remarks and references to Appendices
Basra	1/4/18		To 1st Heavy Mobile Workshop on Peninsular for repairs and on Barracks to 1st Heavy Regt. & transport to Basra. To Equipment Camp – Ammunition & Bombs. Reply to return to Basra.	
	2/4		To 33rd R.M.R. - Shipments & No stores. Spares required. To Base. A map of Basra on stores dumped. Authority for return of disabled received.	
	3/4		To 84th Heavy Field Artillery Brigade and A.C. C. & D Batteries inspecting stores and re general equipment.	
	4/4		To D Battery of 84th A.F.A. Bde.	
	5/4		Inspected stores of Fat Bty and O/5 Regt. 5R. A.F.A. Bde.	
	6/4		To the stores 3 H.K. Bde.	
	7/4		Inspected Revolvers, Rifles 99th Lahore Dy & 1332nd Queen Inspected Lys & all at Corps Troops.	
	8/4		Motor Artillery active. Stores sent on to Amara. Divisible to move Shops to Kazimain.	
Kazimain	9/4		Moved Workshops newspapers to Kazimain. Spares & material arrival for 250 mile lifting to retrieve ground nothing & Artillery O.R. Mountain Arms supplies to Kazimain. Railhead moved from B. Baruna to Baghdad (Kurd encampment F).	
	10/4		Railhead moved from B. Baruna to Baghdad (Kurd encampment). Gave 500 extra of various stores in reserve General Railhead. Ammunition O.R. also requires to large general settling. Head 36K/FAB & 3rd Lu. Bein. for artillery O.R.	
	11/4		To 58 C.E.D. at W.D. 34th Bde (recorded) To HK Qs M.T. Coy. 24K A.F.A. Bde to O.O. march 5K A.F.A.T.	
	12/4		To Railhead Town. 24K A.F.A. Bde to O.O. Left Corps Troops arriving forward march 5K A.F.A.T. To 1st C.T. R.D. received 36 here been to complete supply Btn. to 20 spare each.	

Army Form C. 2118.

WAR DIARY
or
INTELLIGENCE SUMMARY.
(Erase heading not required.)

Instructions regarding War Diaries and Intelligence Summaries are contained in F.S. Regs., Part II. and the Staff Manual respectively. Title pages will be prepared in manuscript.

Place	Date	Hour	Summary of Events and Information	Remarks and references to Appendices
Kemmel	13/4/15		To Railhead. Convoy to Colonel Pigeont returning stores to Base from there – no supplies at Central Shipment	
	14/4		To Railhead. Arranged trucks for returned stores for Base.	
	15/4		Railhead move to Abeele. Finished all general arrangements. Moved stores from Kemmel to Abeele. Arranged steps for sea stores and ammn. stores.	
Abeele	16/4		To Abeele re return to Kemmel at later in. return stores. Arrived all ammunition stores to Railhead moved permanent to Kemmel to Armament. Kent Return to O.C. left for Division for duty.	
	17/4		To Railhead. To 48th Division re sending blankets after return at Armament.	
	18/4		To Railhead. To Brutinne re issue & storage of winter clothing being returned.	
	19/4		To 32nd & 34th M.R. of general returns & equipment stores. To Railhead — to Brutinne re return of stores at Salange. To Bemine re sharing down tents. To D/57 & 111/D.A. re winter stores. Conference at A.D.O.S. office re proposals to have standard quantity of stores for infantry kept in trucks ready for available issue after Armament.	
	20/4		To Railhead and to R.M. stores F. Lister & 3/115 Bde.	
	21/4		To Railhead and to Divnl. Camp at Brutery. Bertram Park for 2 Kadera Lorries for M.G. Para.	
	22/4		To H. Arms re local purchase of Lorries. Walking for 20 Letters. About Mt. Lorry Lee to O.D. at Corps Troops.	

Army Form C. 2118.

WAR DIARY
or
INTELLIGENCE SUMMARY.
(Erase heading not required.)

Instructions regarding War Diaries and Intelligence Summaries are contained in F. S. Regs., Part II. and the Staff Manual respectively. Title pages will be prepared in manuscript.

Place	Date	Hour	Summary of Events and Information	Remarks and references to Appendices
Beaumont	23/4		To Richards maintenance of Winter Clothing. Conversation re stores. To N.T. Dir. M.T. Coy. re intends to ……. To No 2 Ord. M.E. Workshops (Light) re instruction to Area H. Q. B.T. M.S. No O. arrived re 3 A.T. Table.	
	24/4		To Richards to No 1 Heavy Mobile Workshop re allocation to emergency ammunition reserve for 4.5 tons ammunition.	
	25/4		Received revised notice	
	26/4		To Rackeli, Movement of rank of M.G.H.M.(Heavy) re changing Geo regulations, to Rompfurite and accessories re necessity for an Armourer to 1st Corps Troops.	
	27/4		To Rychard, Inspect workshop Company. To K.E.O.H.M.P.(Heavy) for additional carriage boutique at R.S. Ord. N.W.I. Officers Cartons. Confirmed movement of Ord. Units travelling by train per ... Rs.	
	28/4		To Rychard. To 33m B.M.R. to …. to Portinguined position allocated to.	
	29/4		To Richards Boutilion, Paulin. Review Ord Dump at Murphy. Instead not Portuguese Coy. + Portuguese Scheme. Copies marked to N.T. Ros. for Reference.	
	30/4		To Richards. To Portuguese Artillery Wagon Lines. To D.A.C. re Inspection. 17 a.a.Lights red marked to 17th Div. To Q. Head. Geo re starting approach way for Zoo repaired	

J. Crutta Webster Capt. A.O.D.
D.A.D.O.S.
11th Div. 30/4/15

War Diary
DADOS
May 1918

WAR DIARY

INTELLIGENCE SUMMARY

(Erase heading not required.)

Army Form C. 2118.

Instructions regarding War Diaries and Intelligence Summaries are contained in F.S. Regs., Part II. and the Staff Manual respectively. Title pages will be prepared in manuscript.

Place	Date	Hour	Summary of Events and Information	Remarks and references to Appendices
Beaumont	1/5/18		To Railhead. To Portuguese Labour Corps re their requirements. Instructed N.C.O. in routine procedure minutiae. To Portuguese Artillery H.Q. re requirement left instructions for the Reserve Officer to submit demands & push fwd Indents of requirements and deficiencies. Received notification that Non Portuguese units should be transferred for Ordnance services to O.O. 1st Corps. Charges forwarded all correspondence to O.O. Reported to H.R. re completion of handoff of Ammo Dump of 32nd Divn.	
	2/5/18		To Railhead. To O.O. 1st C.T. to save Portuguese units. Routes mile in Beaumont	
	3/5/18		To Railhead. To I.O.M. Nº 26 O.M. Workshops re Technical repairs.	
	4/5/18		General Routine. Checked Gas Reserve with Divl Gas Officer	
	5/5/18		To Railhead. To Nº 1 O.M.M. (Army) to exchange air cylinders for trench stores	
	6/5/18		To Railhead. To MT D.M.T. Coy. To C. Staff re an C.O. re equipment. To Mt MG + Derby R to an C.O. Stores inspected by D.D.O.S (L.P.C.) and A.D.O.S. 1st Corps & Divn Ammo drawn from Gun Park + sent to C.R.E. Inds R. (Pioneers) to complete to new establishment of 12 guns.	
	7/5/18		To Railhead. To Nº 1 O.M.M. (Army) to exchange cylinders. Ann. Laundry supply failed. Demanded supplies from Base through A.D.O.S at 1st Corps.	
	8/5/18 9/5/18		General Routine.	

Army Form C. 2118.

WAR DIARY
or
INTELLIGENCE SUMMARY.
(Erase heading not required.)

Instructions regarding War Diaries and Intelligence
Summaries are contained in F. S. Regs., Part II.
and the Staff Manual respectively. Title pages
will be prepared in manuscript.

Place	Date	Hour	Summary of Events and Information	Remarks and references to Appendices
Bangalore	10/5/18		To Richard. To Jarko Lines. To M.T. Coy. General Routine.	
	11/5/18		To Richard. To 101. O.M.W. (Henry) to exchange afficers.	
	12/5/18		General Routine. Battle units in Reengagement.	
	13/5/18		To 6th Yorks re handing in of equipment. Move following units to O.O. 101 C.T. 110th Innisilling Coy. 3rd Aust. Tunnelling Coy. A.C.E.H. Special Coys R.E. and N°6 Sanitary Section.	
	14/5/18		To Gun Park re additional Runo Guns. Visited R.M. Stores.	
	15/5/18		To Richard. Move - from 30th Divn. to 11th Divn. 2nd Batt Yorks Regt.	
	16/5/18		To Officers Clothing Depot N°1 re accounts. To Gun Park for large indicator. To depot N°1 (A.Coy 2nd Garrison Battalion Oxf & Bucks. L.I.) to Gutsot post detachment at Burko L.I.	
	17/5/18		Collected 36 Runo Guns for increase of establishment of Infantry Battalion to 24 guns each. Posters 4 for A.A. work. Move - from Canadian C.T. to 11th Div.- A. Coy 2nd Garrison Battalion Oxford & Bucks Light Infantry. 6th Yorks returned equipment. Checking civil establishment.	
	18/5/18		Checking stores returned. To Transport Officer 6th Yorks re saddling to be returned. General Routine.	
	19/5/18		" Visited R.M. Stores.	
	20/5/18		" Moved to O.O. at C.T. - A. Coy 2nd Garrison Bn. Ox r Bucks L.I.	

Army Form C. 2118.

WAR DIARY
of
INTELLIGENCE SUMMARY.
(Erase heading not required.)

Instructions regarding War Diaries and Intelligence Summaries are contained in F. S. Regs., Part II. and the Staff Manual respectively. Title pages will be prepared in manuscript.

Place	Date	Hour	Summary of Events and Information	Remarks and references to Appendices
Rouen?	21/5		To Officers Clothing Depot No 1. Tested shirts in Bouagrement. D.D.O.S. inspected stores office	
	22/5		To Railhead. To D/59 Wagon lines - stores. Reports 6th Inds. received from Battle Casualties.	
	23/5		Railhead. Move to Bertin from Rouen. General Routine.	
	24/5		To Railhead. To C.O. Donals, Manchesters. 3,2, L.T.M.B. 57th R.A. M.R. and C.O. 34th Ambulance.	
	25/5		To Artillery Res. Clothing stores. 57th Bde RFA M.R re general clothing. D.A.C. M.R. 57th Bde Wagon Lines - R. Mis Stores - R.A. M.R. re general equipment.	
	26/5		To R.R - 1, 2, 3, + 4 Coys. Div. Train.	
	27/5		General Routine - Checking invoices.	
	28/5		To O.O. at C.T. C.O. L. Offs M.T. Coy. Should not intend to Portuguese Artillery Workshops to O.O. at Corps troops. Received from MC Corps. No further action taken.	
	29/5		To Officers Clothing depot No 1. for stores replacement.	
	30/5		To Railhead re Storage of Blankets. being retained until the 18th June. L. Company ships re new stores. To M.R. Irwin. To 32nd Bde M.R. To O.Co. 32, 33 + 4 L.T.M Bn.	
	31/5		To 24th Div re camp kettles. To MDCS Nth Corps re Layers Stores. To MR Coy Train 2 M/S Bty. R.F.A. To run R. the Store - O. C. of /05.	

F. Costerdale, Capt A.D
D.A.D.O.S. Nth Div.
31/5/18.

Vol 25.

WAR DIARY
DADOS
June 1918

Army Form C. 2118.

WAR DIARY
INTELLIGENCE SUMMARY.
(Erase heading not required.)

Instructions regarding War Diaries and Intelligence Summaries are contained in F. S. Regs., Part II. and the Staff Manual respectively. Title pages will be prepared in manuscript.

Place	Date	Hour	Summary of Events and Information	Remarks and references to Appendices
Rouenpoint	1/6/18		General Routine. Learned 4 known have to 2nd Yorkshire Regt. to complete to war establishment. To Rouen. O.E.D. No 1. re reserve re-equipment. To I.O.M. for 19 feet timber for use in clothing store. + Main Ordnance station for disinfector leaving times.	
	2/6/18		To A.D.O.S. at Corps to discuss outstanding Q'nions. To Corps Camp A.V.R.P. and D.A.S. to D.A.D.O.S. at out 55th Division. re reorganization of Reserve T.M. Bs. Adjutant of Median T.M. Bn. called re divisional question of items to be returned to D.	
	3/6/18		Visited stores + R.Qs. of 33rd Btle.	
	4/6/18		General Routine.	
	5/6/18		To Calais re refit details Lewis furniture. Portuguese Inty (?) workshops from N Corps to DO at C.T.	
	6/6/18		General Routine	
	7/6/18		Visited O.C. OK N Corps. M.T. Coy. No. at Corps Camps. Richard	
	8/6/18		Visited Gun Park, J.A.D.O.S. OK Div. ← OK N Corps. D.D.D.S. re army re A.D.O.S. at Corps visited stores.	
	9/6/18		To Ordnance Heavy details workshops for air cylinders. To officers clothing Depot. To Army Bill. D.O.O.S. office re personnel. O.O. at C.T.	
	10/6/18		Visited R.Os. Stores 3 Grd + 3 2nd Battns.	
	11/6/18		To O/59 stores + wagon lines. To A.O.O.S. at Corps. To M.T. Coy. re general equipment.	
	12/6/18		To Heavy Mobile Workshops for air cylinders. O. No stores Northwood Dunkirk Brouch.	

Army Form C. 2118.

WAR DIARY
INTELLIGENCE SUMMARY.
(Erase heading not required.)

Instructions regarding War Diaries and Intelligence Summaries are contained in F. S. Regs., Part II. and the Staff Manual respectively. Title pages will be prepared in manuscript.

Place	Date	Hour	Summary of Events and Information	Remarks and references to Appendices
Boulogne	13/6/18		General Routine	
	14/6/18		To St Omer & Calais to purchase Summer Hosting.	
	15/6/18		72 Lewis Lenses collected to complete supply Battalions to 32 guns each plus 4 for A.A. defence.	
	16/6/18		To Army Mobile dep for that iron for cleaning purposes + to Officer Cdg Depot. Store destroyed by staffing. 5 Lewis guns through S/Sgt Taylor failed rifle examining the above guns. Council recommends to Units sent in reach to St Army Lewis Park for duty.	
	17/		To Northumberland Fusiliers R.E. & Rainbrook. To H.Q. 33rd Bde to general equipment Lewis Park with Armourer S/S/Sgt F Turberman duty on A.T.B. Instructed Lieut Donaldson to benefit S/Pol for Food purchase it possible of Officer Clothing rept. Inspected Stores of 33rd Bde R.H. 2nd Lorks + Lorks + Lines. Dorsets + Northamptons Fusiliers.	
	19/6/18		To St Omer for bread purchase. Rd. A.R. no general question.	
	20/6/18		To Sun Park — St Pol & to St Eytor Rent. Station. Instructing Lieut Donaldson to arrange Officers in duties to be performed by him during absence of D.A.D.O.S. Chief Clerk instructed to carry out all normal work routines especially to take charge. D.A.D.O.S. Nt Division to advise upon any Armourer questions arising.	
	21/6/18		D.A.D.O.S. commenced leave. Duties taken over by Reserve Officer.	

Army Form C. 2118.

WAR DIARY
or
INTELLIGENCE SUMMARY.
(Erase heading not required.)

Instructions regarding War Diaries and Intelligence Summaries are contained in F. S. Regs., Part II. and the Staff Manual respectively. Title pages will be prepared in manuscript.

Place	Date	Hour	Summary of Events and Information	Remarks and references to Appendices
Jacquenont	24/5/18		To 1st Army Gun Park to review outstanding indents.	
	25th to 27th		General routine.	
	28/5/18		A.D.O.S. Corps wanted officer. To Corps H.Q. Talk with A.D.O.S. on Ordnance matter. Visited the various Corps HQrs in No Area (have no stores of S.D. Coy's held to exchange for grave clothing when necessary).	
	29/5/18		Sergt. Reed sent to A.D.O.S. 1 Corps for temporary duty.	
	30/5/18		General Routine	

Donnellan Lieut
A.D.O.S.
11th Dn.

21/4/18

D.A.D.O.S.
War Diary
July 1918

Vol 26

Army Form C. 2118.

WAR DIARY
or
INTELLIGENCE SUMMARY.
(Erase heading not required.)

Place	Date	Hour	Summary of Events and Information	Remarks and references to Appendices
Bucquemont	1/7/18	—	Usual Routine	
"	2/7/18	—	Usual Routine. Bod 1 rifle fitted for Grenade discharger (pt First report)	
"	3/7/18	—	Usual Routine	
"	4/7/18	—	Party returned from Gun Park for duty	
"	5/7/18	—	S.A.O.O (Major Ellcotte relieved) returned from leave to U.K.	
"	6/7/18	—	Received details to work down at armament. 3 Rifles to Engineers for experiment. 17 pdr gun carriage received to exchange unit for extra Lewis Guns.	
"	7/7/18	—	L. Officer Clothing Depot for Officers	
"	8/7/18	—	L. A.O.A.S. at Corbie. L. local M.G.S. Workshops to repairs to vehicles. L. M.T. Coy on work.	
"	9/7/18	—	L. Richard. Inspected stores of 25th Batt. Ambulance and 9.59 R.F.A. and 32nd I. Bn. Division. C.O. of Manchesters. 33rd Div. R.E. Visited C.O. of 6th Northumberland Fusiliers.	
"	10/7/18	—	L. Edies up supplies of various stores. Received 3 Lewis Rifles to Ordnance	
"	11/7/18	—	Usual Routine	
"	12/7/18	—	Inspected stores of B.E. & D. Batteries of 5th F.A. Bde. Visited O.C. of Bn. Bdes at Officers Clothing depot to exchange stores. Visited 6 Lindsey Ridge and Montague. Received 72 miles roads speed to transport of Lewis Guns to First Report	

Army Form C. 2118.

WAR DIARY
or
INTELLIGENCE SUMMARY.
(Erase heading not required.)

Instructions regarding War Diaries and Intelligence Summaries are contained in F.S. Regs., Part II. and the Staff Manual respectively. Title pages will be prepared in manuscript.

Place	Date	Hour	Summary of Events and Information	Remarks and references to Appendices
Bourgneuf	13/7/18		Inspected stores of Northumberland Fusiliers, M.G. Manchesters. Called O.C. 1st Div. M.G. to orders.	
	14/7/18		In Officers Clothing Depot 101 with stores surplus through casualties. To Gun Park and No.1 Heavy. Wrote to the Workshops.	
	15/7/18		Inspected Train of 32nd S.A.B. Div. Level Clothing Store. Visited 33rd Div. M.G. and the M.G. Divisional Armourer. Wrote Staff, and Statistics. Read & ack'd Bobadilly S.S.	
	16/7/18		To A.D.O.S. Inspected stores of No.4 Coy Trains, 1st Manchester, 1st East Staffs and Londons. Received German Machine Guns for instructional purposes. Hung for M.G. Battalion. 2 sights for Infantry Brigades. Received 70 Templates for Air cylinder.	
	17/7/18		2nd Demonst. attached D.H.Q. attended for instruction in routine of Columns services of the Division. Visited Gun Park and No.1 Heavy. Wrote Workshops for Air cylinder & Spring. Routine.	
	18/7/18		Inspected stores of 32nd 33rd & 34th Bde F.M. Btys. to Railhead. Routine.	
	19/7/18		Usual Routine. Visited O.C. Trains. Correspondence, Comp. Returns	

Army Form C. 2118.

WAR DIARY
or
INTELLIGENCE SUMMARY.
(Erase heading not required.)

Instructions regarding War Diaries and Intelligence Summaries are contained in F. S. Regs., Part II. and the Staff Manual respectively. Title pages will be prepared in manuscript.

Place	Date	Hour	Summary of Events and Information	Remarks and references to Appendices
Rosignano	20/7/18		General Routine. Divisional Conference. Received 10" Howitzer Report "A.A." mountings. Collected 15 cwts of Pickwidding from Army Corps "B". L.L.R. Lieutenant on leaving first Army.	
"	21/7/18		Received details of D.H.R., H.T. Geo Separators, H.R., R.E., Leo Siemen Nightlamps + Monroe Stores.	
"	22/7/18		Received O.C. + R.M. Stores of M.R. and No 1. 2.+ 3. Corps M.T. Divs. Trains. Received H.R. & Lts Lot Land + 2nd York R. Received I.O.M. No 6. Balance 18.7.18 Workshop (Depot) + return from refung it. Received 10 milinhah Supply + A mounting.	
"	23/7/18		General Routine	
"	24/7/18		Visited detachments of 50th F.A.B., Conference at G.D.O.S.+ L Corps officer to witness the report experimentation + elimination of explosives.	
"	25/7/18		Inspected stores of D.A.C. H.R. 1.2.+ 3. actions. Inspected stores of Yorkshire R. and Yorks Lancer. Inspected company bath store of Yorks Lancer. Received 150 Dicks Quintin Anti-Gas.	
"	26/7/18		Inspected stores of 50th Div. R.F.A. Received 160 anti smoke fire ants Eno.	
"	27/7/18		General Routine. Checking returns etc.	
"	28/7/18		Visited Army Med. Off. Walsh. Gen. Rostron.	

Army Form C. 2118.

WAR DIARY
or
INTELLIGENCE SUMMARY.
(Erase heading not required.)

Instructions regarding War Diaries and Intelligence Summaries are contained in F. S. Regs., Part II. and the Staff Manual respectively. Title pages will be prepared in manuscript.

Place	Date	Hour	Summary of Events and Information	Remarks and references to Appendices
	29/7/18		Inspected stores of 32nd Fld. Amb. 33rd Field Ambulance. F. Jacka Bearers. M.S. Battalion	
	30/7/18		To Calais for dental purposes etc.	
	31/7/18		General Conference clearing stations etc. Received 5 new pattern combined tables for Pickers Bears. Received 10 Machray Oxygen & A. mour. Therapy. Received 60 cuits amentation Anti-flu.	

T. Coulb Roberts Major RAMC
D.A.D.M.S. 4th Division
1/8/18.

Army Form C. 2118.

WAR DIARY
or
INTELLIGENCE SUMMARY.
(Erase heading not required.)

Vol 27

Place	Date	Hour	Summary of Events and Information	Remarks and references to Appendices
Bruqueront	1-8-18		Visited all R.M.s & units reference Clothing	
	2.8.18		General Routine. Monthly returns. Received 1 Sample Grenade thrown for issue on Trial for report. Recd 160 Anti combinations Anti gas for Trial.	
	3.8.18		To No 9 Ordnance Depot to obtain stores on loan for use at First Army Communication course on 4th inst. Delivered to Temporary camp at Rinchicourt.	
	4.8.18		General Routine. 5 Trunk shelter collected from D.O. at C.T. & issued to IWT Div. Application for Officer for evening picture area.	
	5.8.18		Returned loaned stores to No 9 Ordnance depot.	
	6.8.18		General Routine	
	7.8.18		To Rinchard comp. To Army Mobile workshop. To 55th Division D.A.D.O.S.	
	8.8.18		Inspected stores of A.B.E.D. Matters. 57th Bde R.F.A. Recd 7 Monkey puzzles A.A. wourting and 53 forward and eight from Army Iron Rate K2!	
	9.8.18		General Routine	
	10.8.18		Visited C.O. & I.K. Staffs and 1st Lincolns. HQ 57th Bde RFA. 32 & 34th Bde R.L. 31st Infy Bde & DTO at C.T. Recd 3 parabellis eye attachments to Vickers Guns.	
	11.8.18		To Rinchard. Visited Lewis M.G. No 4 Gun A.D.O.S. at Corps. No 6. Ord Mobile Workshop (light) on vehicles. D.A.D.O.S. Officer at Division. Inspected stores of 32nd & 33rd & 34th L.T.M.Bn. and Artillery Anti gas cotting store.	

Army Form C. 2118.

WAR DIARY
or
INTELLIGENCE SUMMARY.
(Erase heading not required.)

Instructions regarding War Diaries and Intelligence Summaries are contained in F. S. Regs., Part II. and the Staff Manual respectively. Title pages will be prepared in manuscript.

Place	Date	Hour	Summary of Events and Information	Remarks and references to Appendices
Bruay	12.8.18		Attended exhibition of methods of carrying up Water tins in transport. Inspected intention of methods of packing Limb Lim. limbered wagons S.S.	
	13.8.18		General Routine. Inspected stores of G.T. Rivetone.	
	14.8.18		General Routine. Lt. I.O.M. No.1 Cdn. Mob. Workshop (Heavy) reported for instructions	
	15.8.18		To Divisional Depot Stores of Clothing & Sundries return.	
	16.8.18		General Routine. Inspected stores of 7th S. Staffs. 9th Warwicks Worcester & 3rd Bn. M.H.	
	17.8.18		To Advance & to "B" 1st Division re waiting for D.A.D.V.S. at Division here. Lt. A.D.O.S. at Corps. To Army Supply School to arrange Supplies refits. Rec'd 75 G'cts Returns Roll pro	
	18.8.18		Lt. I.O.M., No.1 Cdn. M. Workshop No.1 ref. exchange	
	19.8.18		Inspected stores of M.R. & No.1. 2. 3. & 4 Coy. 114 Div. Train. 1/577 R.Field. and 357th Field Ambulance	
	20.8.18		General Routine	
	21.8.18		To Gun Park No.1. Lt. I.O.M. D.M. Workshop No.1. Lt. Div'l. Supp. Lt. Supremo 1st Div. Lt. Simmo A.P.D. reported for inspection of boot repairing shops	
	22.8.18		Visited all regimental dumps with Lt. Simmo. Recd. 6 A.R. Unstry Jugs & mountings + 60 French duffers for issue to Tembo in bivouacs.	
	23.8.18		To Tournay area re billets for officer workshops etc. Lt. Simmo detached to 55th Div	
	24.8.18		Moved stores to Hingpanel.	

Army Form C. 2118.

WAR DIARY
or
INTELLIGENCE SUMMARY.
(Erase heading not required.)

Instructions regarding War Diaries and Intelligence Summaries are contained in F. S. Regs., Part II. and the Staff Manual respectively. Title pages will be prepared in manuscript.

Place	Date	Hour	Summary of Events and Information	Remarks and references to Appendices
Bapaume	25.8.18		Moved remaining stores & workshops to Miraumont. Collected 75 rabs Cav. Ernnan Antigas tank Rev. and 75 Returner 157% Div. Received 2 Stores trucks from Rd Corps in replacement of those handed in. S/Sgt. arrived to act C.T. also 3 tents C.S.A. for Advance personnel.	
Miraumont	26.8.18		Moved office to Miraumont. Collected 2 C.S.L. tents from 4th C.T. Issued 1 S.T., R.E. and 5 tents S.A.A. to 2nd D.A.C. Returned Demands through to 4th C.T.	
	27.8.18		Returned 15 sets pack saddlery to 3rd Div. Amm Park B.	
	28.8.18		Collected 30 German rifles from Amm Park B. Received 7 German rifles for transport. Returned R.S.T. stores to Miraumont.	
Miraumont	29.8.18		Moved office to Miraumont. 2 Amm Park, Raised Staff Captain 34th Div. Bde at Hd. at Miraumont. Administration of Div now XVII Corps.	
	30.8.18		Raised A.D.O.S. XVII Corps. Moved Sgt Monk returning to 15th Div. to administer 11th Div. Artillery. Rec'd 500 infantile kits for Kitchen Sum. Rec'd 3 Heavy Lewis M.G's from Amm Park. Rec'd tent pegs for huts with Kitchen Sum. Moved store workshops to Miraumont. Collected 300 Infantry kits from O.O. Army T(B). Railed 100 chargers to Remount Depot.	
	31.8.18		L.D.M.R. at noon. L.A.D.O.S. with particulars of kits to ammunition. Monthly returns released Routine. Arranged to move to Battne.	

1/9/18.

V. Cutts Webster
Major A.O.D.
D.A.D.O.S. 11th Div.

WAR DIARY or INTELLIGENCE SUMMARY

Army Form C. 2118.

Place	Date	Hour	Summary of Events and Information	Remarks and references to Appendices
Arras	1/9/18		Moved office stores & workshops to Arras. To Siege Park for 1 Machine Gun. To Staff Captain 34th Infy Bde. To A.D.G. at Arras.	
	2/9/18		To A.D.O.S. with monthly returns. To 33rd Bde Transport & R.A. stores. To Adv. Ordnance return of loan equipment Berlin.	
	3/9/18		To No. 2 Adv. Mob. Workshops (4/4.E) No. 1 Gun Park (Armourer) and 31st Bde R.M. Stores.	
	4/9/18		General Routine	
	5/9/18		To Transports here & Billets of infantry units. 33rd Inf. Bde. March stores - 31/8/20.	
	6/9/18		Moved office to No.1 Grande Rue du Rivage Arras. General Routine. March 31st.	
	7/9/18		LIH Bde with 14.6.T.M.B. I return of kill ambulance w/4/58 Bde R.F.A. & 10th Cav. Division. To D.A.D.O.S. at Cav. Div. re above move & transfer of personnel & eqpt to assist 11th Cav. Div. re move. Despatched N.C.O. with Armourers Harry & Coster. To 32nd Bde M.R. re move.	
	8/9/18		To 32nd & 33rd Bde R.M. Stores. To M.R. relative to Capt. E. Forbes (Armourer). To 32nd Bde H.R. re general requirements. Red wine of Hith Div. Arty Group (15th Division 15th Div with 115 Div Arty.	
	9/9/18		General Routine. Lt. Club re Armourer returned from Richland on returned stores. To R.A.M.R. w/ 57 & 59 Bde R.F.A. N.R. re equipment.	
	10/9/18		To A.D.O.S. XXIII Corps re returns. General Routine.	
	11/9/18		General Routine.	
	12/9/18		General Routine. A.D.O.S. inspected records office steps & offices	

Army Form C. 2118.

WAR DIARY
or
INTELLIGENCE SUMMARY.
(Erase heading not required.)

Instructions regarding War Diaries and Intelligence Summaries are contained in F. S. Regs., Part II. and the Staff Manual respectively. Title pages will be prepared in manuscript.

Place	Date	Hour	Summary of Events and Information	Remarks and references to Appendices
Arras	13/9		General Routine. Capt Charlton attended office for instruction in Ordnance Services. Visited No 1 Amm. Park. Visited A.R.I Inst. Mobile Workshops, Aircraft Park, Forge waggon, (A.T. Sean Park) for attention. Received 10 Stokes Rampfrom Lubricatingstors Sent O.S.T. Distributed these to Units.	
	14/9		Visited G of D parks. 2 officers and Off. for Bandoliers & Off. pack articles Sent O.ST.	
	15/9		Visited A.B.C.&D. B.Sqs. 57R. 15 R. Q.F.A. re equipment & stores. Met S.T.M.G. instructor.	
	16/9		Visited D.A.Dr.O.S. re Corps re general question of supply and of Other Divisions in fatigues were required to assist in handling stores. Arrange is made of fatigues were reinforced 6 in the demands which is submitted in Quarter were divisions against the Demands of the Divisions to Base area Informed by Asst. D. Director again of the Domain to Base area	
	17/9		General Routine.	
	18/9		Notified by H.Q of the return of the 2nd R. Tele. Sqdn on 20th. Above Cavalry Bd. to move mile to home of no innertaiey personnel. Collected 250 truck filters from G.H.Q. XXII Corps. Delivered 150 to Essex Armament Repair. Received further 15 Stokes Ramps indents from Lewis Park	
	19/9		Moved stores to Aniigornel. Received over 107.	
Aniigornel	20/9		Moved to Aniigornel. Handed over 107. Lunchlocks to D.A.D.O.S. 4th corps.	
	21/9		Received more of 32R. Tele. Troops from V.A.D.O.S. 1st Cavalry Div. Ordnance personnel & Lorry returned for duty with 32R. Tele pre Instns 22/9/17 & 5/10/17. A.T.9a 32R & Sect 15160 will absorbed in 33R. Tele which during his absence.	

Army Form C. 2118.

WAR DIARY
or
INTELLIGENCE SUMMARY.
(Erase heading not required.)

Instructions regarding War Diaries and Intelligence Summaries are contained in F. S. Regs., Part II. and the Staff Manual respectively. Title pages will be prepared in manuscript.

Place	Date	Hour	Summary of Events and Information	Remarks and references to Appendices
Mingoval	22/9		March A/DS Tels. R.F.A. to attending Dumieres. Notified my D.M.S. of early move of 78 Division to Canadian Corps for future time. Visited A.D.C.S. Canadian Corps and A.D.S. XXII Corps re moves of special [illegible] ctve etc.	
	23/9		Visited 3rd B.M.A. and all units of [illegible] Division. All complete. Ambulances of [illegible] arrived but R.T.O. [illegible] not trucks [illegible] to unload & store. All Acres temp engaged in erection. Conference at H.Q. re arrangements for [illegible] advance & Collected [illegible] Fd Ste Pers Hy, 40/pers Pack army, ?35th (Scot arty), and 9 [illegible] 3600 SOR, [illegible] [illegible] (per Bdnl) [illegible] advanced stores.	
	24/9		Chiese Rendez from Rochail to Bremen. [illegible] Leave summary of wounded [illegible] [illegible] [illegible] Collected some Pack artillery from A.D.S. [illegible] [illegible] [illegible] Corps Nro. Stores [illegible] to Arras. and 130 Trench shelters from Gds Corps Nro. [illegible]	
	25/9		A.D.C.S. XXII Corps arrived [illegible] for making stages for wounded & [illegible] Collected 3rd Trench shells from Canadian 4Dr. [illegible] to [illegible] [illegible] to [illegible] [illegible] [illegible] Rochail [illegible] to [illegible]	
Arras	26/9		March to 0.34 b.9.5 (Que H.Q. Arras). Stores [illegible] [illegible] [illegible] Arras. Z A.D.T XXII Corps for move AqK & Sags [illegible] [illegible] for expediting ad under Delivered to [illegible] Refueling Point to A.D.M.S Can. Corps Reps.	
0.34 b 9.5 M.st 51.B.	27/9		March office to Red Cross H.R. General Routine. Red elevent to A Vickers M.Fn. at 7am. Collected from B.R. and delivered to Civil Corps Sp. at 9.30 pm Collected 150 [illegible] [illegible] [illegible] Can Corps Reps.	

Army Form C. 2118.

WAR DIARY
or
INTELLIGENCE SUMMARY.
(Erase heading not required.)

Instructions regarding War Diaries and Intelligence Summaries are contained in F. S. Regs., Part II. and the Staff Manual respectively. Title pages will be prepared in manuscript.

Place	Date	Hour	Summary of Events and Information	Remarks and references to Appendices
O.34 b.8.5 Hut 57 B.	29/9		Inspected Park. Returned stores Divisional charging M.T. Officer at Brielle. Lorries to village women of active troops. Rcvd. instrs. M.T. Officer at 7 months to Railway canteen.	
Brielen Y. 17d. 2.7.	29/9		Moved Officer stores lorries to Brielle. Moved officer at 7 pm to Brielle by road. Instructions from D.M.R.	
	30/9		Moved stores from Brielle 4 to Chateau Brielle. All animals and vehicles to Brielle and accommodated. Chevaillers and Waterers office accommodation at Chateau. General Picture.	

F. Crossarbotte
Major A.O.D.
D.A.D.O.S. NZ Div.
30/9/18.

Vol 29

CONFIDENTIAL.

WAR DIARY
OF
D.A.D.O.S 11TH DIVN

OCTOBER 1918

Army Form C. 2118.

WAR DIARY
or
INTELLIGENCE SUMMARY.
(Erase heading not required.)

Instructions regarding War Diaries and Intelligence Summaries are contained in F.S. Regs., Part II. and the Staff Manual respectively. Title pages will be prepared in manuscript.

Place	Date	Hour	Summary of Events and Information	Remarks and references to Appendices
Bulsaq	1/10/17		Demantled Winter Park & platoform Carriages & waggons. A Lieutenant, 2 Sergts, & corpls and 5 Sappers. 7 hours time wasted F; 2nd Lt 2; npoles Cpl. Waited 1875 Blankets to 32nd Bde.	
	2/10		Lt Munro. Railhead and to stores to arrange about the storehouse & contents unto a returns of L.G. waggons for Burville. Leaves Waggon ammunition to 161 Bde D.A.C.	
	3/10		Moved Office to Burville. Waggon Amm. 18 pdr issued to 161 Bde. D.A.C. F/ Lieut Greenward to Yorks in Burvo. 1 hour time to G.K. Pinaloes.	
Burville	4/10		Lt Am Park of Waggon stall issue ammunition 4.5 How. Lost tring to collect, issued amm to 318 Bde for Pinaoes.	
	5/10		General Routine. Issued 4.5 amm with cartes to 83rd Bde which advanced for 32 Bde. Lost 4 hours time to yards vehicles.	
	6/10		Issued 10 pdr am cart to 314 Bde. No additional park orders. One enquiring Forward Star was actually repaired & wheel consulted the Armourer. Demanded 29 fields Very by ?? who L.R. Armourer Sergt re complained – got too many after twice issued. B.O.O. states no complaints made but all armourers supports. Complaint privately ??? from me & investigated. Corporal who was acting with Pk S/Sgt R.E.A.D. here left detached at St Ruapehu Camp.	

Army Form C. 2118.

WAR DIARY
or
INTELLIGENCE SUMMARY.
(Erase heading not required.)

Instructions regarding War Diaries and Intelligence Summaries are contained in F.S. Regs., Part II. and the Staff Manual respectively. Title pages will be prepared in manuscript.

Place	Date	Hour	Summary of Events and Information	Remarks and references to Appendices
Bapaume	7/10		General Routine. L.D. Reserve open to accommodation. Issued A.S. How + Carriage to D/57 R.F.A. " 2 Wagons R.G.S. to 5th Leicester Foresters " 3" T.M. to 34th Bde h.T.M.B. " 1 Vickers Gun to M.G. Bn.	
	8/10		General Routine. Issued 1 Vickers Gun to M.G. Bn. " 10 Lewis Guns of Dorsets after repairs to 6th Northumberland Fusiliers " 5 Lewis Guns to 34th Bde. " 1500 Blankets to 34th Bde.	
	9/10		General Routine. Visited Railhead at turnes. Arranged with D.A.D.R.T. to offload Kental Laundry 1000 & 7000 and 15,000 draws to winter clothing to rip Laundry. Returned Pontoon parts not required. Visited R.O.O. to return Pres to Base. Issued Wagon L.G.S. to M.G. Bn. 2 Limber pontoon parts for 5th Field Coy " Water Cart to 1/5th Staffordshire Regt.	
	10/10		General Routine. To Mund Railhead re arrangements for drawing + returning stores. To our R.R. side re accommodation. Held office to S.I.F. What 57th Mon cancelled. Returned to Bapaume.	

(Appx): Wt. W12899/M1293. 75,000. 1/17. D. D. & L., Ltd. Forms/C.2118-14

Army Form C. 2118.

WAR DIARY
or
INTELLIGENCE SUMMARY.
(Erase heading not required.)

Instructions regarding War Diaries and Intelligence Summaries are contained in F. S. Regs., Part II. and the Staff Manual respectively. Title pages will be prepared in manuscript.

Place	Date	Hour	Summary of Events and Information	Remarks and references to Appendices
Baralle	11/10/18		General Routine. No cars available. Demands written clothing in want of private received to date. Issued R.E. & Tanks Paper in Chg etc. Issued 1 M.G. Limber to A.T. Gun Bn. Returned 13 riding pack saddles to First Army Depot "G". Cancelled 6" T.M. (matured fire equipment pertains) from M.T. Heavy Rep. Workshop.	
	12/10/18		No cars available. General Routine. Out of Touch with Advance Supply contd. oper-completing issue of Kit necessary winter needs. Received all equipment. Issued these 6011 Rob and 16200 drawers to O/C Laundry at Arras.	
	13/10/18		No cars available. Fell 2 p.m. Instructions from D.H.R. Christmas Box Caps. General Routine. Collected 200 tiered dilution from O.C. 22nd Corps Troops. Issued blankets from Store in Arras for issue to Troops, also magazines & sent down Lines. Issued 1800 blankets to 82nd Bde. 2100 " " 33rd " 550 " " 34th " Visited H.Q. 32nd, 33rd & 34th Bdes with general direction of winter equipment & Service returning at 3pm 14/10/18.	
	14/10/18		Received Account. Arranged despatch of Stores. H.T.Rail Coy busy daily with In Camp. All Stores cleared in handing of returning seasonal demands direct to R.O.O. to save transport. Reported sufficient in obtaining sufficient use of a car for the efficient working of the Balance	

(A7032) Wt. W2839/M333 75,000. 1/17. D.D. & L. Ltd. Forms/C. 2118/14.

Army Form C. 2118.

WAR DIARY
or
INTELLIGENCE SUMMARY.
(Erase heading not required.)

Instructions regarding War Diaries and Intelligence Summaries are contained in F.S. Regs. Part II. and the Staff Manual respectively. Title pages will be prepared in manuscript.

Place	Date	Hour	Summary of Events and Information	Remarks and references to Appendices
Barulla	15/10/18		Services of the Division and about to join the S.O.S. Division. Issued Water 1.G.S. to T.G. Field Coy. 1 lorry lorn to Nº Inf Bgd. Visited 32 Fd MR. 93 Bgde 34 Bgde all Infantry units, M.G. Battalion, E. Forces (Reserve) and Railhead. A.D.O.S. XXII Corps worked Dumps. L.T.M. Bn. and Railhead.	
	16/10/18		Visited M.R. 58 & 59, Bdes. R.F.A. and D.C. & O. Battalions 59. Bde. A.D.O.S. XXII Corps. C Collected lorries from ten Park. 2 lorries to trippers at 8am for D.M.R. Stores. No cars available. Unable to visit Railhead.	
	17/10/18		Demanded Miss Cart for lot Gurkhas. General Routine. Returned 34 Packsaddles and 384 Water Bottles to Army Corps "C" as none required. Issued 1 L.Gun to Manitoba 4th Div for NZ	Sent 2 days LIS
	18/10/18		Car to Railhead. Issued instructions re activity of office. Lt Behenna 4th Div. for NZ Confirm S.B.R. No car afternoon. No visits possible. General Routine Demanded Cart Water tank for 23½ Field Coy R.E.	
	19/10/18		Car at 10.45. 2 cars to Railhead. Lt Gun Park for Triggers 17 pdr. Demanded 500 Blankets No car afternoon. No visits. General Routine. Received wires re moves of Btns.	
	20/10/18		Car 10 am. to H.R. & moves. to Railhead. 2 trucks water tanks received contents. Stores wanted 4500. Jatoria water 6010. Gate Maskotin 775. Issued to Troops Issued 1500 pairs Web Belt to 31st Bde for inside of Kopie & S.B.G for their work with Attempt. To Central ref debilt for Stores Much lorry about t. movie to Miseri. ref debilt for Stores Company to movie to Miseri. Notified H.R. moving to Miseri or Dat. Company to move office up. No car afternoon. No visits. Buses have been from tun Park Issued 2 to 5th Dorsets 2 to 7th Northumberland Fusiliers 1 to 7th Fusiliers	

(A7092). W. W1839/M1393. 75,000. 1/17. D.D. & L., Ltd. Forms/C.2118/14

Army Form C. 2118.

WAR DIARY
or
INTELLIGENCE SUMMARY.
(Erase heading not required.)

Instructions regarding War Diaries and Intelligence Summaries are contained in F. S. Regs. Part II. and the Staff Manual respectively. Title pages will be prepared in manuscript.

Place	Date	Hour	Summary of Events and Information	Remarks and references to Appendices
NAVES	21/10/18		March. Offices to Naves. March offices & stores to Rouvroy. Lorries departed. Rickshaw changed to Marbaix. M.T. Lorries sent from to Watergraft Chatrak 2 trucks x-tending the lines & partains. 4 & 5 the lorries used to clear stores after refilling. Made 600 litres to my dump.	
	22/10/18		Sr. Railhead to dump. Church service & remainder of stores & returned stores from our dicks left in a hopper condition. Berard, Romitre.	Bundles to continue
	23/10/18		In stores to railhead.	
	24/10/18		In stores railhead. Received Books F.S. + 500 Blankets to complete to 1 per man.	Demanded Wgn for R.E.
	25/10/18		In stores railhead. Recd more at A/57 R.F.A. from 1st Cav Div.	
	26/10/18		In stores railhead. Recd 100 Horse Rugs. 2nd consignment. Forked 3yt.	Coke. Kits and at units.
			Railhead at Vergnies. Train very late.	
	27/10/18		In stores railhead with S.S.O. via all refilling points. Train arrived 18.00.	4 M.T. Sup.
			Demand K.T. Baty for Mt Ministers. March Bde Office to Naves.	
	28/10/18		In stores railhead to Raupton Camp. March stores. Sec stores — part of Stepo to Naves.	
			Confirmed arrival of A/57 R.F.A. Demanded K.T. Baty for 6th Russian R.	Rustes 32 G.H.R.
	29/10/18		In Railed stores & Dirol Dump & supples between stations. March returned stores offices & personnel	
			to Naves. Visited 32nd Bde R.A. and infantry units. Visited D.A.D.O.S. 1st Div & 17th Div & Bulk	
			intake & later arrival of stores. Issued from Railhead carts & dual & 17P.K. Field Coy.	1 Tt 2 Pm.
			& A/Limbin R. & Wagon to 9 5 3 Coy. to 67th Field Coy.	

Army Form C. 2118.

WAR DIARY
or
INTELLIGENCE SUMMARY.
(Erase heading not required.)

Instructions regarding War Diaries and Intelligence Summaries are contained in F. S. Regs., Part II. and the Staff Manual respectively. Title pages will be prepared in manuscript.

Place	Date	Hour	Summary of Events and Information	Remarks and references to Appendices
Marie	30/10/18		To Railhead & M.T. Inj. No truck on train. Arrival of Trucks now very irregular. 3 or 4 days from despatch from Base instead of 2 days (normal).	
	31/10/18		To Railhead. Good Count on Sunday. Demanded 1 K.T. lorry for 11th Manchesters. General Routine. To A.D.O.S. Corps re general questions.	

F. Coutts Webster
Major A.O.D.
D.A.D.O.S. 11th Div. 2/11/18

CONFIDENTIAL

WAR DIARY

OF

D.A.D.O.S.

11TH DIVN.

NOVEMBER 1918

Army Form C. 2118.

WAR DIARY
or
INTELLIGENCE SUMMARY.
(Erase heading not required.)

Instructions regarding War Diaries and Intelligence Summaries are contained in F. S. Regs., Part II. and the Staff Manual respectively. Title pages will be prepared in manuscript.

Place	Date	Hour	Summary of Events and Information	Remarks and references to Appendices
Nowes	1/11/17	-	To Rickhed, 22nd Corps Troops. Escorted Gun books for Div. M.T. Coy Forward repair outfit. To Gun Park of carriage for 6" T.M's, Div. Supply Camp. Lt. M.D, D.S. of carriage for T.M's. Bedford issue in view of operations. Received from Base issued to sundry 5000 rds of ammunition, as no warning issued to 7K 3. Staffordshire R. 400 white strips for Bar. Reinforcements. Chinese mentioned, returning etc., issue again 2 days etc.	
	2/10/15		No air morning. Novinski. No truck at Rickheal. Issue for office stoves — stoves. Issued to 8 ATC Corps. 2 p.m. Lt Chayenn v Kissy for Bar. Reinforcements. Demand 4.5" howitzers for D/57R.F.A. Bde downwhile strips for Bar. Reinforcements. Sent lorry at 7.30 pm to Gun Park (Hericé) for Carriage for General Routine. 6" T.M. Arrange with S.E. R.A. To collect from Nowes at 8.30 am 3/10/17. Issued to 93rd Bde H.Q. 50 French shelter to 93rd Bde H.Q. at Fontaine.	
	3/10/17		Moved office v stores to Brefens. Lt Richhead roves	Richhead roves
Brefens	4/10/15		Moved office to Preseau. Lt Stone of Chaynes to arrange move. from Maleroft to Fontaine.	
	5/10/15		Moved stores to Preseau. Demanded G Lewis Guns for 1/K Elwood Transfer. Signals unable to work for Telephone operations. Lt Richhead up, advise Reassigned which to use - Richhead.	
	6/10/13		No rad richhed at evaging. No train arrived.	

Army Form C. 2118.

WAR DIARY
or
INTELLIGENCE SUMMARY.
(Erase heading not required.)

Instructions regarding War Diaries and Intelligence Summaries are contained in F. S. Regs., Part II. and the Staff Manual respectively. Title pages will be prepared in manuscript.

Place	Date	Hour	Summary of Events and Information	Remarks and references to Appendices
Prestage Carpin	7/11/18		Moved Office to Carpin. Dismantled 4 Panhard L.G.S. for 11K M.G. Bn. Vickers out of action. No Telephone communication.	
Carpin	8/11/18		Dismantled R.T. for 11K M.G. Bn. to Rethel & Freiern. Cancelled move of stores to Carpin.	
Rosises	9/11/18		Moved Office to Rosises. No Telephone to Rethel & Freiern. Vehicles included at new stores at Rosises.	
Astmar	10/11/18		Moved Office to Astmar. Moved stores from Freiern. Dismantled 3 Lewis Guns for 2nd Gothas. Issued 3 Lewis Guns from Armourers Shop. to Rethel. Rosises. Clover vickered. Dismantled Kitchen Travelling complete for 11K M.G. Bn. " Limber Wagon " 11K M.G. Bn.	
"	11/11/18		1 R.T. for Ambulation at Rethel. Vickers sent to collect. Armstice signed at 11am. Informed by D.H.R. to Rethel & Rosises. Moved stores to L'Ermitage in 18th.	
	12/11/18		To Rethel & stores at Rosises. Arranged move to L'Ermitage, local reconnaissance. Dismantled 2nd Panhard (11,000). Dismantled 1 Vickers Gun for M.G. Bn.	
	13/11/18		To Rethel & stores at Rosises. Lorry to Rethel 3 with Rifle atores to L'Ermitage. Armd Wagon L.G.S. gone for 11K M.G. Bn. to D.D.O.S. A.O.D.S. & general question leave.	

(A9392) Wt. W3239/M1993 75,000. 8/17. D. D. & L. Ltd. Forms/C2118-14

Army Form C. 2118.

WAR DIARY
or
INTELLIGENCE SUMMARY.
(Erase heading not required.)

Instructions regarding War Diaries and Intelligence Summaries are contained in F.S. Regs., Part II. and the Staff Manual respectively. Title pages will be prepared in manuscript.

Place	Date	Hour	Summary of Events and Information	Remarks and references to Appendices
Artois	14/11/18		Moved office to L'Ermitage. Demanded 100 Rnge Horse. To Richari. To Cantnai for Capt. C. W. Artes actuied for duty instructors unknown. Clean withed. General stores.	
	15/11/18		To Richari. Cleaned general stores. 1 R.T. for 7K.S. Staffs Offload. Wind unit to collect. Demanded 3000 Rnge Horse. Demanded 6000 sets underclothing (replaced destroyed by fire). Demanded 5 tennis line for 9K.N. Yorks R. Demanded 1 R.C. Frd/59 F.a.B.	
	16/11/18	No car.	Demanded 3400 slips 1000 pair drawers 4300 socks to complete replacement of stock restrayed by fire. (Court of Enquiring during hell to sit responsibility for payment &c)	
	17/11/18	No car.	Office moved to Artenois. General routine.	
	18/11/18		General Routine. Stores for refitting. Capt Archer to Richari re Blankets. Motors arrived. Demanded 2 wagons an try C/58 F.A.B. Blankets to 4 O.C. for months special issue. Capt Archer to sit during my absence.	
	19/11/18		General Routine. Capt Archer to Richari. Trucks. Attempts to obtain stores return by 2K. Ordered 11 lorries for 8 am 20K.	
	20/11/18.		Capt Archer to Richari. General Routine. All stores cleared. Units worked to draw Blankets down.	

(A7092). Wt. W12859/M1293. 75,000. 1/17. D. D. & L., Ltd. Forms/C.2118-14

Army Form C. 2118.

WAR DIARY
or
INTELLIGENCE SUMMARY.
(Erase heading not required.)

Instructions regarding War Diaries and Intelligence Summaries are contained in F. S. Regs., Part II. and the Staff Manual respectively. Title pages will be prepared in manuscript.

Place	Date	Hour	Summary of Events and Information	Remarks and references to Appendices
Aulnoir	20/11/18		1. R.S. Sunter took 2 types for M.G. Bgn. at Raichrart. (Unit to collect) Horse Power received. Understanding for laundry arrived. Confusing orders sent in for it at El Ermitage laundry store.	
	21/11/18		Sunders Portera a manual socks etc.	
	22/11/18		do. Attended state entry of Belgian King in to Brussels.	
	23/11/18		do. visited A.D.O.S.	
	24/11/18		do.	
	25/11/18		do. visited Army H.Q. re XXII Corps HQ. also A.D.O.S.	
	26/11/18		Visited new area (Denain) & inspected various premises with a view to finding Offices (also accommodation. Visited Army H.Q. D.A.D.O.S. (Major Anstis Nichols) proceeded to U.K. on one month leave. A/D.A.D.O.S. Capt. Ainsley visited Raichem & Denain. Premises got & date place and day as after visit enquires by 103 Inf. M.G. Corps. Two lorry load of Barrack Stores had therefore to be dumped temporarily. Moved offices from Aulnoir to Denain. Move of Raichem for engine to Prannes cancelled.	
Denain	27/11/18		Moved Armourers, Shoemakers, Tailors & Saddlers Shops for Codonnen to Denain. Am having out of action work broken spring.	
	28/11/18			

WAR DIARY or INTELLIGENCE SUMMARY

Army Form C. 2118.

Place	Date	Hour	Summary of Events and Information	Remarks and references to Appendices
Denain	29/11/18		General features. Established Office at N°. 127. Rue de Villars. No schemes at Railhead. Received telephone message from A.D.M.S. VIII Corps that Corps Cyclists were to proceed to Mely & that a conference dealing with general lines of employment together many other details would be held in a train to commence [illegible] D.M.O.S. that they arranged to air [illegible] to instructions. Informed A.D.M.S. that they would be told if any ambulance is met on D.M.O.S. and to report that the Chief Clerk whenever civil cases reach the station.	
	30/11/18	11-00	Received telegram from A.D.M.S. asking upon whom to impose its duties of instructing forwarded copy to D.H.Q. quoted to Messrs Butts.	
		18-00	A/A.D.M.S. Davis to mix arrangement with 2/Lt Margolis B7S. No re 2/Lt. [illegible] Noble	
	17.45	2/Lt. Noble [illegible]		

(Sgd) John
Capt. RMC
A/D.M.O.S. 11th Div
30/11/18

WR 31

WAR DIARY
of D.A.D.O.S, 11TH DIVISION
DEC 1st to 31st 1918

Army Form C. 2118.

WAR DIARY
or
INTELLIGENCE SUMMARY.
(Erase heading not required.)

Place	Date	Hour	Summary of Events and Information	Remarks and references to Appendices
Denain	1/2/19	09.00	[illegible] M.F.O. inspects Stores in Company Pepôt Arabia. Routine work in office and Chief Clerk.	
"	2/2/19	0900	Tractor Rouleed & lorries load Clearing H.Q. Returns to Railway. 50 tons unloaded. Small boy Interpreter (44) 6 (interior) hired in lieu has been Officer General Routine work in office.	
"	3/2/19	0900 - 1700	1 motor & 3 s.d. 2/1 Pde supply Stores. Headquarters Intelligence Staff/Depot 33rd Inf. Bde. received Stores to Divisions Staff. 4 Divisions Cmdr Clems Received	
"	4/2/19	0930	Deliveries myk A.O.O m.G. H.Stors & demands made by units. Details & Northumberland Fusiliers 1st Ford will Divisions Interpreter (homespaths, clothing) Stone Returns and return slips Received from office Routine	
"	5/2/19	0930	Stores delivered to 33rd Pde. Cmdr Entretten St Amand per lorry. Cleared Routine	
"	6/2/19		Received 260 blankets to complete issue & were 1 visits Received. Clears Routine of Stores	

Army Form C. 2118.

WAR DIARY
or
INTELLIGENCE SUMMARY.
(Erase heading not required.)

Instructions regarding War Diaries and Intelligence Summaries are contained in F.S. Regs., Part II. and the Staff Manual respectively. Title pages will be prepared in manuscript.

Place	Date	Hour	Summary of Events and Information	Remarks and references to Appendices
Seraun	7/17/18	0900	Regular Routine. Visitors:- H.E. Miller, 9th Int. Yorks. Ratters, 2nd Lieuts. Williams & Jack Stewart Harding. Lt. Sherrard 11th Hig. Corps Brandies. R.F.A. St Amand 11th Manchesters. Launched Ara Sgt. Cmdt. left for leave 9/17/18 L- 23/7/18	
do	8/17/18		Received from Lectures:- L. Smith (1st B. Queens 20223) L.Cpl Catterwy Belcher (1/3/25) 1 Loud referring (4 General Hospital) 2 Luts transferred from 1st Army Troops R.E. from 11th But 103 But R.A.C. + 141 But Canadian Railway Troops	
do	9/7/8	0900	2 Privates Reached Reserve (Reserve Camp). Also Supply Dump Gravere	
do	10/17/18	1000	At Reserve attendance as Notaries Public Regt. Cap. at head Gft. Reserve	
Ilsrous	10/17/18	11:00	Office resumed.	
do	11/7/18	1730	Also D.A.O. and C/ 17.30. Proceeded to Regnis Books to attend Lives & Office. Pte Stanlling 11th (3) But Manchester Reg't. Found to be missing on retire from gon. Returned to Reserve 6-30 pm Received recent Equipment Stolen 1, 8 tons.	
do	12/7/18	-	Office Stores noted to various units. Parties received. Inquiries after the discrimination in the issue of fresh meat.	
do	13/7/18		Ordinary routine. Stores to various units.	
do	14/7/18		1 two Received Letters from Railhead. Parties received	

WAR DIARY or INTELLIGENCE SUMMARY

Army Form C. 2118.

(Erase heading not required)

Place	Date	Hour	Summary of Events and Information	Remarks and references to Appendices
Seraucourt	15/7/18		Office Routine. No Stores	
do	16/7/18		10 Lorries general stores from Rosiel. 1 R.E. M.T. lorry limber empties for 11" Signal Cy.	
do	17/7/18		Railhead clearance. 2 trucks containing 9 ton general stores 40-0 rockets returns. 1 truck containing 18 Pdr. Amm. wagr.	
do	18/7/18		Two lorries to Ribsigre at 5 A.M. as per instructions received D.A.D.O. div to return 21.15.18. 1 lorry to rushed to take returns from D.H.Q. also to draw 21 Lorguines + J Dump Somam. Lorry pick up returns + draw 21 Lorguines to D.A.C. & attached units allowing stores to time general stores. 4/5 lorry	
do	19/7/18		1 truck marked containing two line general stores Top lorry left for Ham.	
do	20/7/18		Trucks railhead: No Headquarters Coal. 6" Howitzer full amm. (33") Coal. Railway Cleared. Cmdt. Graham returned to duty. from Base.	
do	21/7/18		Routine took at office	
do	22/7/18		Units joined (5") & 8" Northumberland Fusilier Command	

Army Form C. 2118.

WAR DIARY
or
INTELLIGENCE SUMMARY.
(Erase heading not required.)

Instructions regarding War Diaries and Intelligence Summaries are contained in F. S. Regs., Part II. and the Staff Manual respectively. Title pages will be prepared in manuscript.

Place	Date	Hour	Summary of Events and Information	Remarks and references to Appendices
Douai	23/12/18	—	Attended a meeting 79 C.M. 96 standing W. Manchester Renewal then until 4pm (RAISNES). Case disposed of	
"	24/12/18		To RAISNES. Ord. Canteen for goods for 31st Xmas. Dinner. To Valenciennes Officers Clothing Dept.	
"	25/12/18		Xmas Day. Offices & Stores closed.	
"	26/12/18		Buying Boxing Day allowances — to — Sorting of stores however was proceeded went to Stores Valenciennes to sentis on the 27/12/18.	
"	27/12/18		Rectified. Cleaned.	
"	28/12/18		Major J. Coutts Webster returned from leave & took over the Office &c.	
"	29/12/18 31st		General Routine. No car available therefore visits to units inspection of stores postponed until repairs are completed	

J. Coutts Webster
Major R.A.O.C.
D.A.D.O.S.
IIIth Div.

14/1/9.

WAR DIARY
INTELLIGENCE SUMMARY
(Erase heading not required.)

Army Form C. 2118.

Instructions regarding War Diaries and Intelligence Summaries are contained in F. S. Regs., Part II. and the Staff Manual respectively. Title pages will be prepared in manuscript.

Place	Date	Hour	Summary of Events and Information	Remarks and references to Appendices
DENAIN	1.1.19		New Years Day. Office rotine.	
"	2.1.19		The new arrival of cars 252706 to Capt N/I/ST of 30 type store wrkshps. Reported to D.A.D.R.T. Capt Kennan R.A.O.C. arrived for instruction. Wrkshps stores wrkshops to 51 Div. and Ammunition. Visited M.G.Bn. 6K.2 Tanks. M.I.Coy Lewin. 11K Div Recep Farm Camp. Complaints received of a general shortage of spare wheels particularly sizes 5, 6, + 7.	
"	3.1.19		Visited A.D.O.S. with Capt Kennan. Discussed Part shortage to Ammunition supply of Batteries.	
	4.1.19		Collected 2 Armo Lorries + 5 Rifles from Solesmes. Collected 17 Chickenard from M.I O.M.M.W (Army)	
	5.1.19		Shops + stores now closed on Sundays. Office closed at 1pm	
	6.1.19		Visited M.R. 3rk.L.(5)Bde. 5K Northumberland Fusiliers. 5K Dorset Regt. Demanded 10 17pdr R.P from Base + 2. 4.5 How from Sun Park under authority (Q.M.G.(K.G.I) 27/12/18. 10 Reported to A.O.O.F. rd arrival of Lorries	
	7.1.19		Visited Calais depot re shortage of spares arrived of stores, positions in whether any stores were being installed with general positions. Demand 4.5 cartrige for D/57 R.F.A. from Base.	
	8.1.19		118K Labour Coy moved to 11K Div. from 16K Div. Confirmed wire. 4to Ranglers arrived for instruction. Collected 2. 4.5 Hows (pieces only) from Gun Park + delivered to M. 33. O.M.W (Royal) for front in carriages.	

(A7092) Wt. W12839/M1093 75,000. 1/17. D. D. & L., Ltd. Forms/C21184.

Army Form C. 2118.

WAR DIARY
or
INTELLIGENCE SUMMARY.
(Erase heading not required.)

Instructions regarding War Diaries and Intelligence Summaries are contained in F. S. Regs., Part II. and the Staff Manual respectively. Title pages will be prepared in manuscript.

Place	Date	Hour	Summary of Events and Information	Remarks and references to Appendices
DENAIN	8.1.19		(Continued). Collected 9 flags like those from O/C ☐ C.T.	
	9.1.19		General Routine. Reported on duty & supply of London Electrons.	
	10.1.19		Received 5/175 Recruits from Base. Visited 117th Div. M.T. Coy: re storage of blankets. Sick Report proven re exchanges.	
	11.1.19		Further arrangements re blankets received. Command issued of visited 7th Northumberland Fusiliers 5th/Durham Regt.	
	12.1.19		Office closed. General Routine. Visited 345 Bde No.1 D.M.W.(Army) 103rd M.G. Corps — " —	
	13.1.19		Received 900 F.S. Envelopes from Base for Educational use none rec'd. Demanded 18th Hussar prize for E/5th Bn R.F.A. Visited 33rd Bde re reink & 76th Lumsden Coy R.E. British supplies & A.S.C.	
	14.1.19		Capt Rower reported for 12th Division Truck Blankets received - 9 bales missing. Stores are now being frequently stolen from the trucks in Transit. Reported this matter. Discrepancy reports are sent to Base in every case for investigation. Kaiki 213 Equipment Coy - R.M. & 21 forks of Bde being unequal - Coy applying	

Army Form C. 2118.

WAR DIARY
INTELLIGENCE SUMMARY.
(Erase heading not required.)

Instructions regarding War Diaries and Intelligence Summaries are contained in F. S. Regs., Part II. and the Staff Manual respectively. Title pages will be prepared in manuscript.

Place	Date	Hour	Summary of Events and Information	Remarks and references to Appendices
DENAIN	15.1.19		Sent stores to Douai (49th Div) for Corps Annual Camp. Sent to D.A.D.O.S. executed 1260 prisoners. Visited H.Q. 11th Div. Artillery, units of 57th Bde R.F.A. Complaints still been received as to shortage of boots.	
	16.1.19		Visited all units of 57th Bde R.F.A. Complaints received of shortage of everything. Reported to A.D.O.S. upon shortage of boots.	
	17.1.19		General routine.	
	18.1.19		Visited D.A.T.E., A.D.O.S. VIII Corps ref returns of personnel (Demobilization) re H.R. Returns &c.	
	19.1.19		Sunday. Routine only.	
	20.1.19		1 truck Camp stores arrived. Corps shortage now relieved.	
	21.1.19		Received 300 wagons (20 tons each) from O.T.O. VIII C.T. for instructions. Trial report. Returned 1000 sets first aid to Brunel, taping Camp Valenciennes. Collected Ambulances from Ord Army F.B.	

Army Form C. 2118.

WAR DIARY
or
INTELLIGENCE SUMMARY.
(Erase heading not required.)

Instructions regarding War Diaries and Intelligence
Summaries are contained in F. S. Regs., Part II.
and the Staff Manual respectively. Title pages
will be prepared in manuscript.

Place	Date	Hour	Summary of Events and Information	Remarks and references to Appendices
DENAIN	22.1.19		Visited 2nd Canadian Tramway Coy ref. demobilization. General Routine.	
	23.1.19		"Traffic" up now arrival of Trucks Reported to A.D.O.S. new arrival of Trucks 282702 and 5.6536 to ADC, extract & Tram general stores despatched Calais 3/1/19.	
	24.1.19		General Routine	
	25.1.19		Visited Tramway Coy re their departure.	
	26.1.19		Sunday. Reported further no authority to depts.	
	27.1.19		Moved 2nd Canadian Tramway Coy to Base for Demobilization. Tramway Staff Sgt demobilized. First detachment moved Y.... R.A.O.C. personnel of this Division. Close Indent Accounts	
	28.1.19		General Routine	
	29.1.19		Received per A.M.F.O. Excess of camfor for Return nominal Ro. Collected from O.O. VIII C.T. 60 pairs woollen Trousers + 200 Uniforms (2-nd) + Truckles for distribution Do.	

WAR DIARY
or INTELLIGENCE SUMMARY

Army Form C. 2118.

Instructions regarding War Diaries and Intelligence Summaries are contained in F.S. Regs., Part II. and the Staff Manual respectively. Title pages will be prepared in manuscript.

Place	Date	Hour	Summary of Events and Information	Remarks and references to Appendices
DENAIN	30/1/19		General Routine. Visited H.Q. - N° 1 Coy Train. N° 2 & 3 Coy Train. 6th & 7th Div. Det. Reception Camp, Dining M.T. Coy	
"	31/1/19	1. 4. 5	New camps at Ribécourt for Stores in want of clean precaution being adopted. Visited 32nd Infty Bde M.R. and units of Bde. Visited D.A.D.O.S. 12th Division of Dunkirk on return. Collected 15 Tons oats arrived from Ypres. 5 Lorn Trucks of Oats are awaiting. No Traces of these except two forwarded Generally. Opening this month report of the previous month. There has been a growing shortage of boots, particularly motorcycle oops. The shortage has been enhanced by a shortage of laundry & consequent inability of units to keep boots in a good state of repair. This will usually eventually be much larger means of boots being necessary, as many units at present refurbish will be signed repair will require to be replaced by new boots. The matter has been represented to higher authority & it is stated that all possible action is being taken.	

J. C. W. Webster
Major R.A.O.C.

Army Form C. 2118.

WAR DIARY
INTELLIGENCE SUMMARY
(Erase heading not required.)

WANTS 112 Vol 3 3

Place	Date	Hour	Summary of Events and Information	Remarks and references to Appendices
DENAIN	1.2.19		Confirmed arrival of 325 Quarry Coy. R.E.	
	3.2.19		Continued all work of Bdes. One W.O. on inmate. One W.O. on store again to maintain. One W.O. on main office to relieve Asst Clerk for demobilisation (Civil)	
	4.2.19		Consignment of stores draft [etc] received. Rest quotas now actively wrtg. 2 Wagons L.R.E. received for 97th Field Coy R.E. ~ 11th Div. Signal Coy	
	5.2.19		D.D.O.S. visit postponed. General Routine.	
	6.2.19		Chief Clerk left for demobilisation. M & L Storeman ditto. Worker (a) motor from 12th Div. to 11th Div.	
	7.2.19		D.D.O.S. visit postponed.	
	11.2.19		General Routine. Routine visits.	
	12.2.19		D.D.O.S. visit postponed.	
	13.2.19		D.A.D.O.S. left for duty as A.D.O.S. VIII Corps (Temporarily).	
	14.2.19		General Routine	
	15.2.19		E.O. Wanton returned from leave	
	16.2.19		Enemy aircraft great actions received. Usual precautions issued, all true. returned to Colours	

WAR DIARY
INTELLIGENCE SUMMARY

Army Form C. 2118.

Place	Date	Hour	Summary of Events and Information	Remarks and references to Appendices
Péronne	17/2/19		General Routine	
	18/2/19		Conveyance of Stores general stores received. Major Webster visited office between rounds for B.A.D. to take in surplus stores of unit.	
	20/2/19		Received Stores and Stores, Stores specially sanctioned by Army cleared the Pack Sect Storehouse from order to 9 Divn Sig: Engineers C.R.E. Pte. Hull, Batt. returned to N.E. office for duty.	
	22/2/19		9th Temp Rollers received for VIII Corps	
	23/2/19		Two Precautions received Stores back from M.T.C. Received H.O. temp rollers specially sanctioned by Army. Received Stores good stores and further returned Stores to be sent to India. M. truck journey begun returning Corps Engineers Stores to Wired to know	
	24/2/19		Received Stores good stores. M. trucks - M. trucks began not returned	
	25/2/19		Acknowledged receipt of Army F.W. 168a here by further supply 18/a	
	27/2/19		Received Leave warrant for Engineer Lt/c Wilson. L/c Wilson left 25/2/19 at 2 p.m. for Army Section Sgt Beech started for leave 14 March 19 to take the Divn Section	
	28/2/19		Officers of Corps H.Q. left for leave and to form No. D.O.S.P. Received Stores good stores	

J. Wilson
Major R.E.

Instructions regarding War Diaries and Intelligence Summaries are contained in F. S. Regs., Part II. and the Staff Manual respectively. Title pages will be prepared in manuscript.

WAR DIARY
or
INTELLIGENCE SUMMARY.
(*Erase heading not required.*)

Army Form C. 2118.

DADOS Vol 34

Place	Date	Hour	Summary of Events and Information	Remarks and references to Appendices
Denain	1/3/19		Recd truck containing 100 tubs washing. demanded 200 halters by wire	
	2/3/19		Demanded by wire stents store for CCS.	
	3/3/19		Major Webster returned from Corps, demanded by wire 300 ropes head for animal collecting camp	
	4/3/19		Major A.l. Smith RAOC arrived for duty as DADOS	
	5/3/19		Recd release sub allotment for 4 armourers Gosling Crosby Deering & Seale.	
	6/3/19		Major Webster departed for demobilization	
	7/3/19		The 4 armourers named above departed for demobilization.	
	8/3/19		Major Smith departed for leave to UK 9th to 23rd March. Lt Wise acting as DADOS	
	9/3/19		7 tons genl stores received	
	10/3/19		ADOS visited office & said that 5th Bde RFA will be leaving division on 15th with equipment	
	11/3/19		Railhead changed from Anzin to Ecole Sidon Valenciennes. Armr 1 Sgt [illegible] sent to 5th Bde RFA to inspect rifles	
	12/3/19		Visited 9th Yorks re inspection of unserviceable stores by ADOS – moved 50th labour Co to ordnance 17th Division – 129 labour Co transferred from DO 8 C.T.	
	13/3/19		ADOS inspected stores of 9th Yorks. Two armrs to 7th Yorks to inspect rifles	
	14/3/19		4 tons gen stores from base. Armr Sgts Page & Stapleton left for demob. Transferred 195 & 178 labour Coys to DO IATD. Lt Lovel 6th Yorks acting as DADOS vice Lt Wise proceeding on leave	
	15/3/19		Lt Wise left for leave 17th to 31st. 3 tons of stores from Railhead	
	16/3/19		Usual routine stores & office closed noon	

Army Form C. 2118.

WAR DIARY
or
INTELLIGENCE SUMMARY.
(Erase heading not required.)

Instructions regarding War Diaries and Intelligence Summaries are contained in F. S. Regs., Part II. and the Staff Manual respectively. Title pages will be prepared in manuscript.

Place	Date	Hour	Summary of Events and Information	Remarks and references to Appendices
Dinan				

Army Form C. 2118.

WAR DIARY
or
INTELLIGENCE SUMMARY.
(Erase heading not required)

Instructions regarding War Diaries and Intelligence Summaries are contained in F.S. Regs., Part II. and the Staff Manual respectively. Title pages will be prepared in manuscript.

DADOS 11 D
9 51 35

Place	Date	Hour	Summary of Events and Information	Remarks and references to Appendices
DENAIN	1/4/19		Moved 234 Light Railway Forward Co RE to 40h Bn MT. Recd 1 truck containing 2 Army General Stores from R Read. On way back at Guyffles despatched to SLO Rouen. One lorry load of parcels despatches to SLO Rouen.	
	2/4/19		usual Routine	
	3/4/19 to 5/4/19			
	6/4/19		Moved 103 MG Bn to Basin. Unit left 5AM for port of embarkation. Recd 2 Army General Stores from R Read.	
	7/4/19		usual Routine	
	8/4/19		Recd 5 tons General Stores from R Read	
	9/4/19		usual Routine	
	10/4/19		HQ A B & C D Sq Rde N 20 Lt for port of embarkation. A & G 198 Rds to 100 Sqn B. Reports ared to Co Sqdn at O.1 a.a.o.a	
	11/4/19		usual Routine	
	12/4/19		Recd 1 Lor General Stores from Read	
	13/4/19		Recd 1 lorry General Stores from Read	
	14/4/19		usual Routine	
	15/4/19			

Army Form C. 2118.

WAR DIARY
or
INTELLIGENCE SUMMARY.
(Erase heading not required.)

Instructions regarding War Diaries and Intelligence Summaries are contained in F.S. Regs., Part II. and the Staff Manual respectively. Title pages will be prepared in manuscript.

Place	Date	Hour	Summary of Events and Information	Remarks and references to Appendices
DENAIN	16/4/19		Rec'd 4 Pairs of General Stores from Rhead	
	17/4/19		Usual Routine	
	18/4/19		Good Friday (Sans Office closed)	
	19/4/19		Usual Routine	
	20/4/19		Stores Office closed at noon	
	21/4/19		Easter Monday. Stores Office closed. Rec'd 1 Pair General Stores from Rhead.	
	22/4/19		Usual Routine	
	23/4/19		Inspected U/S Stores of 36 Field Amb.	
	24/4/19		Inspected U/S Stores of Northern Command. Rec'd demolished stores & O.R. Stores from Sw. Zillebeke.	
	25/4/19		Inspected U/S Stores of 5 Dorset R. Rec. Stores Army Lorries, Rec. Stores from	
	26/4/19		Attached York R. and 9th Manchester Regt. Rec'd Stores from 32(A)TMB, 2nd Field Amb, and A/1/8 Brig	
			Rec'd Rehab. Stores from 32(A)TMB, 2nd Field Amb, and A/1/8 Brig	
	27/4/19		Inspected U/S Stores of 58 Bde RFA and 7th D. Staff R. Rec'd Demolition tents from Templeuve R.	
	28/4/19		Placed Office to No 118 Rue de Villars	
	29/4/19		Inspected U/S Stores of 6th Lincoln Regt. Rec'd Demolition Stores & O.R. 9/1/98 from 33 Field Amb. Rec'd 1 Pair General Stores from Rhead	
	30/4/19		Inspected U/S Stores of 1/5 Manchester Regt, 2nd Bn R. & 6th East Yorks (Rec'd) Rec'd Demolition Stores by D.S.C.	

Army Form C. 2118.

**D.A.D.O.S.,
11th DIVISION.**

No. ....
Date 4/6/19

WAR DIARY
or
INTELLIGENCE SUMMARY.
(Erase heading not required.)

Instructions regarding War Diaries and Intelligence Summaries are contained in F. S. Regs., Part II. and the Staff Manual respectively. Title pages will be prepared in manuscript.

Place	Date	Hour	Summary of Events and Information	Remarks and references to Appendices
DENAIN	1/5/19		Inspected up Stores of 11th Bn Ann. Col. and 6th York & Lancs R. Recd Demob Indents of B/57 Brig	
	2/5/19		Inspected up Stores of CRE, 67th, 68th, + 86th Field Coys RE. Indents N.B.M.S. Coy at ANZIN. Received Demob Indents of 6th York & Lancs R. Recd Demob Indents and A.B. Forms from 8th York & Lancs R. Recd 1 Jon General Stores from Railhead.	
	3/5/19		Recd Demob Indents 'A' & 'B' Forms from 8th N. Lancs, CRE, 67th Field Coy. Recd A & B Forms from 68th Field Coy.	
	4/5/19		Recd Demob Indents 'A' & 'B' Forms from 6th York (T.F.). Recd A & B Forms from Sec/78 HQ. Office cleared out.	
	5/5/19		Recd Demob Indents 'A' & 'B' Forms from 33 Emp Coy, HQ. No 1, 2, 3 Sec Section DAC. Recd Demob Indents from 34D TMB	
	6/5/19		Inspected up Stores of No 11 Siege CRMLE	
	7/5/19		Recd Demob Indents from Sec/78HQ	
	8/5/19		Recd 1 Jon general stores from Railhead. Recd Demob Indents A & B Forms from 11th DAG Inspected up Stores of No 1, 2, + 3 Coys 11 Pnr Btn.	
	9/5/19 10/5/19 12/5/19		Inspected up Stores of MG Coy 11 Pnr Btn. General Routine.	

(Ap292). W.t. W12899/M1293. 750,000. 1/17. D. D. & L., Ltd. Forms/C.2118-14

Army Form C. 2118.

WAR DIARY
or
INTELLIGENCE SUMMARY.

(Erase heading not required.)

Instructions regarding War Diaries and Intelligence Summaries are contained in F. S. Regs., Part II. and the Staff Manual respectively. Title pages will be prepared in manuscript.

Place	Date	Hour	Summary of Events and Information	Remarks and references to Appendices
DENAIN	14/5/19		Recd 1 Corps General Orders from Head. Inspected 11th Divn. of 33 C.C.S + 11th Signal Co R.E.	
	15/5/19		Recd 2 Corps General Orders. Read Road A + B Groups + General Orders from 33 C.C.S + 11 Sig. Co R.E.	
	16/5/19		Usual Routine	
	17/5/19			
	18/5/19		Recd Corps General Orders from Head.	
	19/5/19		Inspected Stores of 33 Quarry Co R.E. Recd 1 Engineer Order	
	20/5/19		Usual routine	
	21/5/19			
	22/5/19		Read Engineer Order + a/c Group from 33 Quarry Co R.E.	
	23/5/19		Usual Routine	
	24/5/19		Recd 1 Corps general order from Head	
	25/5/19		Usual Routine. Office + stores closed at noon	
	26/5/19		Usual Routine	
	27/5/19		Recd 2 Corps genl. Orders from Head. Re Goog & Co for leave	
	28/5/19		Hqrs Coyld. left for Cirencester Camp	
	29/5/19		Usual routine	
	30/5/19		Recd 1 Corps General orders from Head	
	3/6/19			

Major D.A.D.Q. 11 Corps Troops

Army Form C. 2118.

WAR DIARY
or
INTELLIGENCE SUMMARY.
(Erase heading not required.)

Instructions regarding War Diaries and Intelligence Summaries are contained in F. S. Regs., Part II. and the Staff Manual respectively. Title pages will be prepared in manuscript.

Place	Date	Hour	Summary of Events and Information	Remarks and references to Appendices
DENAIN	1/6/19		Usual Routine	
	2/6/19		Usual Routine	
	3/6/19		Usual Routine	
	4/6/19		Recd 1 ton General Stores from Base. Yp orders Left F. Duty night 10pm (No 20 D.H.N (9))	
	5/6/19		Inspected m/s stores of Not Signal Construction Co RE. Recd 1 ton General Stores from Base	
	6/6/19		Usual Routine	
	7/6/19		Sent detachments to Base of the following units — 11 Div A, 32, 33, 34 Sig Coy. 22, 13 & 9 Sec L.T.H.D's. 6,7,8,5 & 6 Field R.E's. 11 Div Train. 33,34 & 35 Franks	
	8/6/19		Recd orders of following units to Base — 9 Corps. G.E. Sigs. (C) 9 Sqd.n, 7 Sig Bn Wireless, 9 Chepard F, 5 D.A.C 6, 8 N. Fire, 11 Garr. 55 F.A.B.	
			Stores from Railhead	
	9/6/19		Recd 1 ton Gen Stores	
	10/6/19		Usual Routine	
	11/6/19		Recd 1 ton Gen Stores from Railhead	
	12/6/19		Usual Routine	
	13/6/19		Usual Routine	
			1 ton Gen Stores recd from Base. Pte Golly ret'd from leave	
	14/6/19		Special Railwns to Trains & Sgt Burt left on demob.	
			1 truck of stores arrived	

Army Form C. 2118.

DADOS

WAR DIARY
or
INTELLIGENCE SUMMARY.
(Erase heading not required.)

Instructions regarding War Diaries and Intelligence Summaries are contained in F. S. Regs., Part II and the Staff Manual respectively. Title pages will be prepared in manuscript.

Place	Date	Hour	Summary of Events and Information	Remarks and references to Appendices
DENAIN	15/5/19		General Routine. Vehicles w/s & G.S. Wagons for DAC & Howitzers	
	16/5/19		2 lorry loads Supplies Stores to BPark. 1 lorry load Vehicle Stores to ICS Wagons	
	17/5/19		Usual Routine	
	18/5/19		Inspected stores at Ammn. Columns Parmain. Wanted ICS Wagon, w/s & Pulverised Carts to Rft Books w/s for Rhu. Inspected w/s stores 195 Ton G. RE	
	19/5/19		Wanted ICS Wagon. Inspected w/s stores of 9x Ton G. RE.	
	20/5/19		Collected Stores from Ammn. Column. Returned ICS wagons	
	21/5/19		Vehicles now fit for running and to transit. "DAC. 9 GS:18 Ton G. RPH:21 4 CH:11.G.RE.	
	22/5/19		Usual Routine	
	23/5/19		Usual Routine. Left for 59 Gen. Estab.	
	24/5/19		One 3.5g waggon left to Base. 32 B&v Left for Base. 58 Wag Left for base	
	25/5/19		Load w/s stores to Base. 176 Ton G. RE to MS:T?	
	26/5/19		Lorry stores to ICS Wanted 176 Ton G. RE to MS.T?	
	27/5/19		Stocks w/s stores to Railhead	
	28/5/19		General Routine	
	29/5/19		Vehicles forwarded details for vehicles not to transit...	
	29/5/19		Usual Routine	
	30/5/19		1 load Stores to ICS army.	
			from Railhead	

Jewie
Lt Col.
D.A.D.O.S., 11th DIVISION.

WO 95/45 17991 (Decl. (3)

11TH DIVISION

D.A.D.V.S.

JLY 1916 - MAR 1919

July 1916
ADVS
VOL 1

WAR DIARY
INTELLIGENCE SUMMARY

Army Form C. 2118

(Erase heading not required.)

Instructions regarding War Diaries and Intelligence Summaries are contained in F.S. Regs., Part II. and the Staff Manual respectively. Title Pages will be prepared in manuscript.

Place	Date	Hour	Summary of Events and Information	Remarks and references to Appendices
FLERS	4/7/16	A.M.	Disembarked from H.T. HAVERFORD at MARSEILLES.	
	5/7/16	2 A.M.	Entrained at MARSEILLES	
	7/7/16	11 A.M.	Detrained & arrived at 11th D.H.Q.	
	8/7/16	A.M.	Visits 11th B.A.C.	
	9/7/16	A.M.	Inspects arrival of 11th Sup Train.	
	10/7/16	A.M.	Visits O.C. 32nd Bgde.	
	11/7/16		Went to Corps H.Q. Inspects an animal belonging to a civilian Henri Paulet by order of A.D.V.S. 3rd Army.	
	12/7/16		Called on D.D.V.S. 34th & 19th 3rd Army.	
	13/7/16	A.M.	Accompanies G.O.C. 11th Divn on his inspection of 11th D.A.	
		P.M.	Met 22nd M.V.S. at St Pol.	
	14/7/16	A.M.	Visits 33rd Inf Bde.	
		P.M.	Inspects arrival of 133rd F.A.B. & 11th Sig Coy. Inspects arrival of 59th F.A.B. Cav & 191st Tks & 35th Field Ambulance.	
LE CAUROY	15/7/16	A.M. P.M.		
DUISANS	16/7/16	A.M.	Inspects new horses of 11th Div Train. Calerson O/C M.V.S. Examination of animals. Called on V.O. & 584th F.A.B. Inspects some suspected mange cases at 60th F.A.B.	
	17/7/16	A.M. P.M.	Investigated outbreak of swine fever & advised as to action to be taken. Visits 22nd M.V.S. 11th D.A.C., D.D.V.S. 3rd Army, & Artillery School.	

Army Form C. 2118.

WAR DIARY
INTELLIGENCE SUMMARY
(Erase heading not required.)

Instructions regarding War Diaries and Intelligence Summaries are contained in F. S. Regs., Part II. and the Staff Manual respectively. Title Pages will be prepared in manuscript.

Place	Date	Hour	Summary of Events and Information	Remarks and references to Appendices
DUSANS	18.7.16	Am	Visits 38th F.A.B. in new Billet - Inspects new Howitzer Bn Animals of A.H.S 27/8/13.	
		Pm	Called with O.C. 133rd F.A.B. & Div. Com. Col. Inspects Animals of Div. R.G. Coy.	
	19/7/16	Am	Inspects animals of 33rd Inf 13th & 33rd F.Amb. Found Billet for M.V.S.	
		Pm	Vet Mr. vanushea sick & Billets —	
	20/7/16	Am	Inspects animals of B/Mark Germany.	
	21/7/16	Am	Inspects animals of 38th F.A.B. M.V.S. 35th F.Amb. L.Staff Supply Pioneers.	
		Pm	Took over Billet for M.V.S. D.S.S enters at E.M.O.	
	22.7.16	Am	Conference of V.O. of the Divn — Ordinary Duties	
	23.7.16	Am	Inspects Animals left with farm inhabitants. With a view to getting them removed by M.V.S. Called on Town Major ___ Re attitude of Inhabitants	
			Called at Port Rent Lee & Auxiliary Horse Transport Co.	
	24.7.16	Am	Inspects all the Animals of 33rd Inf Bn	
		Pm	Demonstration in Stno. Smal. Asphodel Mallein Ing at M.V.C.	
	25.7.16	Am	Inspects all horse lines of R.A. Dists	
		Pm	Went to Renikof?.	
	26.7.16	Pm	Visited M.V.S.	
	27.7.16	Am	Inspects Animals of Brigade & D.A.C.	
		Pm	Called on A.D.V.S. in Gem. By. A.D.T. n. D.B.v	

WAR DIARY
INTELLIGENCE SUMMARY
(Erase heading not required.)

Army Form C. 2118

(3)

Place	Date	Hour	Summary of Events and Information	Remarks and references to Appendices
	28.7.16	—	Inspected animals of OMG. Stf g: 1st Line Transport 31st Inf/3rd Colon with Divl. S. Reports arrival of Pte Revait to DADVS 3rd Army.	
	29.7.16	—	Inspected N.V.S.	
WARLUS	30.7.16	—	Changes being arranged with A.C.E 6th Corps to go round Divl area on 31st inst. Re Clothing &c.	
	31.7.16	—	Went round Divl. area with A.C.E 6th Corps. Inspected forelegs of Transport Infantry & Artillery of Div.	

N J Macaulay
Capt. to D...
A D V S ...

1-8-16

Army Form C. 2118.

Vol 3

WAR DIARY
or
INTELLIGENCE SUMMARY.
(Erase heading not required.)

A.D.V.S.
No..........
Date..........
11th DIVISION.

Instructions regarding War Diaries and Intelligence Summaries are contained in F. S. Regs., Part II. and the Staff Manual respectively. Title pages will be prepared in manuscript.

Place	Date	Hour	Summary of Events and Information	Remarks and references to Appendices
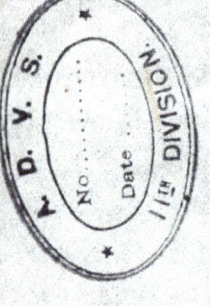				
Le Cauroy	1-9/16	Am	Visits 33rd Inf Bn Horse Lines	
		Pm	Rem: Sgt321 Prevent V.M.V.S.	
Doullens	2.9/16	Am	Left Le Cauroy arr Doullens. Went to Acheux & arrange Billets for M.V.S	
		Pm	Saw O.C M.V.S at Grouches	
Acheux	3.9.16		Arr at Acheux.	
	4.9.16	Am	Visits 58th, 59th & 60th Bns	
		Pm	Called on D.A.V.S. 11th Army	
	5.9.16		O.O. Duties	
	6.9.16		Visits II DAC. OC reports that Lumb Hill Arc has been sent to Hosp. Ophms from Mychmen Prony - self is minister. Called to see Lind Horse at Hos. 2nd Amb Authie. Visits D.D.V.S Res Army & reports occurrence.	
Senlis	7.9/16	Am	Came to Senlis - Saw A.D.V.S out going Bre (12.5.40).	
		Pm	Visits 59th, 60th & 188th Bns R.A.	

Army Form C. 2118

WAR DIARY
or
INTELLIGENCE SUMMARY
(Erase heading not required.)

Instructions regarding War Diaries and Intelligence Summaries are contained in F. S. Regs., Part II. and the Staff Manual respectively. Title Pages will be prepared in manuscript.

Place	Date	Hour	Summary of Events and Information	Remarks and references to Appendices
SENLIS	8.9.16		Troops D.A.C. Divn + M.V.S.	
"	9.9.16		Comm. D.D.V.S. 5th Army — Ordinary duties.	
"	10.9.16	Am	Inspected arrival of 59th, 160th Bde. R.A.	
		Pm	" M.V.S. + 133rd F.A.B.	
"	11.9.16	Am	Inspected arrival of 33rd + 34th Divn — 67, 68, 9, Co. ve	
		Pm	Capt Hamilton reported for duty — Troops M.V.S.	
"	12.9.16	Am	Visited some of 110th, 11th, 112th Bde RFA 33rd Divn	
		Pm	" " 35th Fd. Amb + DAC	
"	13.9.16	Am	Visited Horse lines around BOUZINCOURT	
		Pm	Inspected arrival of 5th Q. Sig. Co. CRE RAH 2nd, 23rd Divn.	
"	14.9.16	Am	Inspected D.A.C.	
		Pm	Visited M.V.C.	
"	15.9.16	Am	Inspected 82nd Infantry line Piompont	
		Pm	" Horse to Evacuation to Bouthop.	
"	16.9.16	—	Ordinary Duties	

Army Form C. 2118.

WAR DIARY
or
INTELLIGENCE SUMMARY.
(Erase heading not required.)

Instructions regarding War Diaries and Intelligence Summaries are contained in F. S. Regs., Part II. and the Staff Manual respectively. Title pages will be prepared in manuscript.

A.D.V.S.
No..................
Date..................
11th DIVISION.

Place	Date	Hour	Summary of Events and Information	Remarks and references to Appendices
Senlis.	17.9.16		Inspected horses of 133rd F.A.B.	
	18.9.16		O.S. duties	
	19.9.16		Inspected animals of 1/5th 2nd Pioneers. SB P.O.'s &c	
	20.9.16		O.S. duties	
	21.9.16		Visited D.A.C. Lines & A.V.S.	
	22.9.16		O.S. duties	
	23.9.16	Am	Inspected animals of 110th, 112th Bns. 2.5th Bn R.A. & one destn 25th T.M.	
		pm	"Martin" M.V.S. & 11th Dn Sig Coy. &c	
	24.9.16		O.S. duties	
	25.9.16		O.S. duties	
	26.9.16		O.S. duties	
	27.9.16		Inspection of Inf. Arnk	
	28.9.16		Inspected animals of 59th & 60th F.A.B &c	
	29.9.16		O.S. duties. Met Capt. 25th Bn. & arranged having no M.V. & Ress &c	

WAR DIARY

of

A.D.V.S, 11th.Division.

for October 1916.

WAR DIARY or INTELLIGENCE SUMMARY

Army Form C. 2118.

A.D.V.S., 11th DIVISION.

Place	Date	Hour	Summary of Events and Information	Remarks and references to Appendices
SENLIS	1-10-16		Left SENLIS for ACHEUX	
ACHEUX	2.10.16		Left ACHEUX for BERNAVILLE	
BERNAVILLE	3.10.16		Remained in "	
BERNAVILLE	4.10.16		Left BERNAVILLE for DOMART	
Domart	5.10.16	A.M.	Inspects animals in M.V.S. at St OUEN. Decides that this place was not fit for Rt. Horses, so arranged billets for this unit at DOMQUEUR, which is about 8 kilometres from St RIQUIER (SP Head)	
"	"	P.M.	Visits hospital in ABBEVILLE	
DOMART	6.10.16	A.M.	Inspects animals of three companies of Division, animals all things considered were in fair & comfortable billets	
"	"	P.M.	Inspects 67 Bn, 88 & 2 Coy Re. the animals of the 67 Coy are in poor condition, those of the other two are carrying well, and of these animals were called on to do much hard work.	
"	"		Inspects animals of 6 Yorks Pioneers. All animals looking well & cared for by C.O. on the officer i/c this animal reserves great praise.	

A.D.V.S. 11th DIVISION.

No. ....
Date ....

Army Form C. 2118

WAR DIARY
or
INTELLIGENCE SUMMARY
(Erase heading not required.)

Instructions regarding War Diaries and Intelligence Summaries are contained in F.S. Regs., Part II. and the Staff Manual respectively. Title Pages will be prepared in manuscript.

Place	Date	Hour	Summary of Events and Information	Remarks and references to Appendices
Domari	7.10.16	A.m.	Inspected M.V.S. with new lieut. Dungavee & found the men in comfortable billets & the animals standing to - clean & in an ocky ard.	
"	8.10.16		On 3rd Duties	
"	9.10.16	—	Inspected the animals of the following units 33rd M.G.C. – 33rd Fd Amb. the four Regts of this Bde. All the animals, with very few exceptions, looking very well, lines clean & everything most satisfactory.	
"	10.10.16		Inspected animals for evacuation at Rail Head. Showing some improvement.	
"	11.10.16		Ordinary Duties	
"	12.10.16		Inspected all the animals of 32nd Inf. Bde. – 32nd M.G.C. 735th Fd Amb. Animals all looking well, stable management, in all Corps, very satisfactory.	
"	13.10.16		Inspected animals of 47th Fd. Park R at P. HAZAR 12 — Visited mules at P. OWEN	

Army Form C. 2118

**A.D.V.S.,
11th DIVISION.**

No.....................
Date...................

WAR DIARY
or
INTELLIGENCE SUMMARY

(Erase heading not required.)

Instructions regarding War Diaries and Intelligence Summaries are contained in F.S. Regs., Part II. and the Staff Manual respectively. Title Pages will be prepared in manuscript.

Place	Date	Hour	Summary of Events and Information	Remarks and references to Appendices
Domart	14/10/16		Inspects animals in St Ouen.	
"	15/10/16		Visits R.A. School Re-Army. Destroys a horse, left there by a Canadian Unit, suffering from an open joint. Inspects horses being entrained by M.V.S. at St LEGER. R.H.Q.	
"	16/10/16		Visits Remt Depot ANSEVILLE & elects a L.D. for M.V.S.	
"	17/10/16	AM	Inspects horses of 116 Bat Sig. Coy. Animals looking of wee. Visit of D.D.V.R. Re-Army. Casting of RemiCorn.	
Domart	18/10/16		Left Domart at St Ouen.	
	19/10/16		Inspects animals of S.A. Co. 11th D.A.C. Animals looking well.	
	20/10/16		Inspects horses of 34th D. Aml. Animals looking well.	
	21/10/16		Proceeds to BEAUMETZ. Investigates outbreak of Horses among Civilian animals there. Visits Mot: Tsp. Sec.	

WAR DIARY or INTELLIGENCE SUMMARY

Army Form C. 2118

A.D.V.S.
11th DIVISION.

Place	Date	Hour	Summary of Events and Information	Remarks and references to Appendices
S:OUEN	22.10.16		With the O.C. M.V.S. locate Depot animals left behind by other Divisions round about Doullens area. Arranged for their disposal. Found that all their animals (5) were being well looked after by the French people in whose charge they were.	
"	23.10.16		Office duties.	
"	24.10.16		Inspects animals of "C" Sig. Co. to —	
"	25.10.16		Visits some animals left behind at several places by Different units. Gather some & arranges for their collection.	
"	28.10.16		Visits M.V.S.	
"	29.10.16		Leave.	
"	30.10.16		"	
"	31.10.16		"	

H.P. Roo[?]
Capt. A.V.C.
f. A.D.V.S. 11 Division
31-10-16.

Vol 5.

WAR DIARY.

~~A.D.V.S. 1st. Div.~~ Vet
22nd Mob. Vet. Section.

WAR DIARY

INTELLIGENCE SUMMARY

(Erase heading not required.)

Army Form C. 2118

A.D.V.S., 11th DIVISION.

Place	Date	Hour	Summary of Events and Information	Remarks and references to Appendices
SOUEN.	7-11-16	—	Returns off leave	
"	8-11-16	—	Visits M.V.S.	
"	9-11-16	—	Inspects Int. Sup. Co. & No. 1 Co. 47 Res. Pk.	
"	10-11-16	—	Inspects S.A.D. DAC	
"	11-11-16	—	Moves to VRIGNEM.	
VRIGNEM	12-11-16	—	Animals of Cav. Div. Train & Staff Sutherland Fusiliers. Dorset Reg. Animals all in good condition. Men comfortably billeted	
"	13-11-16	—	Inspects M.V.S. Animals in good condition.	
"			Inspects animals of Lincoln Reg. & Borderer Reg.	
VRIGNEM	14-11-16	—	Moves to CANAPLES	
"	15-11-16	—	On duties	
"	16-11-16	—	Moves to CONTAY	

A.D.V.S., 11th DIVISION, Army Form C. 2118

WAR DIARY
INTELLIGENCE SUMMARY
(Erase heading not required.)

Instructions regarding War Diaries and Intelligence Summaries are contained in F.S. Regs., Part II. and the Staff Manual respectively. Title Pages will be prepared in manuscript.

Place	Date	Hour	Summary of Events and Information	Remarks and references to Appendices
CONTAY	17.11.16		Moved to HEDAUVILLE. Oan ADVS 63rd Div re taking of over MVS billet.	
"	18.11.16		Ord" duties	
"	19.11.16		Interviews ADVS 19th Div. re location of MVS. CRA 11 Div.	
"	"		Inspected animals of 6 Cyclist Pioneers. Animals all looking well	
"	20.11.16		Inspected animals of the 1st July Bde.	
"	21.11.16		ordinary duties	
"	22.11.16	AM	Inspected Mob. Vet Sec. Animals being Groomed from that unit.	
"	"	PM	Went to FORCEVILLE to see ADVS 37th Div.	
"	23.11.16		Calles on CRA 11 Div. Inspected S.A.C. Bde. 22nd MVS moves into new billet at BOUZINCOURT. Inspected billet in afternoon. Got permission from DDVS. 5th Army for MVS to remain in BOUZINCOURT altho out of 11 Divisional area.	

WAR DIARY
— or —
INTELLIGENCE SUMMARY
(Erase heading not required.)

Army Form C. 2118

A.D.V.S.:
11th DIVISION

Place	Date	Hour	Summary of Events and Information	Remarks and references to Appendices
HEDAUVILLE	24.11.16		Inspects Animals Northam'n. Field Ambulance. Cap't Hodge A.V.C reports him off leave.	
"	25.11.16	A.m	Meeting of T.O's at M.V.S. Demonstration of shoeing with Iron Orb all officers asked to send reports on this from O. Sheds. Horses.	
"	26.11.16	Am	Visited Mob. Vet. Sec.	
		Pm	Went to see A.V.Corps 57th Div. R.E occupation of Reech in Bouzincourt try 2 M.V.S. D.S.v.S. Called in the Eve.	
"	27.11.16		Moved to FORCEVILLE.	
FORCEVILLE	28.11.16		Visits. Not yet see arranges for examination of sick animals this by 2nd M.D.S & 4th Highland F.V.S.	
"	29.11.16	Am	Inspects Animals of 59th & 60th F.A.B. A good many very poor animals still remain in the 59th F.B.de. These are being evacuated to the Base.	
"		Pm	Inspects Sick Animals in M.V.S.	
"	30.11.16		Inspects Civilian horses (3) with mange. Made necessary arrangements.	

WAR DIARY.

A.D.V.S. 11th Div.

~~22nd Mov. Vet. Section.~~

Army Form C. 2118.

WAR DIARY
or
INTELLIGENCE SUMMARY.
(Erase heading not required.)

Instructions regarding War Diaries and Intelligence
Summaries are contained in F. S. Regs., Part II.
and the Staff Manual respectively. Title pages
will be prepared in manuscript.

Place	Date	Hour	Summary of Events and Information	Remarks and references to Appendices
ENGLEBELMER	22.12.16		Inspects horses of 58th Bns. Horses on the very bad standings. But changes on this date to other & better ones. A lot of respiron horses re-gunn dressings.	
	23.12.16		Ord. duties.	
	24.12.16		Visits unit in FORCEVILLE & M.V.S.	
	25.12.16		Writes & etc.	
	26.12.16		Pays calls.	
	27.12.16		Visits 59th Bns horse lines.	
	28.12.16		Visits Mob.Vet.Sec lines.	
	29.12.16		Inspects animals of 32nd Inf.Bde.M.G.Coy. All animals either under cover or on good standings, in fair condition & well looked after.	
	30.12.16		Ord. duties.	
	31.12.16		Inspects Animals of 6 & Yorks Pioneer, all animals in the open & with no shelter. Short in fs.	

W.J. Macaulay
Major A.V.C
A.D.V.S.

1577 Wt.W10791/1773 500,000 1/15 D.D.&L. A.D.S.S./Forms/C. 2118.

WAR DIARY
or
INTELLIGENCE SUMMARY
(Erase heading not required.)

Army Form C. 2118.

ADVS XI? Vol 7

Place	Date	Hour	Summary of Events and Information	Remarks and references to Appendices
ENGLEBELMER	1-1-17	—	Inspects Animals of 32nd & 33rd M.G.Coy. Animals in hard working condition. Three lorries after.	
"	2-1-17		Inspects Animals for Inoculation at 32nd M.V.S. Many Dermatitis Scabetic cases with large areas of Khaki stability. A good many sloughs.	
"	3-1-17		Inspects Animals of 60th F.A. Animals very poor standing in mud up to their knees. Impossible to see anything with their feet or pasterns to skin disease. Then. There no completely immersed in mud. The 60th Animals were in comfortable horses standings in ENGLEBELMER the majority, showing mirrors of the Corner.	
"	4-1-17		Inspects with Col. Dickson Kents M.V.S.	
"	5-1-17		Met Lt Col V DISTA S.V. Army at Malbert see inspection of horses.	

WAR DIARY
or
INTELLIGENCE SUMMARY
(Erase heading not required.)

Army Form C. 2118

Place	Date	Hour	Summary of Events and Information	Remarks and references to Appendices
ENGLEBELMER	6.1.17		Called on Staff Captain 63rd Div R.A. re cases of contagious stomatitis in R.A. units of that Division. Arranged for affected units undergo vetinary inspection. All animals of 11th Div. Train inspected.	
		P.m.	Capt Tinsdeau A.V.C. Called & arranged to inspect the mouths of all the animals in C/317 to Stomatitis	
	7.1.17	-	Visited M.V.S. Inspected animals of No 3 Sec. 63rd D.A.C.	
	8.1.17	-	Inspected animals of A & B Bties 317th F.A.B. 63rd Div. Called on C.R.A. 11th Div.	
	9.1.17	-	Inspected animals of H.Q. Co. 11th Div Train	
	10.1.17	-	Inspected cases of curange in H.Q. Co. Div. Train. Inocks Mr. Co. & arranges for isolation of infected & disinfection of cares at Inf. Inspected animals of 3 Section 63rd D.A.C.	

Army Form C. 2118

WAR DIARY
or
INTELLIGENCE SUMMARY
(Erase heading not required.)

Instructions regarding War Diaries and Intelligence Summaries are contained in F. S. Regs., Part II. and the Staff Manual respectively. Title Pages will be prepared in manuscript.

Place	Date	Hour	Summary of Events and Information	Remarks and references to Appendices
ENCZEZEMER	11/1/17		Meeting of all V.O. att. N.V.S. to see new methods of shoeing with horseshoes to prevent P.U.N.	
"	12.1.17		Inspected animals of 223rd F.A.B. 63rd Div. Division animals (Horses) rather thin - condition very poor for all - healthy tho'.	
	13.1.17		O.S. duties.	
"	14.1.17		Inspected animals of 59th F.A.B. animals on the whole hard hut standing up good. & very dry conditions the convstores a good number of very poor animals, to be traced.	
	15.1.17		Went to Yorench Area to Orders & fields for N.V.S.	
	16.1.17		Rates Mr. E. Two (2000) animals for evacuation	

1875 W¹. W593/826 1,000,000 4/15 J.B.C. & A. A.D.S.S./Forms/C.2118.

Army Form C. 2118

WAR DIARY
or
INTELLIGENCE SUMMARY
(Erase heading not required.)

Instructions regarding War Diaries and Intelligence Summaries are contained in F. S. Regs., Part II. and the Staff Manual respectively. Title Pages will be prepared in manuscript.

Place	Date	Hour	Summary of Events and Information	Remarks and references to Appendices
ENGLEBELMER	17/1/17		Inspects animals of 58th F.A.B. Animals in good dry clean standings. There are a lot of very poor animals to be seen.	
	18.1.17		Inspects animals of 60th F.A.B.	
	19.1.17		Do. Do.	
	20.1.17		Sup ENGLEBELMER AIR MARIEUX	
	21.1.17		Sup MARIEUX " BERNAVILLE	
	22.1.17		Sup BERNAVILLE " YVRENCH	
	23.1.17		Do. Do.	
	24.1.17		Nixe MVS Inspects animals in, Don Que R	
	25.1.17	AM	Bn Ds Duties	
		PM	Inspect animals of 1/4 Pig Coy	

Army Form C. 2118

WAR DIARY
or
INTELLIGENCE SUMMARY
(Erase heading not required.)

Instructions regarding War Diaries and Intelligence Summaries are contained in F.S. Regs., Part II. and the Staff Manual respectively. Title Pages will be prepared in manuscript.

Place	Date	Hour	Summary of Events and Information	Remarks and references to Appendices
YPRENCH	26.1.17		Meeting of all V.Os. Re Lectures to officers. Experiments desiring. Treatment of animals Contagious Stomatitis seen to	
"	27.1.17		A.D.V.S. called with reference to a case of Contagious Stomatitis found in an animal of C/60 Bde. Went with him to their unit & saw the horse. Called on D.D.A.	
"	28.1.17		Proceeded to 60 PA3 horses in C Bty. found 11 cases Stomatitis made arrangements Re- Segregation Disinfection etc. Also Canvas Animals in A59 for this Disease - found none - The mouths of the horses in some Indian Animals suffering from Mange made arrangements about their care.	
	29.1.17		Inspects Nort Col. Div. Farm	
	30.1.17		Inspects Animals of 34th & 33rd Fd Amb.	
	31.1.17		Inspects Animals for evacuation at NIVE.	

W Macaw W
Major +
A.D.V.S.

1875 Wt. W593/826 1,000,000 4/15 J.B.C. & A. A.D.S.S./Forms/C. 2118.

WAR DIARY for month of February, 1917.

A.D.V.S.

22nd Mobile Vet. Section.

Army Form C. 2118

WAR DIARY
or
INTELLIGENCE SUMMARY

(Erase heading not required.)

Instructions regarding War Diaries and Intelligence Summaries are contained in F. S. Regs., Part II. and the Staff Manual respectively. Title Pages will be prepared in manuscript.

Place	Date	Hour	Summary of Events and Information	Remarks and references to Appendices
FRENCH	10.2.17		Inspects Animals of 2 Con. Dn. Trains	
	11.2.17		Inspects Animals of Corps Troops	
	12.2.17		Inspects S-8 & S-9 F.A.B.	
	13.2.17		Inspects H.Q. Co. Dn. Train & S.A.Z.	
	14.2.17		Proceeds on leave.	
	—			
	26.2.17		Returns from leave.	
	27.2.17		Inspects M.V.S.	
	28.2.17		O.D. Duty.	

WAR DIARY.

March 1917.

A.D.V.S.
22nd. Mobile Vet. Section.
****

Army Form C. 2118

WAR DIARY
or
INTELLIGENCE SUMMARY
(Erase heading not required.)

Instructions regarding War Diaries and Intelligence Summaries are contained in F. S. Regs., Part II. and the Staff Manual respectively. Title Pages will be prepared in manuscript.

Place	Date	Hour	Summary of Events and Information	Remarks and references to Appendices
MARIEUX	1-2-17	—	Entes M.S.	
	2-3-17		with A.D.V.S. Durlin	
"	2-3-17		D.A.V.S. inspects 68th Co. R.E. HQ Co. Train. + Doset Regt.	
—	4-3-17		Inspects animals of 33rd Fd. Amb + 116 Bn. Park. 35th K + 134th F. Amb	
	5-3-17		Ordnance whs	
	6-3-17		"	
	7-3-17	—	Inspects Power Batteries of SP 41 + 59 S.A.B.	
	8-3-17		Inspects animals for transfer to MVS.	
	9-3-17	—	Inspects animals 10th Co. Train. Conference at D.V.S. Office	
	10-3-17		Inspects animals of 118 Dy. Co.	
	11-3-17		As walks to Hosp.	

Army Form C. 2118.

WAR DIARY

or

~~INTELLIGENCE SUMMARY.~~

(Erase heading not required.)

Instructions regarding War Diaries and Intelligence
Summaries are contained in F. S. Regs., Part II.
and the Staff Manual respectively. Title pages
will be prepared in manuscript.

Place	Date	Hour	Summary of Events and Information	Remarks and references to Appendices
Mhow(?)			Regimental Sgt for Inspn	
	23.3.17		Returns Division on discharge from Hospital.	
	24.3.17		Inspects Stomatch Cases in 59th FAB. + Inspects DAC	
	25.3.17		Inspects Animals of 58th FAB. Tata M.T.	
	26.3.17		Inspects animals of 3rd Pl Cav. 6th E.Yorks. 32nd r.g.o².	
			for 1, 2, 4, 4th Coy. D.T. Train. 8th N.Staff Staffs. 5/Borders.	
			11th Manchesters. Yorks M.V.T.	
	27.3.17		Inspects animals of 7/Staffs. 1 to 3 Coy Train. 6/Borders 6.6.p.Co	
	28.3.17		Inspects animals of 6/Lincolns Staffords 33rd m.g Co² 67th Bde. & 68th FaCo.	
			3rd m.g Co. - 9/Sherwoods Forresters.	
	29.3.17		Met D.D.V.S. Inspects animes of 3rd H. & Pl Cav. +32nd m.g.Co². Tanks M.V.T.	
	30.3.17		Inspects animals of S.A.P. 35th PAmb. 9 N/Yorks 6/Yorks b/yorks + R.Iron	
	31.3.17		Inspects animals of 33rd Inf.Amb. Sig Co.	

JM Macarthur
Major AVC
A.D.V.S X Div.

1577 Wt. W10791/1773 500,000 1/15 D. D. & L. A.D.S.S./Forms/C. 2118.

WAR   DIARY.

April 1917.

A.D.V.S., 11th.Div.
~~23nd. Mobile Vet. Section.~~

Army Form C. 2118.

WAR DIARY
or
INTELLIGENCE SUMMARY.
(Erase heading not required.)

Instructions regarding War Diaries and Intelligence Summaries are contained in F. S. Regs., Part II. and the Staff Manual respectively. Title pages will be prepared in manuscript.

Place	Date	Hour	Summary of Events and Information	Remarks and references to Appendices
MARIEUX	1-4-17		O.C. Duties	
"	2-4-17		Inspected animals of 33rd Infy Bde	
"	3-4-17		Inspected animals for evacuation at M.V.S.	
"	4-4-17		" 32nd M.G. Co. 3rd F. Amb. No.3 Co. Co. Div. Train	
"	5-4-17		" Border Regt. No.3 Co. D. Train 32nd U.G. Co. 1st Sec. 6. Yorks 67th F.Co. R.E.	
"	6-4-17		" 2nd F. Co. R.E. 32nd M.G. Co. 3rd M.G. Co. "B." Manchester Regt.	
"	7-4-17		M.V.S.	
"	8-4-17		3 Sth F. Amb. No.4 Co. No.2 Co. D. Train 33rd F. Amb.	
"	9-4-17		Cairo on C.R.A.	
"	10-4-17		M.V.S. 67th F.Co. R.E.	
"	11-4-17		Rent at Palee No.2 v 4 Co. Train A.G.C. 3rd F. Ambulance 32nd M.G. Co.	

Army Form C. 2118.

WAR DIARY
or
INTELLIGENCE SUMMARY.
(Erase heading not required.)

Instructions regarding War Diaries and Intelligence Summaries are contained in F.S. Regs., Part II. and the Staff Manual respectively. Title pages will be prepared in manuscript.

Place	Date	Hour	Summary of Events and Information	Remarks and references to Appendices
Acheux	12.11.17		Arrived with D.H.Q. - Ord: Duties.	
	13.11.17		Inspects 3rd & 10th Cavs. & "Manchester" & 8th N.F." & 6th Div. trains.	
	14.11.17		86th R.G. 11th Div. Signals.	
	15.11.17		O.S. duties.	
	16.11.17		Inspection of Remounts at C.a.a. Sec.	
	17.11.17		MVS.	
	18.11.17		Ord. Duties.	
	19.11.17		Went to Bouzincourt. To arrange huts for N.V.S. Inspect Transport of Infantry.	
Ovillers Huts	20.11.17	"	Moves with D.H.Q. to Ovillers Huts	
N.V. Centre	21.11.17		Moves with D.H.Q. to N.V. Centre. Inspects 35th F. Amb. Horses.	

1577 Wt.W10791/1773 500,000 1/15 D. D. & L. A.D.S.S./Forms/C. 2118.

Army Form C. 2118.

WAR DIARY
or
INTELLIGENCE SUMMARY.
(Erase heading not required.)

Instructions regarding War Diaries and Intelligence Summaries are contained in F. S. Regs., Part II. and the Staff Manual respectively. Title pages will be prepared in manuscript.

Place	Date	Hour	Summary of Events and Information	Remarks and references to Appendices
N. Central	22.4.17		Inspects animals of No. 2 4th Co. Train E. Yorks Regt. Yorks Lancs 167th Co. R.E.	
"	23.4.17		" N.F. Lanc. Fus. Scouts	
"	24.4.17		" 58th & 59th F.A.B.	
"	25.4.17		" 11th D.A.C.	
"	26.4.17		" 33rd Inf. Bde. 33rd M.G. Co. 68th F. Co. R.E.	
"	27.4.17		O.S. Rules	
"	28.4.17		Inspects animals of 33rd Inf. Bde. group.	
"	29.4.17		D.D.T. Cases	
"	30.4.17		Meeting about formation of S. Cox. M.V.S.	

J.W. Macaulay
Major ORC
A.D.V.S. X Divn

WAR DIARY.

May 1917.

A.D.V.S.,
  22nd. Mob. Vet. Section.

Army Form C. 2118

WAR DIARY
or
INTELLIGENCE SUMMARY

(Erase heading not required.)

Instructions regarding War Diaries and Intelligence Summaries are contained in F. S. Regs., Part II. and the Staff Manual respectively. Title Pages will be prepared in manuscript.

Place	Date	Hour	Summary of Events and Information	Remarks and references to Appendices
N 11 Central	1-5-17		HedQr Coy, 2, 3 & 4 Coys 11th Devil Train	
"	2-5-17		Inspected M.V.S. and DY.S & DDVS	
"	3-5-17		" S.A.A. Sect and 6th E Yorks (Pioneers)	
"	4-5-17		" 11th Divl Train, 34th Fd Ambulance, 11th Lancashire Regt. 34th M G Coy, 9th LANCS Fusiliers	
"	5-5-17		Ordinary duties	
"	6-5-17		Inspected M.V.S.	
"	7-5-17		Ordinary duties	
"	8-5-17		Inspected M.V.S.	
"	9-5-17 to 13-5-17		Ordinary duties	
"	14-5-17		A.D.V.S. arrived	

1875 Wt. W593/826 1,000,000 4/15 J.B.C. & A. A.D.S.S./Forms/C. 2118.

WAR DIARY or INTELLIGENCE SUMMARY

Army Form C. 2118.

Place	Date	Hour	Summary of Events and Information	Remarks and references to Appendices
Usna Hill	18/5/17		Joined the 11th Division	
"	19/5/17		Forwarded visit D.W.D. & St Jans Cappel	
St Jans Cappel	20/5/17		Visited the M.V.S.	
"	21/5/17		Inspected some arrivals of the D.A.C. D.T.V.S. (called)	
"	22/5/17		Inspected arrival of the 32 M.G. Company " " " 67 Regt " R.E. Visited M.V.S. " A.D.V.S. of the 16th & 36th divisions	
"	23/5/17		Inspected arrival of No 1, 2, 3, & 4 Siv by train " " 56 & 57 Nyrie R.F.A. 34th Field Ambulance 86 " R.E.	
"	24/5/17			

Army Form C. 2118.

WAR DIARY
or
INTELLIGENCE SUMMARY
(Erase heading not required.)

Instructions regarding War Diaries and Intelligence Summaries are contained in F.S. Regs., Part II. and the Staff Manual respectively. Title Pages will be prepared in manuscript.

Place	Date	Hour	Summary of Events and Information	Remarks and references to Appendices
SITANSGABBEL	25/5/17		Inspected arrival of the 10th A.C. Visited the M.V.S. S.O.M.S. College	
			Inspected arrivals of the 33rd & Leinins, 35th Field Ambulance W. Yorks. W. Ridings & 6th Yorks	
	26/5/17		Inspected arrivals of 11th Divisn Signal Coy 6th Lincolns & 6th Borders 36th Divn Visited A.D.V.S.	
	27/5/17		Inspected arrivals of South Staffords, 33 Field Ambulance, 68 Coy R.E. & Sherwood Foresters & inspected equipment Visited the M.V.S.	

Army Form C. 2118

WAR DIARY
or
INTELLIGENCE SUMMARY

(Erase heading not required.)

Place	Date	Hour	Summary of Events and Information	Remarks and references to Appendices
ST JANS CAPPEL	28/5/17		Inspected some arrivals of the S.A.C. & various duties	
	29/5/17		Inspected arrivals of the 5th Dorsets, Stenographers 34th Brigade	
			" " 4th Lancashire Fus.	
			" " 9th Lancashire Fus.	
			" " 34th Machine Gun Co.	
			" " Northumberlands Fus.	
			" some of the arrivals of S.A.C.	
	30/5/17		Inspected some of the arrivals of S.A.C.	
			Visited D.D.M.S. II Corps	
			Visited A.D.M.S.	
	31/5/17		Inspected some arrivals of the 58th Brigade & D.A. and Divn.	Motored to H.Q. A.D.V.S. II Corps
			& 6th York - various dr. V.S.	

1875 Wt. W593/826 1,000,000 4/15 J.B.C. & A. A.D.S.S./Forms/C. 2118.

D.A.D.V.S.
22nd. Mobile Vet .Section.

Army Form C. 2118

WAR DIARY
or
INTELLIGENCE SUMMARY

(Erase heading not required.)

Instructions regarding War Diaries and Intelligence Summaries are contained in F.S. Regs., Part II. and the Staff Manual respectively. Title Pages will be prepared in manuscript.

Place	Date	Hour	Summary of Events and Information	Remarks and references to Appendices
ST JANS CAPPEL	1/6/17		Inspected some animals of the DMC. Horse for evacuation at M.V.S. Conference of V.D. of the Division	
	2/6/17		Inspected horses of the 32 & 33rd Trenchers Sun Co. Horse of 14th Div. Headquarters. Horse lines of A. Battery 58th B. R.S.a.	
	3/6/17		Inspected horses of the 11th Cruechifters & 6th S. York Pioneers. Visited the Sm. V.S.	
	4/6/17		Inspected Remounts - Inspected lines of 16 & 107 Coy. Div. Train	
	5/6/17		Lines of D. Battery 59th Brigade R.F.A. + No 2 Coy Div Train	
	6/6/17		" " " arrival of the 11th DMC. Visited the V.S.	
	7/6/17		Visited m. V.S. & inspected animals for evacuation Inspected horse cases of troops in S.S. & Brigade R.F.a. lines of No 3 Coy Div Train	
	8/6/17		Visited Sm. V.S. D.D.V.S. Called Inspected two lines of Headquarters & Senior Conference of V.O.s. of the Division	

Army Form C. 2118.

WAR DIARY
or
INTELLIGENCE SUMMARY.
(Erase heading not required.)

Instructions regarding War Diaries and Intelligence Summaries are contained in F. S. Regs., Part II. and the Staff Manual respectively. Title pages will be prepared in manuscript.

Place	Date	Hour	Summary of Events and Information	Remarks and references to Appendices
ST JANS CAPPEL	9/5/17		Visited 9th Corps mobile Vety. depot. Arrangs. for evacuation of horse of Bnd. Arrived with DMS from St Jans Cappel to Dranoutre	
DRANOUTRE	10/5/17		Visited in V.S. arranges to move to new location at Dranoutre — ordinary duties.	
	11/5/17		Visited A.V.S. & D.O. Ye 32 & 33 Brigade relieving duties Visited V.C. 11th Div. train	
	12/5/17		Inspected some horses of 35th Field Ambulance to Sherri divisions	
			" " all the horses 8th W. Reays	
			" " the 32nd Bec. Gun Co.	
			" some horses of 9th W. York, Sr Sherri division	
			" remainder of horse trundler of Headquarters & Train	
13/5/17			Inspecting of 6th S. York Sr Sherri division	
			" " Field ambulance "	
			" " Deniz Bos.	

1577 Wt. W10791/1773 500,000 1/15 D. D. & L. A.D.S.S./Forms/C. 2118.

Army Form C. 2118.

WAR DIARY
or
INTELLIGENCE SUMMARY.
(Erase heading not required.)

Instructions regarding War Diaries and Intelligence Summaries are contained in F.S. Regs., Part II. and the Staff Manual respectively. Title pages will be prepared in manuscript.

Place	Date	Hour	Summary of Events and Information	Remarks and references to Appendices
DRANOUTRE	13/6/17		Inspected some lines of the 32nd Machine Gun Co & M. Ellis Murine	
			" " Mew cars of the 58th & 59th Brigades R.F.A.	
	14/6/17		Visited the M.O. of 180 Bajan R.F.A. 16th Divn	
			" " " 197 " 16th Divn	
			" " I.T.C. & 48bly HAC 16th Divn	
			Inspected lines of the 33rd Field Ambulance	
	15/6/17		Inspected lines of "C" Battery 59th Brigade R.F.A.	
			Conference of M.O.s of the Division	
	16/6/17		Inspected lines of "B" Battery 59 Brigade R.F.A.	
			Visited the Dn. R.S. transports arrived for evacuation	
	17/6/17		Visited No 23 Recg. Hospital at Omer	
			Visited the Dn. R.S.	

Army Form C. 2118.

WAR DIARY
or
INTELLIGENCE SUMMARY.
(Erase heading not required.)

Instructions regarding War Diaries and Intelligence Summaries are contained in F.S. Regs., Part II. and the Staff Manual respectively. Title pages will be prepared in manuscript.

Place	Date	Hour	Summary of Events and Information	Remarks and references to Appendices
DRANOUTRE	18/6/17		Inspected manure trenches - Visited the V.O. of 59th Brigade R.F.A. examined case isolated to suspicious mange. Inspected some horse for evacuation in 11th Div. trains.	
" "	19/6/17		Inspected some horse for evacuation - Visited A.D.S. 36th Div. M.V.S. - Inspected cases from H022 M.V.S. to 38th Div. M.V.S. - Visited V.O. of 177 B. R.F.A. 16 Div. + V.O. of 180 B. R.F.A. 16 Div. Inspected some gun shot wounds in the 58 B R.F.A.	
" "	20/6/17		Moved with J.H.A. from Dranoutre to Merris - Visited the M.V.S.	
MERRIS	21/6/17		Visited the A.D.V.S. + D.D.R. Visited the M.V.S.	
" "	22/6/17		Ordinary duties. Visited the Sn V.S. Conference of V.Os. of the Division went to Renescure.	
" "	23/6/17		Served with D.H.Q. from Merris to the V.S. Eberlecques. Velocats sight to the V.S.	
RENESCURE	24/6/17		Moved with D.H.Q from Renescure to Eberlecques. Visited the M.V.S.	

1577 Wt.W10791/1773 500,000 1/15 D. D. & L. A.D.S.S./Forms/C. 2118.

Army Form C. 2118.

WAR DIARY
or
INTELLIGENCE SUMMARY.
(Erase heading not required.)

Instructions regarding War Diaries and Intelligence Summaries are contained in F. S. Regs., Part II. and the Staff Manual respectively. Title pages will be prepared in manuscript.

Place	Date	Hour	Summary of Events and Information	Remarks and references to Appendices
EPERLECQUES	25/6/17		Visited the Sn. V.S. Saw V.Os of the 32nd & 33rd Brigades - Inspected hrs of the 34th Field ambulance	
"	26/6/17		Inspected animals of the 9th Lanc. Inf. 34th Machine Gun Co. - Ashtead Res - Visited the Sn. V.S.	
"	27/6/17		Visited the D.D.V.S. Inspected mange cases of the 32nd Machine Gun Co. & 8th W. Ridings at Houtkerque.	
"	28/6/17		Inspected animals of the 11th Warwicks & 5th Scots Visited the Sn. V.S. Inspected animals for evacuation Inspected & sent 144 Removals	
"	29/6/17		Inspected animals of the 33rd Machine Gun Co. 18 Field & R.E. & 33rd Field ambulance - Conference of V.Os of the Division Visited the Sn. V.S.	

1577 Wt.W10791/1773 500,000 1/15 D.D. & L. A.D.S.S./Forms/C. 2118.

Army Form C. 2118.

WAR DIARY
or
INTELLIGENCE SUMMARY.
(Erase heading not required.)

Place	Date	Hour	Summary of Events and Information	Remarks and references to Appendices
EPERLECQUES	30/6/17		Inspected arrival of the 6th Border Regt. & 7 S. Staffs Regt. " " 1st Lincoln Regt. Visited the Div. W.S. Surgeons annexes for evacuation.	Ostruch Trench art. troops 11-6-17

WAR DIARY.

July, 1917.

D.A.D.V.S. 11th Division.

22nd Mob. Vet. Section.

Army Form C. 2118.

WAR DIARY
or
INTELLIGENCE SUMMARY.
(Erase heading not required.)

Instructions regarding War Diaries and Intelligence Summaries are contained in F.S. Regs., Part II. and the Staff Manual respectively. Title pages will be prepared in manuscript.

Place	Date	Hour	Summary of Events and Information	Remarks and references to Appendices
ETERLECQUES	1/7/17		Inspected arrival of the 9th Sherwood Foresters — Visited the Dn.V.S.	
"	2/7/17		Visited the Dn.V.S. — Inspected sick horse cars in No 304 Coy. Aux: Train	
"	3/7/17		Inspected arrival of the 6th Yorkshire Regt. at HOUTKERQUE — Horse inspection in 9th W. Yorkshire Regt. & No 2 Coy of the train — Inspected arrival of the 67 & 86 Coys. R.E. & 6th S. Yorks. (P) near PESELHOEK	
"	4/7/17		Inspected horse of the 11th Div. School G — Visited the Dn.V.S. Inspected some horse cars at the Horse Lines.	
"	5/7/17		Ordinary duties S.D.V.S. Office	
"	6/7/17		Visits a D.V.S. Inspected horse cars in 32 ber. Jn. Co. at HOUTKERQUE — Visited the Dn.V.S. — Inspected arrival of Headquarters Div. K. Brigade.	

1577 Wt. W10791/1773 500,000 1/15 D. D. & L. A.D.S.S./Forms/C. 2118.

Army Form C. 2118.

WAR DIARY
or
INTELLIGENCE SUMMARY.
(Erase heading not required.)

Place	Date	Hour	Summary of Events and Information	Remarks and references to Appendices
EPERLECQUES	7/7/16		Inspected some sewage carts in the Lawes Sub – Visited No 23 Vety Hospital at OTHER	
	8/7/16		Ordinary duties – Visited Sn. v. S.	
	9/7/16		Visited Nos. of D.A.C. & R.A & went to PERINQE. Called on D.A.D.V.S. 2nd Div. Visited A.D.V.S. 18th Corps – Inspected some mini carts in Visited G.E.W. golds & W. Ridge, yorks & Lancs & No 2 Coy of Train at HOUTKERQE.	
	10/7/16		Inspected horse of evacuation at D.V.S. Inspected some horses of 33 Field Ambulance Inspected horses of 33rd Field Ambulance at No 3 Coy of Train	
	11/7/16		Inspected horses of 87th D. 33rd M.Gun Co & 68 Field Co R.E. Visited Vte Sn. v. S.	
	12/7/16		Inspected horses of 34th M.Gun Co. Visited in v.S. Inspected some cars of D.Rhalonis in S.A. Ascertained & account of Lawes Sub.	

Army Form C. 2118.

WAR DIARY
or
INTELLIGENCE SUMMARY.
(Erase heading not required.)

Instructions regarding War Diaries and Intelligence Summaries are contained in F. S. Regs., Part II. and the Staff Manual respectively. Title pages will be prepared in manuscript.

Place	Date	Hour	Summary of Events and Information	Remarks and references to Appendices
EPERLECQUES	13/7/16		Inspected Gas attacks hors of 105th Inf. Labour Co. in No Relief advanced corps & anti air aff Detain near ST PIERRE BROUCK. Inspected arrival of the Northumberland Inf. & detachment of D.A.C.	
"	14/7/16		attended Conference at Skin of A.D.V.S. 18th Corps — Inspected Some Inspected cars of Stomatitis in 32nd Me. Gun Co near POPERINGE. Visits M.O. in N.S.	
"	15/7/16		Inspected hors of the 85th — Field Ambulance & Goll & Lancs Regt. Inspected some sceneys cars in No 3 Coy of these. Visited on N.S.	
"	16/7/16		ordinary duties	
"	17/7/16		Visited Ho. Yh D.H.E. near POPERINGE — Visits Mr. V.S.	
"	18/7/16		ordinary duties	

1577 Wt. W10791/1773 500,000 1/15 D. D. & L. A.D.S.S./Forms/C. 2118.

WAR DIARY
INTELLIGENCE SUMMARY.

Army Form C. 2118.

Place	Date	Hour	Summary of Events and Information	Remarks and references to Appendices
EPERLECQUES	19/7/17		Inspected arrivals & details at ZENEGHEM & arrival of No 3 section 5th Army Auxiliary Horse to at WATTEN. Inspected Remounts. Inspected sweeps cows in 95th Field Ambulance, 9th W. Yorks & 9th Lancs Fus. Visited No 23 Veterinary Hospital St Omer - carried on tops 5th Corps	
	20/7/17		Visited Sn V.S. & inspected cases of evacuation. Examining & suspicious sweeps cases in Brit. Field Ambulance. Inspected arrival of the W Riding Regt & 9th W. Yorks	
	21/7/17		Ordinary duties	
	22/7/17		Inspected arrivals for evacuation at Sn V.S. Visited area commandant at St JAN TER BIEZEN & arranged with 18th Corps Sn Site for Sn V.S. Inspected sour scurvy cows in Nos. 34 & Company Train at POPERINGHE & two suspected scurvy cows in 5th Army Auxiliary Horse Co at WATTEN	
	23/7/17		Moved with D.H.Q. from EPERLECQUES to WORMHOUDT	

Army Form C. 2118.

WAR DIARY
or
INTELLIGENCE SUMMARY.
(Erase heading not required.)

Instructions regarding War Diaries and Intelligence Summaries are contained in F. S. Regs., Part II. and the Staff Manual respectively. Title pages will be prepared in manuscript.

Place	Date	Hour	Summary of Events and Information	Remarks and references to Appendices
WORMHOUDT	24/7/17		Inspected some supports billets in the 32nd trenchline June Co near Poperinghe -	
"	25/7/17		Moved with S.H.Q. from WORMHOUDT to POPERINGE. Visited to V.S. team camel - visited new Sgt of M.V.S. Called on A.D.V.S. 18th Corps	
POPERINGE	26/7/17		Visited A.D.V.S. 15th Corps, visited Sgt of M.V.S. & V.Os. of 58th & 59th Brigade R.F.A. & S.A.C.	
"	27/7/17		Inspected Average cases in the 58th & 59th Brigade R.F.A. & S.A.C. & 6th S. Yorks (P) Regt. some wounded arriving in the 18th Corps Conference of V.Os. at my office	
"	28/7/17		Attended conference at office of A.D.V.S. 18th Corps Inspected lines of the 86th & 69th Field Coys R.E.	

1577 Wt.W10791/1773 500,000 1/15 D. D. & L. A.D.S.S./Forms/C. 2118.

Army Form C. 2118

WAR DIARY
or
INTELLIGENCE SUMMARY
(Erase heading not required.)

Place	Date	Hour	Summary of Events and Information	Remarks and references to Appendices
POPERINGHE	29/7/17		Visited the M.V.S. & N.O. of 32 & 34 L Inf. Brigades. Visited the corps Mobile Vety de Potmet. Inspected wounded horse of G.E. Foot (?) Regt.	
	30/7/17		Inspected arrival of the D.A.C. & remount camp in the 58th Brigade R.G.A. Visited the M.V.S. & inspects animals in evacuation.	
	31/7/17		Inspected arrival to evacuation at M.V.S. Vety equipment of 11th Div. Train. Horse drawn range cars & horse cars in 34th L Inf. Brigade.	

Godfrey
Senior ALV.
11th Div.

Vol 14.

> D.A.D.V.S.,
> 11th DIVISION.

CONFIDENTIAL

WAR DIARY OF

MAJOR J.W. O'KELLY D.A.D.V.S 11th DIVISION

FROM 1-8-17 TO 31-8-17.

Army Form C. 2118.

WAR DIARY
or
INTELLIGENCE SUMMARY.
(Erase heading not required.)

Place	Date	Hour	Summary of Events and Information	Remarks and references to Appendices
POPERINGHE	1/8/17		Inspected arrivals of evacuation at M.V.S.	
"	2/8/17		Visited H.Q. 4 3rd Duty Brigade & inspected arrival in same. 2nd Visited V.O. & D.A.C. Inspected some Infantry cars of Stretchers in No 2 company of Train – Inspected arrival of evacuation at M.V.S.	
"	3/8/17		Inspected firm shot wounds & weary cases in 58th & 55th Brigades R.F.A. Conference of V.O's at my office – Inspected arrivals of evacuation at M.V.S. Selected new sight of M.V.S.	
"	4/8/17		Attended Conference at Office of A.D.M.S. 18th Corps – Inspected arrivals of evacuation at M.V.S.	
"	5/8/17		Inspected new sight to be Stretchers in No 2 company of train " arrival of evacuation at M.V.S.	
"	6/8/17		Inspected 89 Command of M. Division – visited men evacuated Canvasser site to M.V.S.	

WAR DIARY
of
INTELLIGENCE SUMMARY.

(Erase heading not required.)

Army Form C. 2118.

Place	Date	Hour	Summary of Events and Information	Remarks and references to Appendices
POPERINGHE	7/6/17		Inspected arrival of the 33rd Field Ambulance + 32nd, 33rd + 34th Sanitaire from G.H.Q. Inspected Immobile huts of 6th S. Div (?) Inspected arrival & concentration at M.V.S.	
"	8/6/17		Inspected arrival of the 59th Brigade R.F.A. + B Battery 58th Brigade R.F.A. Inspected arrival of the 67th, 68th Field Coy R.E. + arrival & concentration at M.V.S.	
"	9/6/17		Inspected lines of the 58th Brigade R.F.A.	
"	"		Some transport cases in 401st Field Co. R.E. (57th Div)	
"	"		Arrival of the 37th Machine Gun Co.	
"	"		Inspected concentration at M.V.S.	
"	10/6/17		Inspected lines of 35th Field Ambulance. Directors of M.O. of divisions his Div Office + M.O. attached with 57th Divis. Inspected Removal + Sick Arriving at A.D.S. Arrival & concentration at M.V.S.	

Army Form C. 2118.

WAR DIARY
or
INTELLIGENCE SUMMARY.
(Erase heading not required.)

Place	Date	Hour	Summary of Events and Information	Remarks and references to Appendices
POPERINGHE	11/8/17		Attended Conference at office of A.D.V.S. 18th Corps. Inspected animals for evacuation at Dr. V.S.	
"	12/8/17		Inspected arrivals of 34th Field Ambulance " " Nos. 3 & 4 Corps Reserve " " for evacuation at Dr. V.S.	
"	13/8/17		Inspected arrivals of 32nd trenches from Co. & Nos 1 & 2 Coops of teams — Inspected arrivals for evacuation at Dr. V.S.	
"	14/8/17		A.D.V.S. 18th Corps called. Visited Dr. V.S. with A.D.V.S. & D Battery 59th Brigade R.F.A. & D & B. Batteries 58th Brigade R.F.A. Inspected wounded horses in 6th S. Goal (?) — Visited Dr. V.S. & in Spected arrivals for evacuation	

Army Form C. 2118.

WAR DIARY
or
INTELLIGENCE SUMMARY.
(Erase heading not required.)

Instructions regarding War Diaries and Intelligence Summaries are contained in F. S. Regs., Part II. and the Staff Manual respectively. Title pages will be prepared in manuscript.

Place	Date	Hour	Summary of Events and Information	Remarks and references to Appendices
POPERINGHE	15/6/17		Inspected some trenches change ens in 17/B Royal Scots & 401st & 404th Field Coy R.E. 51st Division.	
	16/6/17		Inspected some huts in A.B. C. & D Batteries 59th Brigade R.F.A. Arrival to inoculation at Sn. V. S.	
	"		Inspected arrival to inoculation at Sn. V. S.	
	17/6/17		Inspected arrival of 32nd Machine Gun Co. Meeting of V.Os. & attaches visits at Army Office. Conference of V.Os. of II Corps. Inspected arrival to inoculation at Sn. V. S.	
	18/8/17		Attended conference at Office of V.O.V.S. IInd Corps. Inspected arrival of No 1 Company 57th Prov. Train. " " for inoculation at Sn. V. S.	
	19/6/17		Inspected arrival of J. W. Jones	

F. W. Jones
A.D.S.S./Forms/C. 2118.

Army Form C. 2118.

WAR DIARY
or
INTELLIGENCE SUMMARY.
(Erase heading not required.)

Place	Date	Hour	Summary of Events and Information	Remarks and references to Appendices
POPERINGHE	20/6/17		Inspected arrival of 282 Army Field Artillery Brigade for evacuation at Sn. V.S.	
"			Inspected arrival of 6th S. Gorks (?) + D. Battery, 59th Brigade R.F.A.	
			" of A + B. Batteries 266th Brigade R.F.A. 53rd Div.	
			" for evacuation at Sn. V.S.	
"	21/6/17		Inspected arrival of A. + B. Batteries 59th Brigade R.F.A.	
			" of D Battery 256 Brigade R.F.A. 57th Div.	
			" for evacuation at Sn. V.S.	
			" of Field ambulance + 6th E. York (?)	
"	22/6/17		Inspected arrival of 35th Field ambulance of 5.A.C.	
			" Sick & wounded arriving for evacuation at Sn. V.S.	
			" Arriving for evacuation at K-X Camps	

Army Form C. 2118.

WAR DIARY
or
INTELLIGENCE SUMMARY.
(Erase heading not required.)

Place	Date	Hour	Summary of Events and Information	Remarks and references to Appendices
X CAMP A.16.C.2.5.	23/8/17		Inspected animals of the 67th & 68th Field Coys R.E. training for evacuation at Div. V.S.	
BORDEN H.30.B.2.3	24/8/17		Drove with D.V.S. to Borden Camps — Inspected animals of B Battery 77th Army Field Artillery Brigade under trevelein test — Inspected heavy animals remount at D.T.C.	
"	25/8/17		Attended conference at office of A.D.V.S. 18th Corps — Inspected animals of J. Battery/77 Army 3.A.B. under trevelein test — Inspected animals of B Battery 282 Army Field Artillery Brigade & C. Battery 282 A.F.A.B.	
"	26/8/17		Inspected animals of 68th Field Coy R.E. & animals for evacuation at Div. V.S. Inspected animals of D Battery 77 Army F.A.B. under the trevelein test — Inspected animals of 11th Div. Signal Co.	
"	27/8/17		Inspected animals of 56th Brigade R.F.A.	

WAR DIARY
or
INTELLIGENCE SUMMARY.
(Erase heading not required.)

Army Form C. 2118.

Place	Date	Hour	Summary of Events and Information	Remarks and references to Appendices
BORDER CAMP A 30 B 2.3	28/8/17		Visited Dn. V.S. & inspected arrival invalids bulletin test Inspected 91 newly arrived Clensiring - for evacuation at Headquarters of train	
	29/8/17		Inspected arrival of A. B & C Batteries 59th Brigade R.F.A. " " " " evacuation at Dn. V.S. " " " 3/3 rd S. Field Ambulance Arrival visit D.H.Q. to X Camp.	
X CAMP A 16 C 2.5	30/8/17		Inspected two injured horses at Hospital Farm Arrival for evacuation at Dn. V.S.	
"	31/8/17		Inspected arrival of 33rd & 35th Machine Gun Co. Kolhark Sir Stansislas Corps. - Meeting of V.Os at my Office - Inspected arrival of B & 92nd, Jor & Lewis & W. Khright - Inspected arrival for evacuation at Dn. V.S.	

Mostwick
Major AVC
ADVS II Corps.

Vol 15.

CONFIDENTIAL

WAR DIARY
OF
MAJOR. J.W. O'KELLY A.V.C. D.A.D.V.S 11th DIVISION.

FROM 1-9-17 TO 30-9-17.

Army Form C. 2118.

WAR DIARY
INTELLIGENCE SUMMARY
(Erase heading not required.)

Instructions regarding War Diaries and Intelligence Summaries are contained in F. S. Regs., Part II. and the Staff Manual respectively. Title Pages will be prepared in manuscript.

Place	Date	Hour	Summary of Events and Information	Remarks and references to Appendices
X CAMP	1/9/17		Attended conference at office of A.D.V.S. 18th Corps. Visits to V.S. & inspected Animals for evacuation	
"	2/9/17		Ordinary duties	
"	3/9/17		Proceeded on leave	
POPERINGHE	13/9/17		Returned from leave	
"	14/9/17		Inspected dismounted Artillery at Proven	
"	15/9/17		Attended conference at office of A.D.V.S. 18th Corps. Inspected & issued Remounts at M.2.Coy of Decin. Visits V.O. of 33rd & 3rd Brigades - Inspected animals for evacuation at M.V.S.	
	16/9/17		Inspected animals of S.W.Midd. 6 York & Lancs. 6th york & 9th W. Yorks. 10th W. Riding 6 York & Lancs. 6th york & 9th W. Yorks. 32nd Machine gun Co. 57 & 58th Fields & R.E. " 6th & 8th York (R.) Inspected animals for evacuation at M.V.S.	

Army Form C. 2118.

WAR DIARY
or
INTELLIGENCE SUMMARY
(Erase heading not required.)

Instructions regarding War Diaries and Intelligence Summaries are contained in F. S. Regs., Part II. and the Staff Manual respectively. Title Pages will be prepared in manuscript.

Place	Date	Hour	Summary of Events and Information	Remarks and references to Appendices
Po PERINGHE	17/9/17		Inspected arrivals of A.B.C. + D Bullrings 59th Brigade R.F.A. S.F.C.	
"	18/9/17		Delivery duties	
"	19/9/17		Inspected arrivals for evacuation at Sr.v.S. Arrived with S.H.Q. to horse honest Visited K.O. of 33rd + 34th Inf. Brigades	
W/o RMHouly	20/9/17		Inspected lorries of 33rd Ambulance Pren Co + 33rd Field Ambulance Visited Sr.v.S. + inspected arrivals for evacuation Inspected arrivals of Nos: 3 + 4 Conference Trains	
"	21/9/17		Inspected arrivals of S. Midland. Fd.A. + 34th Machine Fun Co. " " of 1/1st 9th Lanc's Fus + Headquarters 34th Brigade	
"	22/9/17		Inspected arrivals of Vet 9th Lanc's fus + Headquarters 34th Brigade Called on Brigade General armed - Inspected 1st & 3rd Field Ambulance	

2449 Wt. W14957/M90 750,000 1/16 J.B.C. & A. Forms/C.2118/12.

Army Form C. 2118.

WAR DIARY
or
INTELLIGENCE SUMMARY

(Erase heading not required.)

Instructions regarding War Diaries and Intelligence Summaries are contained in F. S. Regs., Part II. and the Staff Manual respectively. Title Pages will be prepared in manuscript.

Place	Date	Hour	Summary of Events and Information	Remarks and references to Appendices
WORMHOUDT	23/9/17		Visited Veterinary Officer of 34th Inf. Brigade. Visited M.V.S. & inspected arrival for concentration.	
"	24/9/17		Inspected arrival of 5th Dorsets, 6th Lincolns & 9th Cheshires.	
"	25/9/17		Moved with Div H.Q. from WORMHOUDT to BORDER CAMP. Inspected arrival for concentration at M.V.S. Visited H.Q. of 58th & 59th Brigades R.F.A.	
BORDERCAMP	26/9/17		Inspected gun lines of B Battery 59th Brigade R.F.A. Inspected arrivals of B & D Batteries 59th Brigade R.F.A., B & C Batteries 58th Brigade R.F.A. On concentration at M.V.S.	
"	27/9/17		Inspected arrival of A & D Batteries 58th Brigade R.F.A.	

Army Form C. 2118.

WAR DIARY
or
INTELLIGENCE SUMMARY
(Erase heading not required.)

Instructions regarding War Diaries and Intelligence Summaries are contained in F. S. Regs., Part II. and the Staff Manual respectively. Title Pages will be prepared in manuscript.

Place	Date	Hour	Summary of Events and Information	Remarks and references to Appendices
BORDER CAMP	27/9/17		Inspects Force huts in B Battery 59th Brigade R.F.A. & arrival of 7.S. Staff & 6th Border Regt. Visited Div. V.S. & inspected animals for evacuation.	
"	28/9/17		Inspected arrival of 86th Indec to R.E. - Meeting 8 key-officers of Division & 2 attached key-officers of 57th Bn. at my office - Inspected animals arrived in D & C V 253" Brigade R.F.A 57th Distr - Inspected animals for evacuation at M.V.S.	
"	29/9/17		Attended conference at office of G.O.C. 18th Corps - Inspected arrivals of 67th & 68th Siege G.R.E. - Inspected animals for evacuation at M.V.S.	
"	30/9/17		Inspected arrival Personnel— at N.K.C huts - Inspected animals for evacuation at M.V.S.	Norwich Despatches — F.A.D.V.S. 11th Div.

2449 Wt. W14957/M90 750,000 1/16 J.B.C. & A. Forms/C.2118/12.

CONFIDENTIAL

WAR DIARY OF

MAJOR J.W. O'KELLY - D.A.D.V.S. 11" DN.

FROM 1-10-17   TO 31-10-17.

WAR DIARY
or
INTELLIGENCE SUMMARY

Army Form C. 2118

Place	Date	Hour	Summary of Events and Information	Remarks and references to Appendices
BORDER CAMP	1/6/17		Inspected sick arrivals in Nos 1 & 2 Coy Train + wounded arrivals in 51st Divn Train — Visited V.D. Hos 253rd Brigade R.F.A. 51st Divn — Visited An.V.S. & inspected arrivals for evacuation.	
	2/6/17		Inspected Signal Co Hors — Visited An.V.S. & inspected arrivals for evacuation.	
	3/6/17		Inspected Riding Horses in 35th Field Ambulance & wounded horses in 59th Brigade R.F.A. & D.A.C. Inspected Sickly Cows in S Battery 56th Brigade R.F.A. — Inspected arrivals for evacuation at An.V.S.	
	4/6/17		Visited Transport Lines of 34th Brigade (Infy) — Inspected arrivals for evacuation at An.V.S.	
	5/6/17		Inspected 70 Remounts at Steenvoorde — Visited An.V.S & inspected arrivals for evacuation.	

WAR DIARY or INTELLIGENCE SUMMARY

Army Form C. 2118

Place	Date	Hour	Summary of Events and Information	Remarks and references to Appendices
BORDER CAMP	6/6/17		Inspected hommes arrived in D.R.C. Visited D.O. of 256 Brigade R.F.A. 51st Divn. S.A.O.S. 18th Divn. called arrangts to take over site of 22nd Div. V.S. - Inspected arrivals for evacuation at Div. V.S. Capt. O'Donnel to Div. V.S. (returned from leave).	
	7/6/17		Visited Div. V.S. & inspected arrivals for evacuation	
	8/6/17		Inspected sick animals in A & D Batteries 59th Brigade R.F.A. & D Battery 255 Brigade 58th Brigade R.F.A. Inspected horses in A Battery 255 Brigade R.F.A. 57th Divn. Visited Div. V.S.	
	9/10/17		Called on D.H.D.V.S. 18th Divn. Arranges to hand over to 51st Divn. Artillery. 3 Mules & R.E. & 6 E. Yorks (P) Inspected arrivals for evacuation at Div. V.S.	
	10/10/17		Called on A.D.V.S. 18th Corps - Inspected arrivals of 6 E. Yorks (P), 67, 68, & 86 Field Co R.E. Visited Div. V.S.	

Army Form C. 2118

WAR DIARY
or
INTELLIGENCE SUMMARY
(Erase heading not required.)

Instructions regarding War Diaries and Intelligence Summaries are contained in F. S. Regs., Part II. and the Staff Manual respectively. Title Pages will be prepared in manuscript.

Place	Date	Hour	Summary of Events and Information	Remarks and references to Appendices
BORDER CAMP	11/10/17		Called on D.D.V.S. 5th Army. Moved with D.H.Q. from BORDER CAMP to EPERLECQUES	
EPERLECQUES	12/10/17		Visited Sn. V.S. & A.D.V.S. 19th Corps	
"	13/10/17		Visited H.Q. of 34th Infy Brigade & Sn. V. S.	
"	14/10/17		Inspected animals of 9th S. Irelrs., 33rd Machine Gun Co. & 6th Dimont., No 3 Coy Divn. & 33rd Field ambulance	
"	15/10/17		Inspected animals of Northumberland Fus. 34th Machine Gun Co. & Lancashire Fus. Visited Sn. V.S. & inspected animals for evacuation	
"	16/10/17		Inspected animals of 7th D.S. Staffs & 6th Borders. Visited Dn. V.S.	

WAR DIARY or INTELLIGENCE SUMMARY

Army Form C. 2118

Place	Date	Hour	Summary of Events and Information	Remarks and references to Appendices
EPERLECQUES	17/10/17		Visited A.D.V.S. 19th Corps No 23 Veterinary Hospital St OMER	
"	18/10/17		Arrived with D.H.Q. from EPERLECQUES to NORRENT FONTES. Inspected site for Div. V.S.	
NORRENT FONTES	19/10/17		Visited Div. V.S.	
"	20/10/17		Inspected Nos 2 & 3 Sections of D.A.C. Attended Conference at Office of A.D.V.S. 1st Corps - Visited D.H.D.V.S. 6th Divn + arrange to lathe over site for Div. V.S. Visited Div. V.S.	
"	21/10/17		Inspected animals of 6th Yorks + Lancs. Regt. + No 2 Coy Train. Horses of D.H.Q.	

WAR DIARY
or
INTELLIGENCE SUMMARY

Army Form C. 2118

Place	Date	Hour	Summary of Events and Information	Remarks and references to Appendices
NORRENT FONTES	22/10/17		Inspected arrival of 6th Wiltshire Regt. Visited Div. V.S. DADVS. 6th Divn. called	
"	23/10/17		Drove with DDMS from NORRENT FONTES to BRAQUEMONT. Inspected arrival of 68th Field Co RE. Visited Div. V.S.	
BRAQUEMONT	24/10/17		Inspected arrival of 3rd Field Ambulance. Received transport horses of infantry units at M.V.S. Inspected horse transport lines of M.V.S.	
"	25/10/17		Inspected arrival of 86 Field Co RE. Inspected transport and DAC of 34th Infy Brigade + DAC. Visited Div. V.S.	
"	26/10/17		Called on ADVS 1st Corps – Conference of VOs at my office. Visited horse lines of 58th Brigade VICa with ADVS Corps. Inspected 2 cases of Strangles in ADC lines	

Army Form C. 2118

WAR DIARY
or
INTELLIGENCE SUMMARY
(Erase heading not required.)

Instructions regarding War Diaries and Intelligence Summaries are contained in F.S. Regs., Part II. and the Staff Manual respectively. Title Pages will be prepared in manuscript.

Place	Date	Hour	Summary of Events and Information	Remarks and references to Appendices
BRAQUEMONT	27/10/17		Attended Conference at HQrs of A.D.V.S. 1st Corps. Inspected lines of 35th Field Ambulance & B Battery 58th Brigade R.F.A. Visited Sn. V.S.	
"	28/10/17		Inspected arrival of C & D Batteries 58th Brigade R.F.A. Visited Sn V.S. & inspected arrivals for convention. Inspected Stonebrittis cases in H.D.R.C.	
"	29/10/17		Visited Sn.V.S. Arranged for more stabling to be erected. Inspected Ophthalmic cases in Headquarters to Sherier	
"	30/10/17		Inspected horses remounts at MARIES LES MINES. Arrival of A & B Batteries 59th Brigade R.F.A. " 33rd Field Ambulance	
"	31/10/17		Inspected arrival of C & D Batteries 59th Brigade R.F.A. " for convention at M.V.S.	[signature]

Army Form W.3091.

Cover for Documents.

D.A.D.V.S.
11TH DIVISION.

No.
Date

Nature of Enclosures.

CONFIDENTIAL

WAR DIARY OF

MAJOR J.W. O'KELLY - D.A.D.V.S. 11ᵗʰ Dᴵᵛⁿ

FROM 1-11-17   TO. 30-11-17.

Notes, or Letters written.

WAR DIARY or INTELLIGENCE SUMMARY

Army Form C. 2118.

Place	Date	Hour	Summary of Events and Information	Remarks and references to Appendices
BRAQUEMONT	1/11/17		Inspected stomatitis cases in D.H.C. & all animals in No 3 octavo D.H.C. Visited Dr. V.S. Inspected animals of Northumberland Fus., Lancashire Fus, Dorsets & 32nd Machine Gun Co. - Inspected suspicious mange case in 6th Division.	
"	2/11/17		Conference of Veg. Officers at Vety Office - visited Dr. V.S. & inspected animals for evacuation	
"	3/11/17		Attended Conference at Office of A.D.V.S. 1st Corps. - Inspected animals for evacuation at Dr. V.S. Inspected sick animals in Canadian D.H.C. Inspected animals of 52nd Battery Canadian Artillery	
"	4/11/17		Inspected hens of 33rd Machine Gun Co. - Met D.D.V.S. 1st Army in Bethune. D.D.V.S. visited Dr. V.S. Inspected stomatitis cases in D.A.C.	
"	5/11/17		Inspected sick animals in Nos 1, 2, 3 & 4 Corps Trains	

Army Form C. 2118.

WAR DIARY
or
INTELLIGENCE SUMMARY

(Erase heading not required.)

Place	Date	Hour	Summary of Events and Information	Remarks and references to Appendices
BRAQUEMONT	5/11/17		Capt Stowe reported for duty. Visited No. 5. & inspected arrivals. Sn evacuation – Inspected sick arrivals of N.B, C. & D Batteries 59th Brigade R.F.A.	
"	6/11/17		Inspected sample cases in 58th Battery. 11th Brigade Canadian Artillery. Arranges for inspection – Inspected Nos 1 & 2 Sections of 5th Canadian F.A.C. Inspected lines of 61st & 66th F Batteries Canadian Artillery. Visited No. V.S.	
"	7/11/17		Inspected arrivals of 9th A.W. Bridge, 9th A.W. Yorks & 32nd Machine Gun Coy. – Visited No. V.S. Inspected arrivals of the 68 & 57th Field Coy. R.E. recruits arrived in the 6th Dorsets.	
"	8/11/17		Inspected surplus arrived for transfer in D.A.C. Visited No. V.S. & checked equipment being prepared over to been O.C. Inspected sick arrivals in 33rd Field Ambulance – vice arrived in 33rd Field Ambulance.	

Army Form C. 2118.

WAR DIARY
or
INTELLIGENCE SUMMARY
(Erase heading not required.)

Instructions regarding War Diaries and Intelligence Summaries are contained in F. S. Regs., Part II. and the Staff Manual respectively. Title Pages will be prepared in manuscript.

Place	Date	Hour	Summary of Events and Information	Remarks and references to Appendices
BRADUEMONT	9/11/17		Capt Stovel left to No 23 Veterinary Hospital. Conference of T.Os at my Office – Sr. V.S. inspected Sr. V.S. inspected Inspected cow inspected & 5 Slovakhi in P Battery 59 Brigade R.F.A. Called on O.C. Train	
"	10/11/17		Inspected animals for evacuation at Sr. V. S. Called on A.D.V.S. 1st Corps	
"	11/11/17		Inspected animals & lines of the B & D Batteries & A Battery 59 Brigade R.F.A. Sr. V.S. & inspected animals for evacuation Lines of 34th Field Ambulance	
"	12/11/17		Inspected animals of the 30th Dunchie from Co. " " " 67th Field Co R.E. " " " 33rd Dunchie from Co. Visited Sr. V. S. & Rep. officer of 1st Brigade Canadian Artillery	
"	13/11/17		Inspected Dethalania Engs in 58 +59 Brigades R.F.A. Arrival of " Gun Signal Co. – Visited Sr. V.S.	

Army Form C. 2118.

WAR DIARY
or
INTELLIGENCE SUMMARY
(Erase heading not required.)

Instructions regarding War Diaries and Intelligence Summaries are contained in F. S. Regs., Part II. and the Staff Manual respectively. Title Pages will be prepared in manuscript.

Place	Date	Hour	Summary of Events and Information	Remarks and references to Appendices
BEAUMONT	14/1/17		Inspected Blacksmiths and in No 3 Section of B.T.C.	
"			Arrived in No 2 Section B.T.C.	
"			Mrs B 38th Field Ambulance	
			Visited Sa V.S. & inspected & sent to C/o mobile Vety Section	
			I & Spika Service Corps	
"	15/1/17		Inspected arrivals of 86th Field & R.E.	
			" 9th Reserve Park	
			Conference of D.Dos at my office	
			Inspected Stun case in the 6th Lincolns Violet Sn. V.S.	
"	16/1/17		Inspected sick in No 1 Cav Train	
			" " moved to cavalry of Remount Records in Cobbley Leads	
			Visited Sn. V.S. & inspected animals for evacuation	
"	17/1/17		Attended Conference at office of A.D.V.S. 1st Corps	
			Inspected lions of 35th Field Ambulance	
			" arrivals for evacuation at Sn. V.S.	

2449 Wt. W14957/M90 750,000 1/16 J.B.C. & A. Forms/C.2118/12.

Army Form C. 2118

WAR DIARY
or
INTELLIGENCE SUMMARY
(Erase heading not required.)

Instructions regarding War Diaries and Intelligence Summaries are contained in F.S. Regs., Part II. and the Staff Manual respectively. Title Pages will be prepared in manuscript.

Place	Date	Hour	Summary of Events and Information	Remarks and references to Appendices
BRAQUEMONT	18/11/17		Inspected Remounts & sick animals in A Battery 58th Brigade R.F.A.	
"			Sick animals of 33rd field ambulance	
"			Suspicious Strangles Case in A Battery 59th Brigade R.F.A.	
"	19/11/17		Inspected sick animals of B, C, & D Batteries 58th Brigade R.F.A. Inspected lines of No 1 section D.T.C. visited to V.S.	
"	20/11/17		Inspected horse from C Battery 59th Brigade at C.V.S. Suspected Glanders case —	
"			Inspected lines 1st Corps	
"			Inspected lines of 53rd & 33rd Batteries 13th Brigade Canadian Artillery	
"			Inspected lines of 33rd Machine Gun Co.	
"			visited M.VS.	
"	21/11/17		Inspected Standings of D Battery 59th Brigade R.F.A.	
"			" Animals for evacuation at Sn.V.S.	
"			Arranges for sheltering of all animals in C Battery 59th Brigade R.F.A.	
"			Inspected Animals in Nos 2, 3, & 4 Coys Train	

Army Form C. 2118

WAR DIARY
or
INTELLIGENCE SUMMARY

(Erase heading not required.)

Instructions regarding War Diaries and Intelligence Summaries are contained in F.S. Regs., Part II. and the Staff Manual respectively. Title Pages will be prepared in manuscript.

Place	Date	Hour	Summary of Events and Information	Remarks and references to Appendices
BRAQUEMONT	22/11/17		Inspected Animals of 5th Greek-Venezelost Regt.	
"			" " " for Evacuation at Sn. V.S.	
"			" " " of Border Regt. & S. Staffords.	
"			" " " Uncle Maclean led in C Battery 39th Brigade R.F.A.	
"			70 Animal Uncle Maclean led in 39th Field Ambulance	
"			Sick Animal in 39th Field Ambulance	
"	23/11/17		Conference of V.Os at H.Q. Office	
"			Inspected Animals of B Battery 39th Brigade R.F.A.	
"			" " " C " " Uncle Maclean	
"			Test & one case of Stomatitis in Uno Battery	
"			Inspected Animals of D Battery 39th Brigade R.F.A.	
"			Visited Sn. V. S.	
"	24/11/17		Attended Conference at Office of A.D.V.S. 1st Corps	
"			Visited 46th Divn Sn V.S. Kerringes for Evacuation of Cases by Barge	
"			Inspected Stomatitis Cases in 33rd Field Ambulance with A.D.V.S. 1st Corps — Inspected Animals arrived for Evacuation	
"			at Sn. V. S.	

Army Form C. 2118

WAR DIARY
or
INTELLIGENCE SUMMARY
(Erase heading not required.)

Instructions regarding War Diaries and Intelligence Summaries are contained in F.S. Regs., Part II. and the Staff Manual respectively. Title Pages will be prepared in manuscript.

Place	Date	Hour	Summary of Events and Information	Remarks and references to Appendices
BEAUMONT	25/11/17		Inspected animals of the 250 Machine Gun Co	
"			" horse animals of 6th York & Lanc horse lines at Vauchassart	
"			Visited Div. V.S.	
"	26/11/17		Inspected animals of Sherwood Foresters, 6th Lineens, 32 Machine Gun Co. 6th F. Gun (8) & 68th Field 68 R.E.	
"			Inspected animals of "A" Battery 69th Brigade R.F.A.	
"			33rd Machine Gun Co	
"			Visited M.V.S. Inspected animal of evacuation	
"	27/11/17		Inspected horses 95 Remount at 46th Divn Train	
"			" " C, D, & B Batteries 58th Brigade R.F.A. with ADVS & CVPO	
"			Visited 35th field ambulance with ADVS	
"	28/11/17		Inspected horse of century of Remount Receiving in 60th, 61st & 66th Batteries 14th Brigade Canadian Artillery, Infeces all hung in 60th Battery C.F.A. Inspected animals of 88th field & R.E.	

1875 Wt. W593/826 1,000,000 4/15 J.B.C. & A. A.D.S.S./Forms/C. 2118.

WAR DIARY

INTELLIGENCE SUMMARY

Army Form C. 2118

Place	Date	Hour	Summary of Events and Information	Remarks and references to Appendices
BRAQUEMONT	28/11/15		Visited Sn. V.S. Inspected lines of 9th Reserve Park. A.D.V.S. 1st Corps went round 14th Brigade Ammunition Artillery with A.D.V.S. - Inspected lines from C/59th Brigade under treatment lost at Drouvin.	
"	29/11/15		D.D.V.S. 1st Army called & inspected animals of 59th Brigade R.F.A. Visited No. V.S. - Inspected animals of No 2 Section S.A.C. & 33rd Field Ambulance	
"	30/11/15		Inspected animals proposed for casting by Remount Command Nos 1 & 3 Section S.A.C. with A.D.V.S. 1st Corps. Attended P.M. examination on horse destroyed by flanders	

A.D.V.S.
Neufchatel
D.T.D.V.S. 1st Div.

Army Form C. 2118

WAR DIARY
or
INTELLIGENCE SUMMARY
(Erase heading not required.)

D.A.D.V.S.,
11TH DIVISION

Place	Date	Hour	Summary of Events and Information	Remarks and references to Appendices
BRAUVEMONT	1/12/17		Attended conference of A.D.V.S. 1st Corps. Inspected animals & watering at M.V.S. Inspected Elementaire lines in B Battery 58th Brigade R.F.A.	
"	2/12/17		Inspected lines of Strength in Northumberland Hrs. Visited HQ & S- Canadian DAC.	
"	3/12/17		Called on A.D.V.S. 1st Corps. Inspected animals of 52nd, 53rd & 55th Batteries 5th Div Canadian Artillery - Inspected animals of A, B + C Batteries 59th Brigade R.F.A. under Veterinary test - Visited M.V.S.	
"	4/12/17		Called on C.R.A. 5th Canadian Div Artillery - Inspected horse in B Battery 59th Brigade R.F.A. that wanted to Swallow - have been inspected animals for watering - Inspected lines & Cook Sunning Co - Visited Cupet Store - Inspected lines of Headquarters 58th Brigade R.F.A. Inspected lines of 38th Machine Gun Co - Visited A.D.V.S. 46th Divn	

WAR DIARY or INTELLIGENCE SUMMARY

Army Form C. 2118

Place	Date	Hour	Summary of Events and Information	Remarks and references to Appendices
BRAQUEMONT	5/12/17		Inspected horse lines of the 6th Arty & Lines & 6th Yorkshire Regt. Lines of 58th Brigade & 6th R.E. Visited horse lines of 6th Battn. Visited A.V.S. Attended D.V. examination on a horse of "B" Battery. 58th Brigade R.F.A. Destroyer in Flanders. Inspected lines of 38th Field Ambulance.	
"	6/12/17		Inspected arrivals of B & C Batteries & 59th Brigade RFA under Veterinary test – Visited No 23 Vety Hospital at Omer.	
"	7/12/17		Conference of V.Os at Army Office – Called on C.R.A. 11 Division. Inspected lines of C & D Batteries 58th Brigade under Veterinary test. Visited S.V.S.	
"	8/12/17		Attended Conference of ADVS 1st Corps – Inspected arrival of 57th Battery 5th Bde Canadian Artillery & No 1 Coy 5th Canadian Div. Train – Visited Corps mobile Vety Sect.	
"	9/12/17		Inspected horse lines of 58th & 59th Brigades R.F.A. & 11 D.V.C. C.R.A. 11 Div.	

Army Form C. 2118

WAR DIARY or INTELLIGENCE SUMMARY
(Erase heading not required.)

Instructions regarding War Diaries and Intelligence Summaries are contained in F.S. Regs., Part II. and the Staff Manual respectively. Title Pages will be prepared in manuscript.

D.A.D.V.S.
11th DIVISION

Place	Date	Hour	Summary of Events and Information	Remarks and references to Appendices
BRAQUEMONT	10/12/17		Inspected arrival of 6th Yorkshire Regt, Gull & Lewas & 33rd Brigade Headquarters " Strength Coys in Northumberland Div. & King & Kennar Sec. " Lines of lection & 9th Reserve Park " Dairy Mue in 55th Couvrain Siv. Artillery " " " " in 55th Poultry " Loves MH Removals at No 1 Coy Train	
"	11/12/17		Inspected arrival of Dr.V.S & arrival of D.T.C. under Dudlein Inspected arrival of Nos 1 & 2 Coy Train Test	
"	12/12/17		Inspected Animals & 8th W. Riding, 9th W. Yorks, & 32nd Machine gun Co " " hrs of 36th Field Ambulance	
"	13/12/17		Visited Dr.V.S & V.O. % 5th Div Canadian D.T.C. Inspected arrival of 11th D.T.C. under Dudlein Test " hrs of 33rd Field Ambulance - Cases on Ads. 1 Corps	
"	14/12/17		Conference & V.O. at my Office - Visited Dr.V.S & arranged to drive it to Brugnemont - Inspected hrs of S.H.R. & Br.& Fee Ambulance	

Army Form C. 2118.

D.A.D.V.S.
11TH DIVISION.

WAR DIARY
or
INTELLIGENCE SUMMARY
(Erase heading not required.)

Instructions regarding War Diaries and Intelligence Summaries are contained in F. S. Regs., Part II. and the Staff Manual respectively. Title Pages will be prepared in manuscript.

Place	Date	Hour	Summary of Events and Information	Remarks and references to Appendices
BRAQUEMONT	15/12/17		Attended Conference of A.D.V.S. 1st Corps – Called on D.D.V.S. 1st Army. Visited M.V.S.	
"	16/12/17		Inspected Arrivals for evacuation at M.V.S. of "C" Battery 58th Brigade R.F.A.	
"	17/12/17		Inspected Arrivals of 9 Lancashire Fus. Northumberland Ins – 33rd Machine Gun Co – Inspected Animals for evacuation at M.V.S. Inspected Arrivals of 11th Manchesters & 34th Hampshire Pnr Co. Inspected Sick in 55th Battery 3rd Divisional Div. Artillery	
"	18/12/17		Inspected Sick horse terminal of "D" Battery 58th Brigade R.F.A. " horses for evacuation of E Battery 59th Brigade R.F.A. " Arrivals of "A" Battery 58th Brigade R.F.A.	
"	19/12/17		Inspected Animals for evacuation at Br. V.S. Arrival of 11th D.V. Signal Co. Inspected Sick animals in 33rd Field Ambulance Called on A.D.V.S. 1st Corps	

Army Form C. 2118.

D.A.D.V.S.
11TH DIVISION.

WAR DIARY
or
INTELLIGENCE SUMMARY
(Erase heading not required.)

Instructions regarding War Diaries and Intelligence Summaries are contained in F. S. Regs., Part II. and the Staff Manual respectively. Title Pages will be prepared in manuscript.

Place	Date	Hour	Summary of Events and Information	Remarks and references to Appendices
BRAQUEMONT	20/10/17		Inspected animals for evacuation at Sn. V. S. & hers 61c 7th Sn. V. S at Labeuvriere & these arrived in 33rd Field Ambulance	
"	21/10/17		Conference of V.Os at hay Office — Inspected R.O. 7th Sn. V. S. at Hesdigneuil — Visited A.D.V.S. 1st Corps — Visited D.A.D.V.S. 4th → Divn.	
"	22/10/17		Attended conference of A.D.V.S. 1st Corps — Inspected sick horse lines of 6th Border Regt. 34th Field Ambulance. Lame sub & sickened sub.	
LABEUVRIERE	23/10/17		Drove with D.H.Q. from BRAQUEMONT to LABEUVRIERE. Inspected sick horse standing of 33rd Brigade, No 2 Coy train. 11th Stonshiers + 5th Dorsets — Visited Sn. V. S.	
"	24/10/17		Visited Sn. V. S. Inspected animals of D Battery 35th Brigade R.F.A. Inspected sick animals of 33rd Field Ambulance	
"	25/10/17		Visited Sn. V. S. & inspected animals for evacuation — Inspected animals 6th Lincoln Regt. 33rd Machine Gun Co + 7th S. Staffords. Inspected her horse lines of 65 R field & RE 32 + 34 Machine Gun Co	

WAR DIARY or INTELLIGENCE SUMMARY

Army Form C. 2118.

D.A.D.V.S.
11th DIVISION.

Place	Date	Hour	Summary of Events and Information	Remarks and references to Appendices
LA BEUVRIÈRE	26/12/17		Inspection of horses by Remounts at Aire. Remount return Murder to Wing. Arrivals of 30th Artn. to V.S. & the 6th E. York. (9)	
"	27/12/17		Inspection Arrivals of Nos 1,2,3 & 4 Coys. Brigns. - finished day V.S. T. Inspected Animals for evacuation - Visits Corps Vet. O.	
"	28/12/17		Inspected Arrivals of 230 Machine Gun Co. & B Battery 59th Brigade R.F.A. " " " of 67th Divn. to V.E.	
"	29/12/17		Attended Conference at Office of Hours of Corps.	
"	30/12/17		Visits Div. V.S. & inspected Animals for evacuation.	
"	31/12/17		Inspected hres of B. Battery 59th Brigade R.F.A. & others sent in & Battery 59th Brigade R.S.A. - Visits Div. V.S.	

Chadwick
D.A.D.V.S. 11th Divn.
5HSTB 1/1/18

Army Form W.3091.

Cover for Documents.

Vol 19

Nature of Enclosures.

Confidential
War Diary of
Major J.W. O'Kelly
D.A.D.V.S. - 11th Division
1-1-18 to 31-1-18.

Notes, or Letters written.

WAR DIARY or INTELLIGENCE SUMMARY

Army Form C. 2118

Place	Date	Hour	Summary of Events and Information	Remarks and references to Appendices
LABEUVRIERE	1/1/18		Visited the V.S. Took over duties of A.D.V.S. 1st Corps during absence of A.D.V.S.	
"	2/1/18		Inspected sick animals in "A" & "C" Batteries 59th Brigade R.F.A. Arrivals for evacuation at the V.S. Arrivals of 33rd Divisional Train Co. Starting of Officers horse in Bethune. Visited 46th Div. Mob V.S. Arrivals of 32nd Machine Gun Co. – Visited Corps Mob V.D.	
"	3/1/18		Inspected arrivals of 68th Siege Co. R.E. & 7th S. Staffords	
"	4/1/18		Inspected Arrivals of 8th Northumberland Fus, Lancashire Fus & 34th Machine Gun Co. – Visited Corps Mob V.D. Visited the V.S. & inspected arrivals for evacuation. Seen conference of V.Os at my office	
"	5/1/18		Sick conference of S.D.V.S. 1st Army – Inspected arrivals of 11th Manchester. Visited S.D.V.S. 1st Army.	
"	6/1/18		Inspected arrivals for evacuation at Corps Mob V.D.	

Army Form C. 2118

WAR DIARY
or
INTELLIGENCE SUMMARY
(Erase heading not required.)

Place	Date	Hour	Summary of Events and Information	Remarks and references to Appendices
LABEUVRIERE	7/1/18		Suspects some men cars in 124 Heavy Battery at Houchin + in 17th Heavy Battery at Drouvin - visited in V.S. Suspects arrived of 5th Dorset Regt. + 86th Field Co R.E., 250 Machine Gun Co + No 1 Section D.A.C.	
	8/1/18		Suspects visited 39 Remounts at Hesdin-les-Mines " Arrivals of Evacuation at No V.S. " Arrival of 6th Field Lance + 67 Field Co R.E. Called on SDVS. " " " " Battalion cars at Corps Hr. V.D.	
	9/1/18		Suspects see Battalion cars at Corps Hr V.D. " Nos 2 + 3 Sections D.A.C.	
	10/1/18		Suspects arrival in Evacuation at No V.S. + some Mni cars in "D" Battery 59th Brigade R.F.A.- Suspects arrived of 6th Dorset Regt. - Remounts of Sherwood Foresters -	
	11/1/18		Held Conference of M.Os at Army HQrs - Suspects Removal of 6th E. Yorks (P) + 6th Lincolns - Suspects visited 3 horse clip at Bethune visited Corps Hr V.D.	

1875 Wt. W593/826 1,000,000 4/15 J.B.C. & A. A.D.S.S./Forms/C. 2118.

WAR DIARY
INTELLIGENCE SUMMARY

Army Form C. 2118.

Place	Date	Hour	Summary of Events and Information	Remarks and references to Appendices
LA BEUVRIERE	12/1/18		Attended Conference of D.A.D.V.S. Divisions at 1st Corps. ADVS Ophthalmic cure in Corps Bn. V.D. Visited Mr V.S.	
"	13/1/18		Inspected Animals of "C" Battery 59th Brigade & C Battery 58th Brigade. ADVS 1st Corps returned cases to act as ADVS 1st Corps. Animals for evacuation visited Mr V.S. & inspected	
"	14/1/18		Inspected Animals of "B" & "D" Batteries 59th Brigade R.F.A. " " for evacuation at Mr V.S. Inspected animals of 34th & 35th Field Ambulances. Visited ADVS 46th Division re arranged taking over site for Mr V.S.	
"	15/1/18		Inspected Animals of 11th Divn Signal Co. & 33rd Field Ambulance. " " for evacuation at Mr V.S. " 65th Field Co R.E. visited Mr V.S at Bethune	
"	16/1/18		Inspected Animals of 9th Sherwood Foresters, 6th Yorkshire Regt, 6th W. Yorks. Called on A.D.V.S 1st Corps	

Army Form C. 2118.

WAR DIARY
or
INTELLIGENCE SUMMARY

(Erase heading not required.)

Instructions regarding War Diaries and Intelligence Summaries are contained in F. S. Regs., Part II. and the Staff Manual respectively. Title Pages will be prepared in manuscript.

Place	Date	Hour	Summary of Events and Information	Remarks and references to Appendices
LABEUVRIERE	17/1/18		Inspected sick animals in A. & B. Batteries 58th Brigade R.F.A. Held conference of Arrivals for evacuation at Sn.V.S. Vets at Bdy office –	
"	18/1/18		Inspected arrivals of A & D Batteries 58th Brigade R.F.A. – Visited Sn.V.S. Of 33rd Machine Gun Co.	
"	19/1/18		Attended conference at office of A.D.V.S. 1st Corps – Inspected animals of 2nd W. Riding Regt. Visited H.Q. Ye 58th Brigade R.F.A.	
"	20/1/18		Inspected Arrivals of 'B' Battery 58th Brigade R.F.A. & A Battery 59th Brigade R.F.A. Visited Sn.V.S. & inspected arrivals for evacuation – Visits H.Q. Ye 3rd Inf. Brigade	
"	21/1/18		Visited Sn.V.S. – Called on A.D.V.S. 1st Corps	
"	22/1/18		Handed over duties of A.D.V.S. to Capt Scott	
"	23/1/18		Proceeded on leave –	

War Diary.

of Major J.W. O'Kelly. AVC.
     DADVS. 11. Divⁿ.

February 1918.

WAR DIARY
INTELLIGENCE SUMMARY

(Erase heading not required.)

Army Form C. 2118.

Place	Date	Hour	Summary of Events and Information	Remarks and references to Appendices
SAILLY LABOURSE	6/2/18		Returned from leave	
"	7/2/18		Ordinary duties	
"	8/2/18		Held conference of Vety Officers at my Office - Inspected animals of 8th S.W. Derby regt. + 6th E. Yorks. (P) + sick animals of 5th S. Staffs + 9th W. Yorks - Inspected animals of 32nd + 34th Machine Gun Coys - Visited the V.S. + inspected animals for evacuation	
"	9/2/18		Attended conference of A.D.V.S. 1st Army - Inspected animals of 33rd Machine Gun Co + 62nd Porter Regt.	
"	10/2/18		Inspected animals of 68th Siege Co R.E. + sick animals in "C" + "D" Batteries 58th Brigade R.F.A. Inspected + viewed 138 remounts at D.A.C. lines - Inspected sick animals in No 1 + 2 Sections 257th Kennelly Coy. + Visited the V.S. Inspected horse of 257th Kennelly Coy.	

Army Form C. 2118.

WAR DIARY
or
INTELLIGENCE SUMMARY
(Erase heading not required.)

Place	Date	Hour	Summary of Events and Information	Remarks and references to Appendices
SAILLY LABOURSE	11/2/18		Inspected Animals of 6th Yorkshire Regt., 6th York & Lancs, 9th W. Yorks. Headquarters 55th Brigade R.F.A. & 32nd Infantry Brigade. Inspected Sick Animals in "B", "C" & "D" Batteries 55th Brigade R.F.A. " Animals of 9th Lancer Fus. & 8th Northumberland Fus. Visited the v.S. Collect or M.D.V.S. 1st Corps	
"	12/2/18		Inspected animals of 7th L.S. Staff, 6th Lincoln, & 9th Sherwood Foresters " " of "C" Battery 56th Brigade R.F.A.	
"	13/2/18		Inspected Animals of the 86th Field Co R.E. 56D Heavy Hospo Co R.E. & 116 Labour Co. Inspected Animals for evacuation at the v.S. Headquarters Inspected Animals of "B" Battery 58th Brigade R.F.A. & Headquarters 58th Brigade R.F.A.	
"	14/2/18		Inspected animals of the 5th Dorsets & 11th Dorsetshire Regt. " " of "B" Battery 55th Brigade R.F.A.	

Army Form C. 2118.

WAR DIARY
or
INTELLIGENCE SUMMARY

(Erase heading not required.)

Instructions regarding War Diaries and Intelligence Summaries are contained in F. S. Regs., Part II. and the Staff Manual respectively. Title Pages will be prepared in manuscript.

Place	Date	Hour	Summary of Events and Information	Remarks and references to Appendices
SAILLY LA BOURSE	15/2/18		Visited M.V.S. & inspected Animals for evacuation	
"	16/2/18		Steel conference of V.Os at my Office	
			Attended Conference of A.D.V.S. 1st Corps — Went with A.D.V.S. to select site for Veterinary Casualty Clearing Station	
"	17/2/18		Inspected Animals of B, D & C Batteries 59th Brigade R.F.A.	
			" " of 250th Machine Gun Coy	
"	18/2/18		Inspected Animals for evacuation at M.V.S. met A.D.V.S. 1st Army	
			" Site Aviines in No 2 Coy Train	
			" Animals of A & D Batteries 58th Brigade R.F.A.	
			" " of 34th Field Ambulance	
"	19/2/18		Inspected Animals of 67th Selen C.R.E. & 33rd Field Ambulance	
			" of Nos 1 & 2 Sections S.A.C.	
"	20/2/18		Inspected Animals of "A" Battery 55th Brigade R.F.A.	
			" " of Nos 3 & 4 Coy Train	
			" " at M.V.S.	

Army Form C. 2118.

WAR DIARY
or
INTELLIGENCE SUMMARY
(Erase heading not required.)

Place	Date	Hour	Summary of Events and Information	Remarks and references to Appendices
SAILLY LABOURSE	21/2/18		Inspected arrivals of 35th Field Ambulance + lines of No 3 Section D.A.C. Inspected arrivals of Nos 1 & 2 Corps Train	
"	22/2/18		Inspected Sick arrivals in 86 Field Co R.E. Visited M.V.S. Inspected arrivals for innoculation – held conference of Sgts at own office	
"	23/2/18		Inspected arrivals of 11th Divn Signal Co. Attended conference at office of A.D.V.S. 1st Corps	
"	24/2/18		Inspected sick arrivals in "B" Battery 39th Brigade R.F.A. Visited No. 4 5th Army Field Artillery Brigade & inspected horses. Debelt-Coos in 73rd Battery 5th Army F.A.B. Inspected arrivals of 68th Field Co R.E. Visited M.V.S.	
VERQUIN	25/2/18		Moved with D.H.Q. from SAILLY LABOURSE to VERQUIN. Inspected arrivals of "A", "B" & "D" 5th Batteries 5th Army Field Artillery Brigade. " " " 468 Field Co R.E. (46th Divn) " " for innoculation at M.V.S. which arrived of 33rd Field Amb.	

2449 Wt. W14957/M90 750,000 1/16 J.B.C. & A. Forms/C.2118/12.

Army Form C. 2118.

WAR DIARY
or
INTELLIGENCE SUMMARY
(Erase heading not required.)

Instructions regarding War Diaries and Intelligence Summaries are contained in F. S. Regs., Part II. and the Staff Manual respectively. Title Pages will be prepared in manuscript.

Place	Date	Hour	Summary of Events and Information	Remarks and references to Appendices
VERDUIN	26/2/18		Inspected sick arrivals in Dorset Regt. Inspected horse lines of 67th Field Co. R.E. Inspected arrivals of 32nd, 33rd & 34th Machine Gun Coys. " " 6th Border Regt. & 33rd Brigade Headquarters " " No 3 Section D.A.C.	
"	27/2/18		Visited the V.S. Inspected sick arrivals in 11th Div. Signal Coy.	
"	28/2/18		Inspected arrivals for evacuation at the V.S. " " 7th N.S. Staffords. " & issued 103 Remounts at No 2 Coy D.A.C. Called on A.D.V.S. 1st Corps	J.O'Reilly Lieut/Col. D.A.D.V.S. 11th Div.

DADVS/11 D

War Diary
of
D.A.D.V.S. & 22nd Mob. Vet. Section
for March, 1918
11th Division

Army Form C. 2118.

WAR DIARY
or
INTELLIGENCE SUMMARY.
(Erase heading not required.)

Instructions regarding War Diaries and Intelligence Summaries are contained in F.S. Regs., Part II. and the Staff Manual respectively. Title pages will be prepared in manuscript.

Place	Date	Hour	Summary of Events and Information	Remarks and references to Appendices
VERQUIN	1/3/18		Visited sen V.S. & inspected Arrival of evacuation. Held Conference of Vety-Officers at my Office	
"	2/3/18		Ordinary duties	
	3/3/18		Inspected Arrivals of 6th Battery, 5th Army Sick Ashley Purse & 468 Area C.R.E. 46th Divn Inspected Arrivals of B.A.C. 5th D.A.B.	
	4/3/18		Inspected Arrivals of 73rd Battery 5th Army S.A.B. Visited sen V.S. Inspected Arrivals of evacuation.	
"	5/3/18		Visited sen V.S. Inspected Arrivals of 6th E. Yorks (P). 8th P.W. Ridings & Stagonothis 32nd Brigade. Inspected Arrival of No 102 Section D.A.C. Called on A.D.V.S. 1st Corps	
	6/3/18		Attended Casting board by D.D.R. Ste Anny - Inspected Arrival of 81st Battery 5th Army D.A.B. Inspected units of 64th Battery R.F.A.	

Army Form C. 2118.

WAR DIARY
or
INTELLIGENCE SUMMARY.
(Erase heading not required.)

Instructions regarding War Diaries and Intelligence Summaries are contained in F. S. Regs., Part II. and the Staff Manual respectively. Title pages will be prepared in manuscript.

Place	Date	Hour	Summary of Events and Information	Remarks and references to Appendices
VERQUIN	7/3/18		Inspected arrival of 2/5- Batty 5th Army F.A.B.	
"	8/3/18		" " 73rd " "	Held conference
"			of D.D. at my office	
"	9/3/18		Inspected arrivals for evacuation at Fn. V.S.	
			Inspected arrivals of 6th Division, 7th S. Staffs, 6th Border. 9th Sherwood Foresters, Headquarters 33rd Inf. Brigade. attended conference of A.D.V.S. 1st Corps.	
"	10/3/18		Inspected arrivals of 11- Div. Signal Coy & 11- Div. Signal Coy	
"	11/3/18		Inspected arrivals of A & B Batteries 59th Brigade R.F.A. for evacuation at Fn. V.S. 11- British Machine Gun Coy	
"	12/3/18		Inspected arrival of A.B. & C Coys 11- British Machine Gun Coy & D Batty 59th Brigade R.F.A.	

WAR DIARY
or
INTELLIGENCE SUMMARY.

Army Form C. 2118.

Place	Date	Hour	Summary of Events and Information	Remarks and references to Appendices
VERQUIN	13/3/18		Inspected arrivals of 11th Stevedore Coys. 67th Field Coy R.E. 5th Dorset Regt. Visited burrs & inspected arrivals of evacuation. Inspected arrivals of 330th Field Ambulance & some Officers Camps in Nos 1 & 3 Corps areas.	
"	14/3/18		Inspected sick cases in Nos 1 & 2 Stationary DHQ. Visited the N.S. & inspected arrival of evacuation. Inspected lines of "A" "B" & "C" Batteries 58th Brigade R.G.A.	
"	15/3/18		Inspected arrivals of 7th W. Yorks. & lines of 68th Field Co R.E. & No 2 Coy Irwin. Visited the N.S. & A & B Batty 57th Brigade R.G.A. & Pay Office - Inspected lines of A & B Batty 59th Brigade R.G.A. & 1st Corps 11th Batt. Sunshine Gun Cops. net N.O.V.S. 1st Corps	
"	16/3/18		Inspected equipment of M.V.S. Allanies Conference of Aosts Septs & 6th Yorkshire Regt & C Battery 59th Brigade R.G.A.	
"	17/3/18		Inspected arrivals of visited the N.S. & inspected arrival for evacuation.	

Army Form C. 2118.

WAR DIARY
or
INTELLIGENCE SUMMARY.
(Erase heading not required.)

Place	Date	Hour	Summary of Events and Information	Remarks and references to Appendices
VERQUIN	18/3/18		Inspected Arrival of the 86th & 68th Field Coy R.E. - Inspected Harness of the 64th, 73rd & 81st Batteries 5th Army B of R.F.A. Inspected Wounded Animals in No 3 cat. D.H.S.	
"	19/3/18		Arrival for Evacuation at Ser. V. S. Inspected reserve Harness at No 1 Coy Trains. Visited Ser. V. S.	
"	20/3/18		Inspected D.H.Q. Horses & arrival for Evacuation at Ser V. S. Inspected Animals of 8th North. Sub. 9th Lewis Inf. 2nd Lewis Inf. Headquarters	
"	21/3/18		III Brigade & 6 E. Yorks (P) & No.s 1 & 3 Corps Reserve. Attended Conference held by D.V.S. at	
"	22/3/18		Visited Ser. V. S. Sillers.	
"	23/3/18		Inspected Animals of A & B Batteries 59th Brigade R.F.A. for Evacuation at Ser V. S.	
"	"			

Army Form C. 2118.

WAR DIARY
or
INTELLIGENCE SUMMARY.
(Erase heading not required.)

Place	Date	Hour	Summary of Events and Information	Remarks and references to Appendices
VERQUIN	24/3/18		Inspected Slices lines at Verquigneul & lines of 86th & 67th Field Coys R.E. Inspected Sick animals in 5th Divnl - Inspected arrival of 8th W. Ridings & 6th York & Lancs.	
	25/3/18		Inspected arrival of B & C Batteries 58th Brigade R.F.A. Pekited No V.S. called in ADVS 1st Corps	
	26/3/18		Inspected arrival of 31st Field Ambulance took arrival in 5th Divnl wounded in St Bretay 5th Army Bde R.F.A. Inspected arrival of No 3 Cav. S.H.C Kanninal sh Lancashire Inspected arrival of No 1 2nd Corps Hreion at Mt. V.S. Inspected arrival of 5th Army Bde R.F.A. Sick in 73 Bdy.	
	27/3/18		Visited Divs. Inspected wounded animals in No 3 Cav. S.H.C & St Bretay 5th Army Bde R.F.A. Inspected arrival of 34th Divl Vet. Lant.	
	28/3/18		Inspected arrival of A Batty 58th Brigade R.F.A. Inspected & Issued 90 Remounts at No 1 Coy Hreion - Inspected arrival of No 1 Sect. S.A.C.	

WAR DIARY or INTELLIGENCE SUMMARY

Army Form C. 2118

Place	Date	Hour	Summary of Events and Information	Remarks and references to Appendices
VERQUIN	29/3/18		Inspected Animals of "D" Battery 58th Brigade R.F.A. & animals of 9th Sherwood Foresters - Inspected animals of No 4 Special Coy R.E. + 251 Tunnelling Coy -	
"	30/3/18		Attended Conference of A.D.V.S. 1st Corps - Visited Sec. V.S. - Inspected Animals for inoculation -	
"	31/3/18		Ordinary duties - Visited Sec. V.S. -	

Boswell
Veterinarian -
A.D.V.S. 11th Div.

(6339) Wt. W160/M3016 1,500,000 10/17 McA & W Ltd (E1898) Forms W3091.   Army Form W.3091.

Cover for Documents.

Nature of Enclosures.

Confidential

War Diary of
Major J. W. O'Kelly. A.V.C.
D.A.D.V.S. 11th Div.

from 1/4/18 — 30/4/18

Notes, or Letters written.

Army Form C. 2118.

WAR DIARY
or
INTELLIGENCE SUMMARY
(Erase heading not required.)

Instructions regarding War Diaries and Intelligence Summaries are contained in F. S. Regs., Part II. and the Staff Manual respectively. Title pages will be prepared in manuscript.

Place	Date	Hour	Summary of Events and Information	Remarks and references to Appendices
VERQUIN	1/4/18		Inspected Arrivals of 116th Labour Coy = 86th Field Coy R.E. Inspected Lines of 64th Batty 5th Army Bde R.F.A. Inspected detachment of M.V.S. at Bethune. Inspected Horse Lines in 73rd Batty 5th Army Bde R.F.A.	
"	2/4/18		Inspected with A.D.V.S. 1st Corps. Arrivals of 81st 305th 362nd & 473rd Batteries 5th Army Bde R.F.A.	
"	3/4/18		Inspected Arrivals of "A" & "D" Batteries 84th Army Bde R.F.A. " " 116th Labour Co. & 7th Field Survey Coy " of B.A.C. 84th Army Bde R.F.A. & Headquarters " Inspected Arrivals of Advanced in D Batty 59th Bde R.F.A. 58th Reserve R.F.A. Inspected wounded Animals in D Batty 59th Bde R.F.A. on V.S.	
"	4/4/18		Inspected Arrivals of "C" & "B" Batteries 82nd Army Bde R.F.A. " " of 67 & 68th Field Coys R.E. " " " " for evacuation at M.V.S.	

Army Form C. 2113.

WAR DIARY
or
INTELLIGENCE SUMMARY.
(Erase heading not required.)

Place	Date	Hour	Summary of Events and Information	Remarks and references to Appendices
VERDUN	5/4/18		Inspected Arrivals of 11 & 12 Bolby Machine Guns Corps. Held conference of Los at HQ Offices. Visited the M.S. & Inspected Arrival for Evacuation treatment & Gatherines – Under treatment & Gatherines –	
"	6/4/18		Inspected transport lines of 33rd Infy Brigade attached conference of A.D.V.S. 12 Corps	
"	7/4/18		Called on A.D.V.S. 11 Corps. & arrangement about evacuation by train. Visited No 23 Veterinary Hospital at Orier. Also A.D.V.S. Corps & 35th Field Ambulance	
"	8/4/18		Inspected Arrivals of 5 Utrecht & Ambulances. "C" Bulley 59 Brigade R.F.A. & 231 Armoury Sec Lab & S.	
"	9/4/18		Inspected lines of 46 & 107 Army R.F.C. 5 E Army Bde R.F.A. Inspected Service of 33rd Field Ambulance Mob. Pthsy & Disc. Inspected Arrival for Evacuation at M.V.S. Visits No 113 Cry & 2 & Remount Sqn & F.W. Bulley	
"	10/4/18		Review – Inspected Arrivals F 7 & 8 Review & Roman 2	

Army Form C. 2113.

WAR DIARY
or
INTELLIGENCE SUMMARY

(Erase heading not required.)

Instructions regarding War Diaries and Intelligence Summaries are contained in F. S. Regs., Part II. and the Staff Manual respectively. Title pages will be prepared in manuscript.

Place	Date	Hour	Summary of Events and Information	Remarks and references to Appendices
VERQUIN	11/4/18		Inspected Arrivals of 81st Bde + Headquarters 5th Army R.F.A. Brigade. Visited A.D.V.S. 1st Corps - Visited detachment of Bn. V.S. at Bethune + "A" Batty 5th Army R.F.A. Brigade - Inspected Animals for evacuation at Bn. V.S.	
"	12/4/18		Inspected Animals infected with Lice in No 1 Rest D.T.C. Visited Bn. V.S. Held Conference of Vety Officers at my Office	
"	13/4/18		Attended Conference at Office of A.D.V.S. 1st Corps. Inspected Animals for evacuation at Bn V.S.	
"	14/4/18		Inspected lines of "A" + "B" Batteries 59th Brigade R.F.A. Arrivals of 81st + 73rd Batteries 5th Army R.F.A. Brigade	
"	15/4/18		Inspected Arrivals of Northumberland Hus, 5th Dorsets + Headquarters of 34th Infy Brigade - Inspected received 28 accounts at No 1 Cvy Train Brouin - Passed with D.H.Q. from Verquin to Braquemont.	
BRACQUEMONT	16/4/18		Inspected Arrivals of H.Q.rs. 33rd Inf Brigade, 6th Lincoln, 9th Sherwoods + 7th S. Staffs. - Inspected Arrivals for evacuation at Bn V.S.	

Army Form C. 2118.

WAR DIARY
INTELLIGENCE SUMMARY.
(Erase heading not required.)

Instructions regarding War Diaries and Intelligence Summaries are contained in F. S. Regs., Part II. and the Staff Manual respectively. Title pages will be prepared in manuscript.

Place	Date	Hour	Summary of Events and Information	Remarks and references to Appendices
BRACQUEMONT	17/4/18		Inspected "A" + "B" Coys 115th Battn Machine Gun Coy - Inspected lines of 33rd Field Ambulance - Inspected arrival of R.W. Gowns, 1st Gordon Lowry + lines of 86th Field Coy R.E. - Inspected arrival of Headquarters 32nd Bty Brigade + their arrival in D.A.C. Visits A.D.V.S. 1st Corps	
	18/4/18		Inspected arrival of "C" + "B" Batteries 58th Brigade R.F.A. + lines of No 2 Section D.A.C. + C. Bty 59th 4th Brigade R.F.A. Inspected arrival of Headquarters 58th 2nd Brigade R.F.A. -	
	19/4/18		Inspected arrival of C + D Coys 1st Battn Ambulance from Coy. 35th Field Ambulance. " " D W.O.S at day Office - Inspected arrival for Held Conference of M.V.S. evacuation at M.V.S.	
	20/4/18		Attended Conference of A.D.V.S. 1st Corps - Inspected horses arrival in 6th Battery 5th Army R.F.A. Brigade -	
	21/4/18		Inspected arrival of "A" Battery 58th Brigade R.F.A. visit of 73rd Battn 5th Army R.F.A. Bde. Visits Veth Evacuating Station at Berlin	

WAR DIARY or INTELLIGENCE SUMMARY

Army Form C. 2118.

Place	Date	Hour	Summary of Events and Information	Remarks and references to Appendices
BRACQUEMONT	22/4/18		Inspected Animals of A & B & D Batteries 59th Brigade R.F.A. & 34th Field Ambulance - Visited Sen. V.S.	
"			" of 2 Co. Train Brown - Inspected	
	23/4/18		Inspected, viewed Remounts at No.1 Coy Train Brown - Inspected Nos 1 & 2 Rest/vin S.T.C. Visits Remount Section at Marles les Mines Crossed on 4 D.V.S. 1st Corps - Inspects arrived for remounts at Sen. V.S.	
	24/4/18		Inspected Animals of 67th & 68th Siege Coys R.E. & No.3 Section S.T.C. " " for remounts at Sen. V.S. Visited Veterinary Evacuating Station at Burbine	
	25/4/18		Inspected Lines of Nos 1, 2, 3 & 4 Coys Trains - Visited Sen. V.S.	
	26/4/18		Inspected lines of B & D Batteries 58th Brigade R.F.A. & "B", "C", & "D" 59th Brigade R.F.A. Selected site for Sen. V.S. Held conference of Vety Officers at Brigade -	

Army Form C. 2118.

WAR DIARY

~~INTELLIGENCE SUMMARY~~

(Erase heading not required.)

Place	Date	Hour	Summary of Events and Information	Remarks and references to Appendices
BRACQUEMONT	27/4/18		Attended conference of ADMS 1st Corps - Visited 16.23 left Hospital St Omer -	
"	28/4/18		Inspected arrivals of 88 Field Co. R.E., Macquencourt OH.D. Infmd Coy for concentration at Seyus.	
"	29/4/18		Inspected arrivals of D Batty 58th Anysons R.F.A & C Batty 58 A/Anysone R.F.A. Nos 1 & 3 Corps Review	
"	30/4/18		Inspected arrivals of 64th Sqdn. Nos 2 & 4 Corps Review. Green Border 11th Public trenches from Corps - Called on ADMS 1st Corps - Visited 6 & K.S.	

Absolutely
Major etc
ADMS 11 Div

War Diary
DADVS
May 1918

Army Form C. 2118.

WAR DIARY
INTELLIGENCE SUMMARY.
(Erase heading not required.)

Place	Date	Hour	Summary of Events and Information	Remarks and references to Appendices
BRACQUEMONT	1/5/18		Inspected Lines of S.A.C. Visited Sen. V.S.	
"	2/5/18		Inspected Lines of 34th Divl Train. Visited Sen. V.S. & inspected animals. Visited Remount Section at Menenlau les Soins for evacuation.	
"	3/5/18		Inspected animals of the 4th Batty & the 4th Batty of the 4th Group Portuguese Artillery. Also 3rd Batty. Held conference of Vety Officers at Hrq Office. Inspected animals for evacuation at Sen. V.S.	
"	4/5/18		Attended conference of A.D.V.S. 1st Corps. Visited Sen. V.S. & inspected Lines of 1st Port Cav Squad.	
"	5/5/18		Inspected animals of No1 Batty 4th Group Portuguese Artillery	
"	6/5/18		Inspected Lines of 32nd & 33rd Divl Brigades & "C" Batty 55th Trench Bty. Visited Sen. V.S. & inspected animals for evacuation.	
"	7/5/18		Inspected animals of Headquarters & No 6th Group Portuguese Artillery. Visited A.D.V.S. 1st Corps. Inspected horse & mules ambulance	

Army Form C. 2118.

WAR DIARY
INTELLIGENCE SUMMARY.
(Erase heading not required.)

Instructions regarding War Diaries and Intelligence Summaries are contained in F. S. Regs., Part II. and the Staff Manual respectively. Title pages will be prepared in manuscript.

Place	Date	Hour	Summary of Events and Information	Remarks and references to Appendices
BRACQUEMONT	8/5/18		Visited Nieurpont Section Mons. Co. Divns - Inspected lines of "A" & "B" Batteries 59th Brigade R.F.A. Inspected animals & lines of Nos. 1 & 2 S. Section	
"	9/5/18		Inspected lines of 60th Bties & R.E. & lines of "A" Bty, 58th Brigade R.F.A.	
"	10/5/18		Inspected lines of "B" Bnty 59th Brigade R.F.A. Inspected animals & horses at M.V.S. Interviewed & left papers at Army Office	
"	11/5/18		Attended conference of A.D.V.S. Corps	
"	12/5/18		Called on O.C. 4th Group Divisional Artillery	
"	13/5/18		Inspected animals & horses in 4th Group Divisional Artillery & 217 A.T. Coy R.E. Handed in ranches at M.V.S. 1st Corps	
"	14/5/18		Inspected animals of 6th Yorks, 9th W. Yorks, 6th Durhams & Lancs & Hampshire 32nd Infantry Brigade. Inspections of O Bty, 58th Brigade R.F.A. Wested Stores	
"	15/5/18		Inspected animals of 6th Lincolns, 9th Sherwood Foresters, 7-8 Buffs, 8th Norfolk & Headquarters 33rd Inf. Brigade.	

WAR DIARY
INTELLIGENCE SUMMARY
(Erase heading not required.)

Army Form C. 2118.

Place	Date	Hour	Summary of Events and Information	Remarks and references to Appendices
BRAIQUEMONT	16/5/18		Inspected arriving of 11th Dressing Stn + 5th Sanitary Section, 33rd + 34th Field Ambulances. Inspected line of 11th Div Train. Sir Green - Inspector arrived for inspection at 10am. Called on ADMS I Corps	
"	17/5/18		Inspected arriving of 86th + 67th Field Amb'cs Coy RE + 85th Field Ambulance. Line of "A" Batty 58th + "A" Batty 55th Brigades RFA. Held Conference of Reps Officers at HQ Office.	
"	18/5/18		Inspected arriving of the 86th Field Amb Coy RE. 6th F. Batt. (9) + 2nd Yorkshire Regt.	
"	19/5/18		Inspected arriving of C + D Coys 11th Batt. Machine Gun Corps " 2nd Yorkshire Regt.	
"	20/5/18		Inspected arriving of A + B Coys 11th Batt. Machine Gun Corps. 6th EYR (9) + "B" + "D" Batt. 58th Brigade. R.F.A. - Inspected line of DAC Inspected arriving of 1st + 2nd Batts Essex Regt. Inspected arriving for inspection at 10.4.5.	

Army Form C. 2118.

WAR DIARY
INTELLIGENCE SUMMARY.
(Erase heading not required.)

Instructions regarding War Diaries and Intelligence Summaries are contained in F. S. Regs., Part II. and the Staff Manual respectively. Title pages will be prepared in manuscript.

Place	Date	Hour	Summary of Events and Information	Remarks and references to Appendices
BRACQUEMONT	21/5/18		Inspected Equipment of 2nd F.S. 58th Brigade R.F.A.	
"	22/5/18		Inspected Horse Lines of 2nd Army Brigade R.F.A. Arrived of "C" Battery 58th Brigade R.F.A.	
"	23/5/18		Inspected Lines of "A" & "B" Batteries 59th Brigade R.F.A. 2nd Gallop for transport at M.D.S. Called in A.D.S. 1st Corps	
"	24/5/18		Inspected Arrival of 58th O.R.s by H.E. went rounds of West Officers at Army Office	
"	25/5/18		Inspected Arrival of "B" Battery 59th Brigade R.F.A. Attended Conference of A.D.V.S. 1st Corps - Visited Horse V.S. & Inspected Arrival of Evacuation	
"	26/5/18		Inspected Arrival of 33rd Field Ambulance - Inspected Horse Remounts at D.A.C. line	

Army Form C. 2118.

WAR DIARY
INTELLIGENCE SUMMARY.
(Erase heading not required.)

Instructions regarding War Diaries and Intelligence Summaries are contained in F. S. Regs., Part II. and the Staff Manual respectively. Title pages will be prepared in manuscript.

Place	Date	Hour	Summary of Events and Information	Remarks and references to Appendices
BRACQUEMONT	27/5/18		Inspected arrival of B.C. Party 59th Brigade R.F.A. + N° 2 Section of DAC.	
"	28/5/18		Inspected arrival for evacuation at S1 U.S.	
"	29/5/18		Inspected arrival of 82 Bde + 68 Bde Sec Coy R.E. + N° 1 + 3 Section D.A.C.	
"	30/5/18		Inspected arrival of Headquarters 11 DivN + Signal Coy R.E., N° 1, 2, + 3 Coys Train	
"			Visited S1 U.S. + inspected arrival for evacuation	
"			Visited S1 U.S. with G.O.C. who inspects it - inspectz. arriving of Headquarters 33rd + 34th Brigade R.F.A.	
"	31/5/18		Inspected arrival of 2nd Bn, 4 Groups Divisional Artillery	

Archives Campagne
64 DPS. w.t. Div.

WAR. DIARIES.
DADVS & 22nd Mob Vet Section
June 1918

Army Form C. 2118.

WAR DIARY
or
INTELLIGENCE SUMMARY.
(Erase heading not required.)

Instructions regarding War Diaries and Intelligence Summaries are contained in F. S. Regs., Part II. and the Staff Manual respectively. Title pages will be prepared in manuscript.

Place	Date	Hour	Summary of Events and Information	Remarks and references to Appendices
BRACQUEMONT	1/6/18		Inspected lines of 8th Northum Fus. 6th E. Yorks (2) & 2 Yorks. Attended Conference of A.D.V.S. 1st Corps	
"	2/6/18		Ordinary duties	
"	3/6/18		Inspected animals of "B" "C" & "D" Batteries 82nd Army Brigade R. F. A. " " " for evacuation at Rn V.S. " " " B 4th Bdy 3rd Grp Portuguese artillery " " " "B" Coy 11 Battn Scaforths Grn Up	
"	4/6/18		Inspected animals of 33rd Field ambulance " " " " for evacuation at Rn V.S.	
"	5/6/18		Visited Bio [?] to Vety Hospital Calais	
"	6/6/18		Inspected animals of 67th Field Coy R.E. 34th & 35th Field Ambulances Visited Field Remount Section. Inspected animals for evacuation at Dvs. Inspected animals	
"	7/6/18		Held Conference of Vety Officers at Dn Office of 9th & W. Yorks. Visits Divs.	

Army Form C. 2118

WAR DIARY
INTELLIGENCE SUMMARY
(Erase heading not required.)

Instructions regarding War Diaries and Intelligence Summaries are contained in F.S. Regs., Part II. and the Staff Manual respectively. Title Pages will be prepared in manuscript.

Place	Date	Hour	Summary of Events and Information	Remarks and references to Appendices
BRACQUEMONT	8/6/18		Ordinary duties.	
"	9/6/18		do.	
"	10/6/18		Inspected arrival of 66 & 86th Field Coy R.E., 2nd Yorkshire Regt & God & Lanes.	
"	11/6/18		Medical British Officer attached - Substitute Artillery - Inspected line of "D" Batty 59th Bngde R.F.A. Inspected arrival for evacuation at Hos	
"	12/6/18		Inspected arrival of "B" & "D" Batteries 59th Brigade R.F.A. Inspected arrival of substitute artillery - evacuation at Sn. v. S. hers to Substitute artillery	
"	13/6/18		Inspected arrival of 7th D.S Staff, 6th Divisione - 6th D.S. Lynds (P.) Vicenti Sn. v. S. & inspected arrival for evacuation	
"	14/6/18		Held conference of hosp. officers at Divy Office. Inspected lines of "A" Batty 55th Bde R.F.a. - B Batty 58th Bde R.F.a. Inspected arrival of 77th & 89th Labour Corp & 27th Labour Group for evacuation at Sn. v. S.	

WAR DIARY
INTELLIGENCE SUMMARY
(Erase heading not required.)

Army Form C. 2118.

Instructions regarding War Diaries and Intelligence Summaries are contained in F. S. Regs., Part II. and the Staff Manual respectively. Title pages will be prepared in manuscript.

Place	Date	Hour	Summary of Events and Information	Remarks and references to Appendices
BRACQUEMONT	15/6/18		Inspects arrival of the 11th Manchesters + 5th Dorsets & some arrivals in 8th Army Bde R.F.A.	
	16/6/18		Inspects arrival of the 9th Sherwood Foresters, 8th Northumberland Fus. & lines of 35th Field Ambulance	
	17/6/18		Inspects sheep views to D.A.O. Inspects arrival of D. Bdy. 8th Army Bde R.F.A. examined the evacuation at arrival	
	18/6/18		Inspects arrival of "B" Batty. 59th Brigade R.F.A. views to D.A.E. views P.O. of 8th Army Bde R.F.A. Inspects running to evacuation	
	19/6/18		Inspects sick in No 2 Coy Divn Cyclos on A.D.V.S. & cyclo views in V.S.	
	20/6/18		Inspects arrival of 3rd Fd. Amblees — views Pr. V.S. & cyclos arrived to evacuation arrival of "A" Batty 55 I Brigm R.F.A. Calls on A.D.V.S.	
	21/6/18		Inspects views in V.S. & inspects arrival to evacuation 1st Cav.	

WAR DIARY
INTELLIGENCE SUMMARY.
(Erase heading not required.)

Army Form C. 2118.

Instructions regarding War Diaries and Intelligence Summaries are contained in F. S. Regs., Part II. and the Staff Manual respectively. Title pages will be prepared in manuscript.

Place	Date	Hour	Summary of Events and Information	Remarks and references to Appendices
BRACQUEMONT	22/6/18		Inspected Arrival of "D" Batty 58th Brigade R.F.A.	
			" " " " " " " for evacuation at M. & S.	
			Attended conference of A.D.V.S. 1st Corps	
	23/6/18		Ordinary duties	
	24/6/18		Inspected arrival of B + C Batteries 58th Brigade R.F.A.	
			" Nos 1 + 2 Sections D.A.C.	
			Visited H.Q. of 59th Brigade R.F.A.	
	25/6/18		Inspected arrival of "A" Batty 84th Army Bde R.F.A.	
	26/6/18		Inspected line of 59th Brigade R.F.A. training for evacuation at M. & S.	
	27/6/18		Inspected arrival of A, C, + D Batteries 59th Brigade R.F.A.	
	28/6/18		Ordinary duties	
	29/6/18		Ordinary duties	
	30/6/18		do	

W.Siddely
Major...
ADVS 11th Divn

DADVS & ~~22nd~~ Mobile Vet Section

War Diary
July 1918

11th Division

WAR DIARY
or
INTELLIGENCE SUMMARY

Army Form C. 2118.

Place	Date	Hour	Summary of Events and Information	Remarks and references to Appendices
BRACQUEMONT	1/7/18		Inspected animals of 34th Field Ambulance. Visited Mr. V.S. & Inspected animals for evacuation. Visited Vety Officer of 59th Brigade R.F.A. Inspected sick animals in "C" Battery 59th Brigade R.F.A.	
"	2/7/18		Ordinary duties	
"	3/7/18		Inspected sheep used for Antitoxin Serum S.A.C. Vierte, also V.S. T inspected animals for evacuation	
"	4/7/18		Ordinary duties	
"	5/7/18		do. do.	
"	6/7/18		do. do.	
"	7/7/18		do. do.	
"	8/7/18		Inspected animals Suspected of Mine disease in No 3 section S.A.C. Visited Mr. V.S. & inspected animals for evacuation. Called on A.D.V.S. 1st Corps	
"	9/7/18		Inspected sick animals of 59th Brigade R.F.A. & animals for evacuation at Mr. V.D.V.S. Called on A.D.V.S. 1st Corps.	

Army Form C. 2118.

WAR DIARY
or
INTELLIGENCE SUMMARY.
(Erase heading not required.)

Instructions regarding War Diaries and Intelligence Summaries are contained in F. S. Regs., Part II. and the Staff Manual respectively. Title pages will be prepared in manuscript.

Place	Date	Hour	Summary of Events and Information	Remarks and references to Appendices
BRACQUEMONT	10/7/18		Inspected arrival of 2nd Yorkshire Regt. visits see V.S. & inspected arrivals for evacuation	
"	11/7/18		Inspected arrival of 35 F. field ambulance at 217 F Field G.A.J. " for evacuation at M.V.S.	
"	12/7/18		Inspected animals of H.C. Batty, 59 F Brigade R.F.A. visits conference of Veterinary Officers at army office	
"	13/7/18		Inspected animals of Sherwood Foresters. 8 Northumberland Fus. & Headquarters of 3rd Infy. Brigade. attended conference of A.D.V.S 1st Corps — called on A.D.V.S. 1st Army	
"	14/7/18		Inspected arrivals of 11th Devonshires & 5th Dorsets. Inspected arrivals for evacuation at M.V.S. & 8th Vet. conv. Dep M.B.3 section BAC	
"	15/7/18		Called on D.D.V with A.D.V.S. 1st Corps & visited Nos. 10 – 13 Veterinary Hospitals & No 2 Convalescent horse Depot.	

WAR DIARY or INTELLIGENCE SUMMARY

Place	Date	Hour	Summary of Events and Information	Remarks and references to Appendices
BRACQUEMONT	16/7/16		Inspected arrivals of the 67th, 68th & 86th Field Coys R.E. Visited Mr V.S. & inspected arrivals of remounts — Inspected arrivals of 34th Field Ambulance + No 3 Section D.A.C. Inspected arrivals of "A" Batty 59th Brigade R.F.A. + 470 ", wounded arrivals to " , Field C.R.E.	
" "	17/7/16		Inspected arrival of 33rd Siege Ciencebulence + arrivals of No 1 section D.A.C. & civil arrivals in Lievin + B. Stephen Pugto. Visited Mr V.S. & inspected arrivals to evacuation	
" "	18/7/16		Inspected arrivals of 11th Bombs Cheshire Queen Corps — " with A.D.V.S. 1st Supp A.B. a + D Britanis 84th Army Bryant — Visited Mr V.S. R.J.a. + Potapane Artillery.	
" "	19/7/16		Inspected line of "B" + "D" Batteries 59th Brigade R.F.a.	
" "	20/7/16		Inspected wounded arrivals in "A" Batty 59th Brigade R.F.a. Visited Mr V.S. & inspected arrivals to evacuation	

Army Form C 2118.

WAR DIARY
or
INTELLIGENCE SUMMARY.
(Erase heading not required.)

Instructions regarding War Diaries and Intelligence Summaries are contained in F. S. Regs., Part II. and the Staff Manual respectively. Title pages will be prepared in manuscript.

Place	Date	Hour	Summary of Events and Information	Remarks and references to Appendices
BRACQUEMONT	21/7/16		Ordinary duties	
"	22/7/16		Inspected arrival of the 6th Lancers & 7. S. Staff & No 2 Cavln S.A.C.	
			" wounded arrival of 470 files & V.E. - Inspected Arrival	
			The convention at M.N.S	
			A.D.V.S. 1st Corps called	
	23/7/16		Inspected Arrival of 6th E. York (?)	
	24/7/16			
	25/7/16		Inspected arrival of C Battey 55th Brigade R.F.A. & 9th W. Sussex	
			" lines of 55th Brigade R.F.A. Inspected were arrival in No 1	
			C3 Shew returning the evacuation at No N.S.	
	26/7/16		Inspected arrival of "C" & "D" Batteries 55 Brigade R.F.A	
			Held Conference of Vets at Army Office	
	27/7/16		Attended Conference of A.D. V.S. 1st Corps	

Army Form C. 2118.

WAR DIARY
or
INTELLIGENCE SUMMARY

(Erase heading not required.)

Instructions regarding War Diaries and Intelligence Summaries are contained in F. S. Regs., Part II. and the Staff Manual respectively. Title pages will be prepared in manuscript.

Place	Date	Hour	Summary of Events and Information	Remarks and references to Appendices
BRACQUEMONT	28/9/16		Inspected & issued 58 Reinforcements at No 1 Coy. Stores	
"	29/9/16		Inspected Animals of "D" & "B" Batteries 59th Brigade R.F.A. & Brigade R.F.A. Vertes lines of "B" & "C" Batteries 81st Army Brigade R.F.A. Visited H.Q. &c. Inspected Animals of reinforcements at 2nd V.S. — 58th Brigade R.F.A. & Inspected lines of "B" Battery	
	30/9/16		Inspected Animals of "A" Battery, 59th Brigade R.F.A. arrived of Nos 1 & 2 Coys. Rein. — Inspected Animals of reinforcements at 2nd V.S.	
	31/9/16		Inspected Animals of A Battery 58th Brigade R.F.A. Remounts of Nos 3 & 4 Coys. Rein —	Closing, troops are stops & Rain

Army Form C. 2118.

WAR DIARY
or
INTELLIGENCE SUMMARY.
(Erase heading not required.)

Instructions regarding War Diaries and Intelligence Summaries are contained in F.S. Regs. Part II. and the Staff Manual respectively. Title pages will be prepared in manuscript.

DADYS 11 2
9fSC 26

Place	Date	Hour	Summary of Events and Information	Remarks and references to Appendices
BRACQUEMONT	1/8/18		Inspected horses of transporters coin.	
"	2/8/18		Ordinary duties	
"	3/8/18		Inspected arrival of depual by animals of exercution at M.V.S.	
"	4/8/18		Ordinary duties	
"	5/8/18		Inspected sick animals in No 1 Coy Thenin. training for evacuation at M.V.S. Visited 1st Army Vets Remount Section	
"	6/8/18		Ordinary duties	
"	7/8/18		do do	
"	8/8/18		Visited M.V.S. & inspected animals for evacuation	
"	9/8/18		Ordinary duties	
"	10/8/18		Inspected animals for evacuation at M.V.S.	
"	11/8/18		Inspected arrival of the 11th tramanaphim. 5th Divnel & Workino Ins	
"	12/8/18		Ordinary duties	
"	13/8/18		Visited M.V.S. & inspected arrival of the 68th & 86th Field Amps R.E.	
"	14/8/18		Inspected arrival of the 68th & 86th Field Amps R.E.	

D. D. & L., London, E.C.
(A10266) Wt W3500/P713 750,000 2/18 Sch. 83 Forms/C2118/16.

WAR DIARY
or
INTELLIGENCE SUMMARY.
(Erase heading not required.)

Army Form C. 2118.

Instructions regarding War Diaries and Intelligence Summaries are contained in F.S. Regs., Part II. and the Staff Manual respectively. Title pages will be prepared in manuscript.

Place	Date	Hour	Summary of Events and Information	Remarks and references to Appendices
BRACQUEMONT	15/8/18		Inspected arrival of 67th Ares & R.E., C & B Batteries 59th Brigade R.F.A. & 34th Field Ambulance. Visited No. V.S.	
" "	16/8/18		Held Conference of Veterinary Officers at Army Offices	
" "	17/8/18		Inspected sick animals in 58th Brigade R.F.A. Attended Conference of A.D.V.S. 1st Corps	
" "	18/8/18		Inspected wounded animals in "D" Batty 59th Brigade R.F.A. Arrival of 35th Field Ambulance.	
" "	19/8/18		Lame horse cases in "C" Batty 59th Brigade R.F.A. Horse Lines	
" "	20/8/18		Ordinary duties	
" "	21/8/18		Inspected & issued Remounts at No 1 Cav Division. Arrival of Remounts at M.V.S.	
" "	22/8/18		Inspected arrival of "D" Batty 58th Brigade RFA. Headquarters 58th Brigade. arrival of A/58th Bde at Army School. Called on ADVS 1st Corps	

Army Form C. 2118.

WAR DIARY
or
INTELLIGENCE SUMMARY.
(Erase heading not required.)

Instructions regarding War Diaries and Intelligence Summaries are contained in F. S. Regs., Part II. and the Staff Manual respectively. Title pages will be prepared in manuscript.

Place	Date	Hour	Summary of Events and Information	Remarks and references to Appendices
BRACQUEMONT	23/8/18		Took charge of Adv. office of Ambulance arrival at Lancashire at HQrs	
"	24/8/18		Visited near Divisional area	
"	25/8/18		Selected site for Ad. v. S. - Advance arrived for evacuation of sick	
"	26/8/18		Moved with A.D.D. from BRACQUEMONT to VILLERS CHATEL	
"	27/8/18		Selected site for Main Advanced Div. r. S.	
"	28/8/18		Inspected Arrival of No 2 Coy Train & arrival of 2nd 2-York	
"	29/8/18		Visited Ad. r. S. Inspected Adv. arrived in S.A. & Motor Amb moved into St. A.D from Villers Chatel to MAROEUIL - Visited Adv. r. S.	
"	30/8/18		Visited 33rd Inf. Field ambulance & 67th Field Amb R.E.	
"	31/8/18		Inspected Arrival of No 3 Coy Train - Inspected sick in No 2 Coy Train Visited 33rd & 34th Field ambulances	

WAR DIARY
INTELLIGENCE SUMMARY.
(Erase heading not required.)

DADVS 11 D.

Place	Date	Hour	Summary of Events and Information	Remarks and references to Appendices
MAROEUIL	1/9/18		Selected site for Mn.V.S.	
"	2/9/18		Moved with D.H.Q. from MAROEUIL to ARRAS. Inspected Animals of the 32nd & 33rd Infty Brigades	
ARRAS	3/9/18		Inspected Animals of 11th Manchesters & S. Staffs. Visited Mn.V.S.	
"	4/9/18		Called on A.D.V.S. 22nd Corps - Inspected Animals for evacuation at Mn.V.S.	
"	5/9/18		Visited Hdy Officers of 55th & 57th Brigades R.F.A. & D.A.D.V.S. 15th Divn. Inspected Animals for evacuation at Mn.V.S.	
"	6/9/18		Inspected Animals of 33rd Fld. Ambulance + Animals for evacuation at Mn.V.S.	
"	7/9/18		Inspected Animals of 8th Devonshire Inf. Bn. - Visited 22 Corps Hty Remounty Station - Visited Mn.V.S. Called on G.O.C. 34th Infty Brigade	
"	8/9/18		Ordinary duties.	
"	9/9/18		Proceeded on leave.	

Army Form C. 2118.

WAR DIARY
INTELLIGENCE SUMMARY.
(Erase heading not required.)

Place	Date	Hour	Summary of Events and Information	Remarks and references to Appendices
VILLERS CHATEL	24/9/18		Returned from leave	
"	25/9/18		Visited Sn. V. S. & inspected animals for evacuation	
"	26/9/18		Moved with D.H.Q. from VILLERS CHATEL to ARRAS. Visited new site of Sn. V. S. Called on A.D.V.S. Canadian Corps. Inspected animals of "A" Battery, 5th Brigade R.F.A.	
ARRAS	27/9/18		Visited Sn. V.S. Called on A.D.V.S. Canadian Corps.	
"	28/9/18		Moved with D.H.Q. from ARRAS to BARALLE	
"	29/9/18		Visited Sn. V.S. & inspected animals for evacuation.	
BARALLE	30/9/18			

Yours truly
[signature]
A.D.v.S. 11th Div.

WAR DIARY
INTELLIGENCE SUMMARY

Army Form C. 2118.

Place	Date	Hour	Summary of Events and Information	Remarks and references to Appendices
BARALLE	1/10/18		Inspected arrival of 4 Battery 58th Brigade R.F.A. Convoys on A.D.V.S.	
"	2/10/18		Inspected arrivals of Nos 2, 3 & 4 Corps trains + 35th Field Ambulance. Visited A.D.V.S. & inspected arrivals of remounts.	
"	3/10/18		Inspected arrivals of remounts at M.V.S. Convoys on AC. 11th Div. trains.	
"	4/10/18		Inspected arrivals of remounts at A.D.V.S.	
"	5/10/18		Inspected arrival of 33rd Field Ambulance & arrival of remounts at A.D.V.S.	
"	6/14/18		Inspected arrival of 11th Div. Special by horse arrival of 15/27 11th Div. trains - visited A.D.V.S. & inspected remounts for remounts.	
"	7/10/18		Inspected arrival of remounts at A.D.V.S.	

Army Form C. 2118.

WAR DIARY
or
INTELLIGENCE SUMMARY.
(Erase heading not required)

Instructions regarding War Diaries and Intelligence Summaries are contained in F. S. Regs., Part II. and the Staff Manual respectively. Title pages will be prepared in manuscript.

Place	Date	Hour	Summary of Events and Information	Remarks and references to Appendices
BARALLE	8/10/18		Inspected & wrote to Dir Artillery 88 Divn. Inspected arrival & concentration at Br. R. S.	
"	9/10/18		Inspected arrival of No 3 Section S.T.C. arriving for concentration at Br. R. S. Inspected Hors of Headquarters 11 Div.	
"	10/10/18		Inspected arrival & concentration at same. Reconn'd Roits & inspected arrival for concentration	
"	11/10/18		do.	
"	12/10/18		do.	
"	13/10/18		do.	
"	14/10/18		Inspected arrival of "A" "B" "C" & "D" Batteries 55th Brigade R.F.A. Reconn'd for concentration at Br. R. S.	
"	15/10/18		Inspected arrival of B, D & C Batteries 58th Brigade R.F.A. arrival of Headquarters 58th Brigade R.F.A. Visited Br. R. S.	

WAR DIARY
or
INTELLIGENCE SUMMARY
(Erase heading not required.)

Army Form C. 2118.

Instructions regarding War Diaries and Intelligence Summaries are contained in F. S. Regs., Part II. and the Staff Manual respectively. Title pages will be prepared in manuscript.

Place	Date	Hour	Summary of Events and Information	Remarks and references to Appendices
BARALLE	16/8/18		Inspected arrival of No. 1 & 2 Section D.A.C.	
"	17/8/18		Inspected arrival of the 68th & 86th Field Coy R.E., Divisional Staff, Sherwood Foresters — Called on A.D.V.S. 22nd Corps	
"	18/8/18		Inspected arrival of 69th Field Coy R.E. Visited Mr. V.S. & Inspected arrivals for evacuation	
"	19/8/18		Inspected arrival of the 9th W. Yorks, Green & Lanark & 2nd Yorkshire Regt.	
"	20/8/18		Visited Mr. V.S. & inspected arrivals for evacuation	
"	21/8/18		Moved with D.H.Q. from Baralle to Naives – Visited Mr. V.S. at new location Naives St. Remy	
NAIVES	22/8/18		Inspected arrivals of "B" Coy 11th Battn. Machine Gun Coy, Divisional Section, Sherwood Foresters, 1st & 2nd Staffordshire Regts. Visited V.O. of 32nd Batty Brigade	

Army Form C. 2118.

WAR DIARY
or
INTELLIGENCE SUMMARY.
(Erase heading not required.)

Instructions regarding War Diaries and Intelligence Summaries are contained in F. S. Regs., Part II. and the Staff Manual respectively. Title pages will be prepared in manuscript.

Place	Date	Hour	Summary of Events and Information	Remarks and references to Appendices
NAIVES	23/6/18		Inspects Animals of the 8th Northumberland Fus. 5th Brigade. 11th Manchester - visits Sn.V.S. Inspects animals of the 6th E. York (R.) & 86th Field Coy R.E.	
"	24/6/18		Inspects animals of "C" "D" + "A" Coys 11th Battn Machine Gun Coy	
"	25/6/18		Selects sick H Sn.V.S. Visits Sn.V.S. + inspects animal Evacuation - Inspects animals of 11th Div. Signal Coy	
"	26/6/18		Inspects animals of "A" "C" + "D" Batteries 59th Brigade R.F.A. Visits Sn.V.S.	
"	27/6/18		Inspects sidings & Remount at #1 Coy train line - visits Sn.V.S.	
"	28/6/18		Visits lines of 9th Brigade + 9th Shrwood - Inspects animals of 32. R. Fus. Ambulance arrived for evacuation at Sn.V.S.	
"	29/6/18		Inspects & 68th 4th Divn R.E. + 6th Divisn Det.	
"	30/6/18		" 11th Manchester + No 14 Coy Train + Headquarters 34th Staff Brigade	
"	31/10/18		No Draft-Strength ADVS 11 Divn	

WAR DIARY or INTELLIGENCE SUMMARY

Army Form C. 2118.

DADV S. (L) 30

Place	Date	Hour	Summary of Events and Information	Remarks and references to Appendices
NAVES	1/11/18		Inspected animals of the 7 7th Bn. Staff & Headquarters 33rd Inf. Bde. Inspected animals for evacuation at Iwuy.	
"	2/11/18		Selected site for M.V.S. at HASPRES - Inspected animals of 35th Field Ambulance & Civil. by No 2 Coy. Inspected animals of 35th Field Ambulance. Visited M.V.S.	
HASPRES	3/11/18		Arrived with DHQ from NAVES to HASPRES. Inspected animals of 3rd & 4th Field Ambulances & No 1 Coy. Grenier Visited M.V.S.	
PRESEAU	4/11/18		Moved with DHQ from HASPRES to PRESEAU - Inspected animals for evacuation at M.V.S.	
" "	5/11/18		Selected site for M.V.S. - Visited M.V.S.	
" "	6/11/18		Ordinary duties	
" "	7/11/18		Moved with DHQ from PRESEAU to CURGIES. Inspected remount details at Haspres - Called on A.D.V.S. 22 Corps - Visited Divnl. & inspected animals for evacuation	

Army Form C. 2118.

WAR DIARY
or
INTELLIGENCE SUMMARY.
(Erase heading not required.)

Instructions regarding War Diaries and Intelligence Summaries are contained in F. S. Regs. Part II. and the Staff Manual respectively. Title pages will be prepared in manuscript.

Place	Date	Hour	Summary of Events and Information	Remarks and references to Appendices
CURGIES	8/11/18		Inspected lines of Bn & duty Brigade & No 3 Section R.T.C. Inspected animals for evacuation at HQrs.	
ROISIN	9/11/18		HQrs & keys & inspected animals for evacuation arrived from Curgies to Roisin. Moved with DHQ from Curgies to Roisin	
AULNOIS	10/11/18		Inspected animals for evacuation at HQrs. Moved visit DHQ from Roisin to Aulnois	
"	11/11/18		Inspected wounded horses of 16th Lancers	
"	12/11/18		Ordinary routine	
"	13/11/18		Selected site for horse DHQrs / Army Called	
"	14/11/18		Attended Conference of Div Commander at DHQ	
"	15/11/18		Belivery duties	
"	16/11/18		Inspected animals for evacuation at HQrs - wrote list of horses A & B Coy. Inspected horses from Battn & 67 & Sec 2 R.E.	

WAR DIARY
or
INTELLIGENCE SUMMARY.

Army Form C. 2118.

Place	Date	Hour	Summary of Events and Information	Remarks and references to Appendices
AULNOIS	17/11/18		Ordinary duties	
"	18/11/18		do. do.	
"	19/11/18		Inspected arrival for concentration at Aulnois	
"	20/11/18		Inspected arrival of 18 Army Bylmr Res for concentration	
"	21/11/18		do.	
"	22/11/18		Visited R.A.P. & inspected arrival for concentration	
"	23/11/18		Inspected training of 67th & 68th Field Coys R.E.	
"	24/11/18		Inspected arrival of 4th Div. Signal Coy	
"	25/11/18		Ordinary duties	
"	26/11/18		do. do.	
"	27/11/18		Moved into billets from AULNOIS to DENAIN	
"	28/11/18		Inspected line of 4th Div. Signal Coy, 5th Hussars & 8th Northumbd Fus	
"	29/11/18		" 3rd Field Ambulance - Kinder Coys 11th Batt. M.G. Corps	
"	30/11/18		Inspected lines of 11th Batt. M.G. Corps	

WAR DIARY / INTELLIGENCE SUMMARY

Army Form C. 2118.

DADVS 1/72

Place	Date	Hour	Summary of Events and Information	Remarks and references to Appendices
DENAIN	1/12/18		Inspected arrival of 58th & 59th Brigades RFA. Visited Lines.	
"	2/12/18		Inspected arrival of 6th Gun Lancs & 9th W. Yorks.	
"	3/12/18		Inspected arrival of Nos 1, 2 & 3 Secs DAC. 6th Lincs, 33rd field ambulance, B/57 RFA, Sherwoods & 7th S. Staffs. Visited Lines.	
"	4/12/18		Inspected arrival of 3rd & 4th feed ambulance & 8 Inskilling Ings.	
"	5/12/18		Visited M.V.S. & inspected arrival for evacuation.	
"	6/12/18		Inspected lines & arrival of 67, 68 & 86 field ambs RE & 75th field ambulance & 11th Div Train.	
"			Called on DDVS 1st Army.	
"	7/12/18		Inspected lines of No 2 Canadian Sherwoods, 5th Dorset & 2nd Yorks	

WAR DIARY

INTELLIGENCE SUMMARY

(Erase heading not required.)

Army Form C. 2118.

Place	Date	Hour	Summary of Events and Information	Remarks and references to Appendices
DENAIN	8/12/18		Ordinary duties	
" "	9/12/18		Inspected moves with Selection Committee of the 55th Div RE	
	10/12/18		" " 59th Fld Coy	
	11/12/18		" " 34th Army Troops Coy V R.E. & M.V.S.	
	12/12/18		" " 33rd Army Troops & 35th Fld Coy	
	13/12/18		" " 32nd " " 67 & 68 Sig Coy R.E.	
	14/12/18		Inspected animals of 5th Divsl & 2nd Canadian Stationary Coy & arrived for evacuation at once.	
	15/12/18		Inspected animals of Wireless Sec & 24th Fld ambulance & Mobile Veterinary 9 & 86th Divsl Troops R.E.	
	16/12/18		Inspected animals of 11th Div Signal Coy	
	17/12/18		Called on Staff 1st Army. Inspected animals of coronation at vet Inspection line of 12th/13th & 58th Div R.E.	

Army Form C. 2118.

WAR DIARY
INTELLIGENCE SUMMARY
(Erase heading not required.)

Instructions regarding War Diaries and Intelligence Summaries are contained in F. S. Regs., Part II. and the Staff Manual respectively. Title pages will be prepared in manuscript.

Place	Date	Hour	Summary of Events and Information	Remarks and references to Appendices
DENAIN	18/10/18		Inspected arrival of A & B Batteries 58th Brigade RFA. Visited Rents.	
	19/10/18		"	
	20/10/18		Inspected arrival of C & D Batteries 58th Brigade RFA	
	21/10/18		" " Brigade Ammunition Column "	
	22/10/18		" " Main Cards in C/59 RFA.	
	23/10/18		Inspected Police huts	
	24/10/18		" " 11th Ambulance	
	25/10/18		Arrival of C/59 RFA returned to Convention at Front	
	26/10/18		" " " Do	
	27/10/18		delivery on the Do	
	28/10/18		Do	
	29/10/18		Inspected arrival of E Brigade Ams & 31st Field Ambulance	

Army Form C. 2118.

WAR DIARY
INTELLIGENCE SUMMARY
(Erase heading not required.)

Place	Date	Hour	Summary of Events and Information	Remarks and references to Appendices
DENAIN	30/10/18		Antpertas arrived of 6th Gren & Hussars.	
	31/10/18		Antpertas arrived for preventive at units. Cases on estate 1st Army.	

Motucly
Captain
DADVS 11th Army

WAR DIARY
OF
INTELLIGENCE SUMMARY.
(Erase heading not required.)

Army Form C. 2118.

DADVS 11D.

Place	Date	Hour	Summary of Events and Information	Remarks and references to Appendices
DENAIN	1/1/19		Inspected arrival for classification of 67th & 86th Field Coys R.E.	
"	2/1/19		" Headquarters Divn & Police Long	
"	3/1/19		" 2nd Field Ambulance & Northumb. Inf.	
"	4/1/19		" 6th D.S. Goths (P.) & 22nd Bn V.S.	
"	5/1/19		" 5th Scouts & Northumberland Inf	
"	6/1/19		" 12 Bn musketeers	
"	7/1/19		" "D" Batty 55th Infantry R.F.A.	
"	8/1/19		" "A" Batty 55th Infantry Rota R	
"	9/1/19		" "B" Batty " "	- 733 Inspected
"	10/1/19		" 11 Div. Signal 6 R.E.	
"	11/1/19		" do.	
"	12/1/19		" 32nd Inf. Brigade	
"	13/1/19		" "	

WAR DIARY
or
INTELLIGENCE SUMMARY
(Erase heading not required.)

Army Form C. 2118.

Instructions regarding War Diaries and Intelligence Summaries are contained in F. S. Regs., Part II. and the Staff Manual respectively. Title pages will be prepared in manuscript.

Place	Date	Hour	Summary of Events and Information	Remarks and references to Appendices
DENAIN	14/1/19		Infants. arrived & concentration of 58th Brigade R.F.A. Hqrs. & C.R.A. Hqrs. "C" Batty 58th Brigade R.F.A.	
"	15/1/19		Batteries arrived & concentration. "D" & "B" Battys 58th Brigade R.F.A.	
"	16/1/19		" " "A" & "B" " " & Hqrs Brigade	
"	17/1/19		"C" Batty 58th Brigade R.F.A. & No.1 Sect. D.A.C.	
"	18/1/19		No 1 & 2 Sects D.A.C.	
"	19/1/19		Do.	
"	20/1/19		Headqrs. D.A.C. & No 3 Sect. D.A.C.	
"	21/1/19		11th Battn. Machine Gun Corps	
"	22/1/19		Do. & Hqrs 34th Infy Brigade	
"	23/1/19		67, 68 & 87 Questns R.E.	
"	24/1/19		33rd Infy Brigade	
"	25/1/19		"	

Army Form C. 2118.

WAR DIARY
or
INTELLIGENCE SUMMARY.
(Erase heading not required.)

Instructions regarding War Diaries and Intelligence Summaries are contained in F. S. Regs., Part II. and the Staff Manual respectively. Title pages will be prepared in manuscript.

Place	Date	Hour	Summary of Events and Information	Remarks and references to Appendices
DENAIN	26/1/19		Ordinary duties	
"	27/1/19		Inspected two king clearings "C"	
"	28/1/19		Inspected & Clearpatin arrived ? 2nd Div Train	
"	29/1/19		do do ~ (A.S. York (J.)	
"	30/1/19		Ordinary duties	
"	31/1/19		Called on A.D.V.S. 3" Corps & D.D.V.S. Army view duty	

Maxwell
Major
D.A.D.V.S. "

WAR DIARY
INTELLIGENCE SUMMARY
(Erase heading not required.)

DADVS Vol 33

Place	Date	Hour	Summary of Events and Information	Remarks and references to Appendices
DENAIN	1/2/19		Railway duties	
"	2/2/19		MTS inspected. Horse with doubtful mallein reaction destroyed COMRE	
"	3/2/19		do	
"	4/2/19		"	
"	5/2/19		Visited Advnd Camp. Deputy duties 678 dos ADVS VIII Corps Railway duties	
"	6/2/19		"	
"	7/2/19		"	
"	8/2/19		Visited MVS & inspected animals 82nd Bde. Inspected 200 animals at Corder's Camp previous to Boulogne	
"	9/2/19		Railway duties	
"	10/2/19		Visited 76 & S. Inspected Donnels 2 Sq FF+B 33 Fd Amb 87 Fd + 66 Fld Coys RE.	
"	11/2/19		Inspected & classified animals of the 163 & 112 M. G. Coy.	
"	12/2/19		Railway duties	
"	13/2/19		Visited Corder's Camp	
"	14/2/19		Corder's Camp + MVS	
"	15/2/19		Inspected animals 5g F2+B	

G Neville Capt
a/ DADVS
11th Division

Army Form C. 2118.

WAR DIARY
INTELLIGENCE SUMMARY.
(Erase heading not required.)

Place	Date	Hour	Summary of Events and Information	Remarks and references to Appendices
DENAIN	16/2/19		Sister Barnes Camp No 865 Railway sidings	
"	17/-			
"	18/-		Inspected No 3 Prees Barnes Camp	
"	19/-		Visited M.I.S. Prisoners Camp 19 a 96.	
"	20/-		Inspected mule lines M.I.C.	
"	21/-		Collected 100 Bovril tablets for use extensively in Denain considerable drop in attendance at sick parades since use	
"	22/-		Administrative duties	
"	23/-		" "	
"	24/-		Visited M.I.S. Prisoners Camp Inspected mules	
"	25/-		" "	
"	26/-			
"	27/-		Sick horses inspected Indian Convoy	
"	28/-		Chinese Labour Camp St Amand	

BlockBarl
a/DADVS 1st Division

Army Form C. 2118.

WAR DIARY
or
INTELLIGENCE SUMMARY.
(Erase heading not required.)

Instructions regarding War Diaries and Intelligence Summaries are contained in F. S. Regs., Part II. and the Staff Manual respectively. Title pages will be prepared in manuscript.

Place	Date	Hour	Summary of Events and Information	Remarks and references to Appendices
DENAIN	1/3/19		On leave	
	21/3/19		Returned from leave	
	22/3/19		Relieving duties	
	23/3/19		do	
	24/3/19		do	
	25/3/19		Attended bath & zinfield. Arrived at Somain	
	26/3/19		Visited to C.S.	
	27/3/19		Relieving duties	
	28/3/19		Visited to N.S.	
	29/3/19		Relieving duties	
	30/3/19		do	
	31/3/19		Inspected zinfield. Arrived fr bath	

www.ingramcontent.com/pod-product-compliance
Lightning Source LLC
Chambersburg PA
CBHW081431300426
44108CB00016BA/2349